P9-CQV-474

BEFOR   AND AFTER HINCKL   EV
ALUAT   \EFO
RM

DATE DUE

STEAD   HENRY J

KF92

**This item is Due on
or before Date shown.**

NW

BEFORE AND AFTER HINCKLEY: EVALUATING INSANITY DEFENSE REFORM

Before and After Hinckley: Evaluating Insanity Defense Reform

Henry J. Steadman, Margaret A. McGreevy,
Joseph P. Morrissey, Lisa A. Callahan,
Pamela Clark Robbins, and Carmen Cirincione

THE GUILFORD PRESS
New York   London

© 1993 The Guilford Press
A Division of Guilford Publications, Inc.
72 Spring Street, New York, NY 10012

All rights reserved

No part of this book may be reproduced, stored in a retrieval system, or transmitted, in any form or by any means, electronic, mechanical, photocopying, microfilming, recording, or otherwise, without written permission from the Publisher.

Printed in the United States of America

This book is printed on acid-free paper.

Last digit is print number: 9 8 7 6 5 4 3 2 1

Library of Congress Cataloging-in-Publication Data

Before and after Hinckley : evaluating insanity defense reform / Henry
   J. Steadman . . . [et al.].
     p. cm.
   Includes bibliographical references and index.
   ISBN 0-89862-280-8
   1. Insanity—Jurisprudence—United States.   2. Law reform—United
States.   I. Steadman, Henry J.
KF9242.B44 1993
345.73'04—dc 20
[347.3054]   93-15172
                                                       CIP

*This book is dedicated
to the memory of*

Saleem Shah, Ph.D.

*May he rest in peace knowing
how well he shaped his field
and nurtured those he left
behind to labor in it and to try to
uphold his high standards.*

About the Authors

Henry J. Steadman, Ph.D., is President of Policy Research Associates, Inc., Delmar, New York Previously, he directed a research bureau for 17 years for the New York State Office of Mental Health. His work has resulted in more than 80 journal articles, 18 book chapters, and 5 books. He has received the Amicus Award from the American Academy of Psychiatry and the Law in 1987 for his "numerous contributions over many years," and the Philippe Pinel Award from the International Academy of Law and Mental Health in 1988 for his exceptional contribution to research on aggression among the mentally ill.

Margaret A. McGreevy, M.A., over the past 15 years has worked on a wide variety of research projects on issues at the interface of the criminal justice and mental health systems at Policy Research Associates and the New York State Office of Mental Health.

Joseph P. Morrissey, Ph.D., is Deputy Director of the Sheps Center for Health Services Research and Professor of Administrative Medicine at the University of North Carolina, Chapel Hill. He directs an NIMH-funded postdoctoral training program there in mental health services research. His recent work has focused on quantitative studies of mental health services research with special emphasis on interorganizational networks.

Lisa A. Callahan, Ph.D., was the Field Director for the research project reported here while at Policy Research Associates and the New York State Office of Mental Health. She is currently Assistant Professor of Sociology at Russell Sage College, Troy, New York. Her current research is on conditional release programs for persons acquitted by reason of insanity who are eventually released to the community.

Pamela Clark Robbins, B.A., is Vice President of Policy Research Associates. Currently she is the Project Coordinator for the John D. and Catherine T. MacArthur Foundation Violence Risk Assessment Study, a 3-year prospective study of 1,000 mentally ill persons after their release to the community.

Carmen Cirincione, Ph.D., is an Assistant Professor in the Political Science Department at Clemson University. His major current work is in the area of risk assessment and decision theory.

Preface

There remain a few fields of endeavor where modern technology has yet to supplant the burdens of manual labor: unfortunately, research on insanity defense pleas is one. The data reported in this book demanded countless hours of work in dusty, poorly lit, and cramped record rooms in county courthouses and the basements of state mental hospitals across the United States. Looking back, we wonder whether it is possible to communicate just how grueling this work was. If we fail to indicate the extent of our labors, the ultimate value of the data in this book will not be properly appreciated. As we were completing our work, one of our research team said, "No one will ever do this again." We hope this prediction proves wrong, but the complexities of multijurisdictional research that relies on manual records certainly will dissuade many researchers from carrying out similar studies, and will continue to perplex and hamper anyone who follows in our footsteps.

We were on the verge of running out of steam at different points in this research over the six and a half years we were funded by the National Institute of Mental Health, but the commitment of a remarkable project staff enabled us to persist. There was no fast or easy way to gather the data for this study. Lisa A. Callahan and Pamela Clark Robbins spent weeks on the road, exercised incisive judgment in choosing field staff, deftly gained access to the records we needed, and were unyielding in their demand for quality data.

A number of our state coordinators warrant mention for their personal and professional investments in this project: Deborah R. Baskin (New York); Paul Ford (Ohio and Washington); Patrick T. MacDonald (California); Mary

Herring Munro (Georgia); Ellen H. Steury (Wisconsin); Stella Z. Theo-
doulou (California); and Twila Voorhees (Montana).

One member of our field research staff, Lanning Trueb, deserves
special note for his extraordinary efforts in data collection in multiple counties in Ohio, Montana, Washington, and California. He literally followed
our research across the United States.

We also owe a great debt to the many clerks of court and medical
record librarians who provided us with access to their records and offices,
often for weeks at a time.

No task on a research project such as this is more important than
coding and checking the thousands of forms obtained. Over the life of the
project we were fortunate to have a group of careful, thoughtful coders
who included Diane Cohen, Brian Morrissey, Sharon Steadman, and
Stephanie Valvo.

The complexities of the data set and the challenge of managing most
of it in the early analytic stages in a PC environment were more than
matched by the ingenuity and skill of Deborah Chard and Eric Silver. We
are especially indebted to Eric Silver for his proficient management of the
data throughout the project, and for his willingness to proofread early drafts
of the chapters and offer us insightful comments and ideas. The produc-
tion of this manuscript through its many drafts and rewrites was greatly
facilitated by the wordprocessing talents of Theresa Flansburg.

The legal research reflected throughout this book is the product of
two project consultants, Connie Mayer and Joseph Wierschem, both of
whom proved to have deep insight into this branch of mental health law.

Feedback throughout the project was provided by a distinguished
Advisory Board comprised of Alex Brooks, Eliot Hartstone, John Monahan,
Loren Roth, and David Wexler. It is wonderful to have such brilliant and
thoroughly enjoyable colleagues and friends.

The constructive comments on an earlier draft by two Advisory Board
members, John Monahan and Loren Roth, and the highly regarded legal
scholar Christopher Slobogin greatly improved the final product. We hope
their poorly compensated time, which they willingly gave, is somewhat
rewarded by the greater sophistication and smoother presentation of this
final version.

A special word of thanks is due Steven Banks, who was a statistical
consultant for all of the thorny analytical problems this data set posed. He
has a gift for understanding and communicating, and was always ready to
educate us. What warrants even greater note is the fact that Steve's assistance in answering the Review Committee's questions following their 1984
site visit probably made the difference in the decision to give us the funding to do this research.

Often government project officers are little more than "checker-
uppers." Not so with our project. We were blessed with a true colleague

as our NIMH project officer. Saleem Shah attended every Advisory Board meeting, read and thoughtfully critiqued every page of memo or text we ever sent him, and contributed major substantive insights throughout this project. As this manuscript was being prepared to go to press, tragedy struck. Our dear friend and colleague was killed in an accident in which the other driver was drunk. To those of us who had heard, over the years, Saleem's frequent comparison of the very limited danger posed by persons with mental disorders in contrast to the high degree posed to all of us by persons driving under the influence of alcohol, it was a horrible irony. He was a very special person. His was a unique place in the field he helped create. We will miss him deeply.

H.J.S.   April 8, 1992
M.A.M.
J.P.M.
L.A.C.
P.C.R.
C.C.

Contents

1 The Rush to Reform: From Hinckley to Dahmer 1

2 Insanity Defense Reform from a Systems Perspective 11

3 The Course of Insanity Defense Reform: 1978–1990 32

4 Effects of Changing the Insanity Test in California 45

5 Changing the Burden and Standard of Proof:
   Georgia and New York 63

6 Changing the Conditions of Confinement and Release
   in New York 86

7 The Impact of Adopting a Guilty but Mentally Ill
   Verdict in Georgia 102

8 The Impact of Abolishing the Insanity Defense
   in Montana 121

9 The Next Wave of Reform 138

References 153

Case References 161

Appendix A: Research Methodology 165

Appendix B: Data Abstraction Form 183

Appendix C: Criminal Procedure Laws: Applicable Sections
   from the Four Study States 189

Index 212

1

The Rush to Reform:
From Hinckley to Dahmer

The picture in the February 13, 1992, issue of *Time* said it all. The largest frame offered Jeffrey Dahmer, on trial for the murder, dismemberment, and cannibalization of 15 men in Milwaukee. The top right-hand frame pictured David Berkowitz, the "Son of Sam," who terrorized New York City for 13 months in 1976–1977 while killing six people and wounding seven others. The bottom right-hand frame showed John Hinckley, the would-be assassin of President Ronald Reagan in 1981.

What linked these three notorious persons was the insanity defense, a criminal defense characterized by *Newsweek* (Mathews, Springen, Rogers, & Cerio, 1992:49), as "one of the most maddening areas of the law—an isthmus where legality, morality, and medicine vie for dominance." In the same month an editorial in the highly respected scientific journal *Science* (Koshland, 1992:777) called the insanity defense "a kind of legal monstrosity." Jeffrey Dahmer did plead "not guilty by reason of insanity," but he was found guilty and sentenced to 15 consecutive life sentences without chance of parole. David Berkowitz was examined by psychiatrists for fitness to proceed with his trial. The examination found him competent to proceed, whereupon he pleaded guilty. So neither the Dahmer nor the Berkowitz cases incited an outcry calling for revision of the insanity defense. After their convictions, the press, the public, and legislators moved on to other issues.

But the John Hinckley case was another matter. As one observer (Tighe, 1983:224) noted, "When would-be Presidential assassin John W.

1

Hinckley pleaded not guilty by reason of insanity in answer to the indictment for his March 1981 attack on Ronald Reagan, he rejuvenated a movement which has become almost a tradition in the United States: that of reforming the insanity defense." Actually, it was not so much Hinckley's plea that set these processes into motion as it was his acquittal by reason of insanity in June 1982.

Throughout the 1980s, few activities were more popular in U.S. mental health legal circles than tampering with the insanity defense. Hinckley's insanity acquittal sparked a flurry of legislative rhetoric and public inquiry about how to stop such "abuses" in the future. As *Time* (Boyce & Jackson, 1982:61) reported during Hinckley's trial, "An acquittal would undoubtedly spur new efforts for change and abolition; many would find it unthinkable for a Presidential assailant to go unpunished." This judgment carries considerable historical precedent.

In the 182 years between the establishment of the insanity defense with the Criminal Lunatics Act of 1800 and Hinckley's acquittal, few comparable outcries had occurred. This is not to say that negative public reactions to insanity acquittals were uncommon. As Tighe (1983:235) observed, "highly publicized trials involving possibly insane defendants like Hinckley have been a regular feature of American life since the early nineteenth century and have just as regularly resulted in legal reform campaigns." Again, because of Hinckley, the public wanted to know how the American system of justice could be protected from repetitions of such apparent abuse. How could they avoid letting such criminals "get off"? How could they be protected from a mental health system that might well release dangerous mentally ill patients into the community?

These are the public policy issues at the core of the debates about the insanity defense. As Ellis (1986:962) perceptively noted, "the public's concern is less with ascertaining whether blame properly can be assigned to a particular defendant than with determining when he will get out. And the delusions of law professors and mental disability professionals to the contrary notwithstanding, it is the public's concern that drives the debate on possible changes on the insanity defense."

In response to these public concerns in the early 1980s, state and federal legislators, buttressed by professional associations' resolutions for reform, proposed a wide array of statutory changes or reforms for the insanity defense. Nearly all of the proposed reforms were designed to restrict use of the insanity defense or to make it a less-attractive option for defendants. These statutory changes or reforms were generally intended to correct perceived flaws in the defense that were instituted during the mental health advocacy movement of the 1960s and 1970s (see Chapter 3). At its 1983 Annual Meeting, the American Bar Association promulgated a position to drop the volitional component in the insanity test. In December 1983 the American Medical Association recommended abolishing the insanity defense. When Edward Meese was nominated as U.S. Attorney General in early 1984, in a national television news interview he espoused federal proposals to make the insanity defense less attractive. Clearly, as a result of John Hinckley's insanity acquittal, political capital could be gained by expressing outrage at the workings of the insanity defense.

Did all of this political rhetoric produce substantial change? If change is defined simply as statutory enactments, considerable change did indeed take place. Fully 34 states made some type of alteration to their insanity defenses between 1982 and 1985 (Callahan, Mayer, & Steadman, 1987). But if change is defined in terms of how many people entered insanity pleas, how many were acquitted, who the people were who pleaded insanity and were found not guilty by reason of insanity (NGRI), or how long people were institutionalized after their NGRI verdicts, the picture is much less clear. The systems dealing with these issues are complex. County, state, and federal levels of government are involved. Both within and across these levels, information is often not shared. County level information on insanity pleas, for example, is rarely, if ever, aggregated to the state level, meaning that almost nothing is known about the earliest stages of the insanity defense process. This situation should not be surprising. For the day-to-day operations of the system, such data are not really needed. If an insanity plea is unsuccessful, the state has no need to report it for any reason. It is merely another criminal case disposed of in a county court; the defendant is convicted and becomes a criminal justice statistic, not a mental health statistic. If the insanity plea is successful, the defendant is usually committed to a state mental hospital, at that point becoming a state statistic. As a result, the effort required to compile the necessary information to foster a broader understanding and perspective on the operation of the insanity defense is prohibitive for information systems and most researchers.

In the years immediately following John Hinckley's insanity acquittal, legal reform rumbled along unchecked by any empirical data on what results actually could be expected from various types of reform. As is usually the case, the prominent questions about the insanity defense were political ones, not empirical ones. Even if they had been empirical ones, precious little information was available to be used in intelligent debate about issues. The recurring public outcries of indignation about perceived abuses of the insanity defense have not precipitated much factual information about what is actually going on.

THE INSANITY DEFENSE IS POLITICALLY DYNAMIC

Many historical observers see the insanity defense as a critical component of criminal law. As Moran (1985a:10) said, "the insanity defense raises to relief and makes graphic the inherently complex and often ambiguous character of criminal responsibility." It functions as a set of legal-psychiatric procedures for establishing the culpability of defendants and diverting those judged not responsible for their actions to the mental health system, rather than to the criminal justice system. The actual process under which the insanity defense operates is subject to change. As Brooks (1985:134) observed, "blameworthiness is in the eye of the beholder and not a constant. During a period characterized by humaneness toward offenders, fewer offenders are considered blameworthy; in a period of fear and punitiveness, many are blameworthy."

In the past, insanity acquittees often spent many years (even whole lifetimes) locked in institutions for the criminally insane (Steadman & Cocozza, 1974). Under such conditions, they were never a major source of public concern. However, over the last two decades there has been a more rapid release of NGRI cases from hospitals in many states. This has been a byproduct of two factors: civil libertarian court rulings that insanity acquittees are entitled to the due process rights of civil patients, and advances in psychiatric treatment, particularly the use of psychotropic medications that permit the seeming restoration of sanity for many defendants, even if it cannot be established with certainty whether such acquittees remain dangerous (American Psychiatric Association [APA] Insanity Defense Work Group, 1983). Increasing public concern over the use and abuse of the insanity defense has been fueled during the past two decades by releases of notorious defendants who, once free, have again committed heinous crimes, and by NGRI verdicts that the public saw as enabling highly visible defendants to avoid proper punishment for their criminal behavior. In fact, the insanity defense was expanded as recently as the late 1950s to include a broader category of offenders based on new concepts and developments in the psychiatric field. More recently, however, the impetus for reform has come mainly from dissatisfaction with the diversionary aspect of the insanity defense in the context of recent changes in the mental health system.

Accordingly, the core objectives of almost all recent efforts to reform the insanity defense have been either an increase in perceived public safety, the reduction in the number of insanity acquittees, or the prevention of their early release from mental hospitals. These intents are clearly evident in commentaries from the early 1980s on the insanity defense in both the popular and professional media:

> The public's perception that mentally ill offenders are being processed through a revolving-door system that rapidly returns to the streets those acquitted on grounds of insanity has provoked calls for reform. (Appelbaum, 1982:14)

> Edwin Meese, President Reagan's top advisor, has called for abolition of the insanity plea in criminal cases as a means of "ridding the streets of some of

the most dangerous people that are out there." (*New York Daily News*, April 23, 1981)

Along with professional debate over the insanity defense comes a public out-cry against "criminals getting away with murder." (*Frontiers of Psychiatry*, 1982:1)

The exodus of insanity acquittees in some states has alarmed both the public and the psychiatric profession, which traditionally has been expected to play some continuing role in the social control of persons found not guilty by reason of insanity. The public's perception that a successful plea of insanity is a good way to "beat the rap" contributes to a belief that the criminal insanity defense is not only fundamentally unfair ("for afterall, he did do it") but also that insanity is a dangerous doctrine. (APA Insanity Defense Work Group, 1983)

MISPERCEPTIONS REGARDING THE INSANITY DEFENSE

Because of sporadic but highly publicized cases such as those involving John Hinckley, David Berkowitz ("Son of Sam"), and Mark David Chapman (in the latter two cases insanity was expected to be the plea, but was not used), the public and its legislators' perceptions of the insanity defense are badly skewed. Pasewark and Seidenzahl (1979) found that college students overestimated the number of insanity pleas by a factor of 800 and Pasewark and Pantle (1979) found that legislators overestimated the number by a factor of 400. In fact, for 1980, the most recent year for which national data are available, only 2,542 persons were found NGRI and admitted to mental hospitals in the entire United States (Steadman, Rosenstein, MacAskiel, & Manderschied, 1988). In New York there were only two insanity *pleas* for every 1,000 felony *arrests* in 1978 (Steadman, 1980), and in California there were only five insanity *acquittals* for every 1,000 felony *convictions* in 1980 (Jordan, 1982).

The policy significance of the misperceptions of the public and legis-lators is at least threefold. First, inaccurate ideas are likely to result in stat-utes that produce a detention and treatment system that is both inappropri-ate and damaging for the vast majority of insanity acquittees. The American Bar Association (ABA), in its *Criminal Justice and Mental Health Standards*, calls for special, more restrictive procedures for insanity acquittees involved in murder, rape, manslaughter, robbery, and arson precisely to avoid such changes (American Bar Association, Standing Committee on Association Standards for Criminal Justice, 1984). By specifically designating only serious crimes for special security reviews, the ABA hoped that legislative attempts to more securely detain the small number of insanity acquittees involved in serious offenses would not result in overly restrictive, retro-gressive changes in civil commitment standards for other insanity acquittees or persons in state mental hospitals on involuntary commitments.

Second, reforms initiated in the absence of scientific information about their likely consequences may lead to illusory change. One example is Michigan's 1975 guilty but mentally ill (GBMI) statute. As Smith and Hall (1982:77) pointed out, "The primary purpose behind the Michigan GBMI verdict was to decrease the number of insanity acquittals. Michigan legislators hoped to use the new verdict to prevent the early release of dangerous NGRI acquittals by offering Michigan juries a substitute for the insanity verdict." In the 3 years prior to the introduction of the GBMI plea, there was an average of 60 NGRI acquittals per year. In the first 7 years (1975–81) after the GBMI statute was passed, there was an average of 53 NGRIs each year and an average of an additional 33 GBMIs (B. Meyer, personal communication, 1982). Thus, as opposed to the goal of reducing the number of insanity acquittals, this number remained fairly constant. Further, the number of insanity *pleas* more than doubled over the same period (Blunt & Stock, 1985). The effect of this legal reform appears to have been merely to create a new category of mentally ill offender whose incumbents were identified for treatment within the prison system rather than within the state mental hospital system. In this case, statutory change soothed the "true justice" demands of the public, but it failed to address the uses and any potential abuses of the NGRI plea.

Third, insanity defense reforms may result in a disproportionate investment of scarce resources not only in the reform process itself, but also in the creation of institutional arrangements that will draw critical resources away from the larger mental health system, a system already fiscally distressed and underfunded. A crucial policy issue is whether insanity defense reform is cost-effective given the press of other service demands on the mental health and criminal justice systems. In fact, cost issues are a major rationale for undertaking research on insanity defense reforms. The low base rate of insanity acquittals led the APA Insanity Defense Work Group (1983:682) to conclude, "While philosophically important for the criminal law, the insanity defense is *empirically unimportant* (involving a fraction of 1 percent of all felony cases)."

Nonetheless, consideration of insanity defense reforms consumes enormous time and effort for congressional and state legislative committees, state mental health agency staff, and special committees of various professional associations. Further, GBMI statutes, for example, mandate mental health treatment in prisons which are widely recognized as having huge shortfalls in professional staff and resources for such care. State mental hospital authorities, in turn, are now facing a mandate to reallocate institutional resources to community-based mental health services. Yet lengthening hospitalization for NGRI acquittees will surely add to the maintenance costs of specialized institutional facilities.

Many of these types of expenditures represent costs of overreacting to the perceived problems associated with the insanity defense. As such, they may replicate the failings of mental health reform in this country over the past 150 years (Morrissey & Goldman, 1985). That is, costly systems of care are created to deal with one or another perceived problem without due regard to their longer term consequences for the system as a whole.

REAL INFORMATION FOR REAL DECISIONS

This book is about how research can inform policy debates over reforming the insanity defense. It is about the actual operation of the insanity defense in real life. It is about how judicial decisions on insanity are made and how the people who enter insanity pleas are processed. Ultimately, it is about how the actual operations of legal and mental health systems differ substantially from the public's and legislators' perceptions of these systems.

As we explain in much greater detail in Appendix A, we originally chose ten states for study: seven states that had enacted major statutory reforms, and, for comparison purposes, three states that had instituted no reforms. Before data collection began two states were eliminated due to multiple, simultaneous statutory changes that could not be disentangled; more realistic costing out of the data collection; and the expunging from court records of data essential for our research.

In the remaining eight states, five change states (California, Georgia, Montana, Ohio, and New York) and three comparison states (New Jersey, Washington, and Wisconsin), we examined nearly 1 million indictments in 49 counties to unearth 8,953 insanity pleas. These cases were tracked in regard to court, mental health, and correctional status. The data on which this book is based are from four of the change states. Ohio was dropped as a reform state after a more careful statutory analysis conducted after data collection indicated some additional subtle legal changes in insanity proceedings that meant the particular 1980 reform on which we had planned to focus had too brief a period of effect to be studied. The three comparison states were also dropped because, after analyzing six years of data from these states, we felt the data could not be pooled to reflect national trends, and believed further that no individual state provided an appropriate comparison with any one of the four change states.

Accordingly, the data reported here are drawn from four states: California, Georgia, New York, and Montana. Across these four states, five major types of reforms were introduced around the time John Hinckley was found not guilty by reason of insanity. One of the changes, shifting the burden and standard of proof, was made in two states: Georgia and New York.

These states afforded a unique opportunity to study insanity defense reforms. The four states all adopted major statutory changes in their insanity codes, plus each had enough insanity pleas each year so that we had sufficient cases to study over time. In most U.S. jurisdictions so few defendants plead insanity that there is no way to effectively study trends in the use of the insanity defense and how these are impacted by major reforms. In fact, Montana, which is included in our study, barely met our standard for enough cases. However, because it has the largest volume of cases of the three U.S. states that have attempted to abolish the insanity defense, we finally decided to include Montana for its significance regarding the abolition issue.

In addition to abolition, the other major insanity defense reforms we will analyze involve changes in the test for insanity (California, 1982); changes in the burden and standard of proof (Georgia, 1978, and New York, 1984); changes in conditions of confinement and release (New York, 1980); and the introduction of a new plea, "guilty but mentally ill" (Georgia, 1982). As we will explain further in the next chapter, these five changes represent the main types of reform introduced by states during the 1980s and early 1990s. They offer an opportunity to assess the likely consequences of reform relative to the goals that prompted the public and legislators to act in the first place. In other words, did the public get what it wanted in these efforts to reform the insanity defense?

In general, we were surprised at how many states actually did implement statutory changes after Hinckley's insanity acquittal. Much of the literature suggests that while numerous bills are introduced after notorious cases such as Hinckley's, few are ever passed and implemented as the push to reform looses it oomph over time.

Of the changes we studied, we correctly predicted that changing the test for insanity would make little difference. California's 1982 shift from an American Law Institute (ALI) test to a very restrictive McNaughtan standard (see Chapter 4) altered nothing in the volume of insanity pleas, their success rate, the characteristics of who pleaded insanity or who was acquitted, or how long those acquitted by reason of insanity stayed in confinement.

Across the other four types of insanity defense reforms, we found much more real change than we expected. While the specific shifts in our key measures varied by the type of reform, the four types of reform produced measurable effects on at least one or two of our measures. For example, the rate of insanity pleas went down in Georgia and New York after these states shifted the burden of proof to prove insanity from the state to the defendant. Georgia's guilty but mentally ill statute was disproportionately used for the most serious criminal charges, and those who were found GBMI received longer sentences and had longer confinements than "sane" defendants found guilty of similar charges. New York's 1980 changes in the conditions of confinement were associated with the creation of a group of acquittees (12% of all acquittees) who were released immediately after postverdict psychiatric evaluations. The 1978 "abolition" by Montana turned out to be a euphemism for business as usual; after that reform, defendants who previously would have been found NGRI were found incompetent to stand trial (IST) and then committed indefinitely to the same wards in the same maximum security mental hospital as NGRIs before the reform.

Clearly, the legal landscape in which the insanity defense operates in the United States has changed substantially since 1982 in ways that appear to have resulted from John Hinckley's insanity acquittal. In demonstrating how things have changed, we rely heavily on county-level data on insanity *pleas*. This has rarely, if ever, been done before for multiple jurisdictions. We feel our focus on the *county* is a major strength of our effort to understand how attempts at reform actually have an impact on insanity proceedings.

In the past decade a much wider variety of data on NGRI cases has become available. Information has been developed by various investigators on the characteristics of insanity acquittees, their criminal and hospitalization histories, their types of offenses, their institutional careers, and their recidivism (Steadman, 1985). Although a substantial body of knowledge about persons *acquitted* by reason of insanity has been developed in the last 10 years, there is surprisingly little information about persons who *pleaded* "not guilty by reason of insanity." Very few researchers have studied insanity *pleas*, and existing studies on pleas offer sketchy information at best (see Boehnert, 1989; Janofsky, Vandewalle, & Rappeport, 1989; Jeffrey, Pasewark, & Beiber, 1988; Phillips, Wolf, & Coors, 1988; Packer, 1987; Pasewark, Jeffrey, & Beiber, 1987; Steadman, Keitner, Braff, & Arvanites, 1983). Even some journal articles whose titles include the term "insanity pleas" are actually based almost exclusively on *acquittal* data, not *plea* data (McGinley & Pasewark, 1989; Hawkins & Pasewark, 1983).

The omission of data on insanity pleas is certainly not due to a lack of interest in the subject or its insignificance (McGinley & Pasewark, 1989). Rather, this gap is primarily the result of one major practical problem: data on insanity pleas are not centrally or systematically compiled.

Information on all those defendants who entered an insanity plea and who were either unsuccessful or who were not hospitalized upon acquittal remains at the county court house, the district attorney's office, and with the examining psychiatrists. This means that to study insanity pleas one must go to *every* county in a state to gather complete information for even *one* state. Once there, finding the few insanity pleas among all arrests is a daunting, if not impossible, task.

Fairly comprehensive information about insanity *acquittals* has been much easier to obtain because most persons found NGRI are committed to state mental health facilities for some period of time, and state-level information systems are usually easier to access than county-level record systems where the plea data are maintained. Further, NGRIs are usually identified as such at the receiving facility because of their special legal status. Insanity acquittal information is, in effect, centralized and reasonably accessible. Researchers have been able to access these data in many states; consequently, we know quite a lot about persons who *successfully* pleaded NGRI.

Where we fall short in our understanding of the full process of pleading and/or being acquitted by reason of insanity is with *unsuccessful* insanity pleas. Recently, McGinley and Pasewark (1989) called attention to this deficit in their national survey of the 51 forensic directors in the United States. Few of the respondents were able to provide information about insanity pleas, and those who did generally provided gross estimates. These researchers note that accurate data are needed on NGRI pleas, and they ask why these data are not more readily available. As the research currently stands, there is not even one cross-jurisdictional study on both "unsuccessful" and successful pleas.

Because we felt it was impossible to adequately address insanity defense reforms without plea data, we invested 5 years in collecting the necessary data. The dominant public policy issues concern the insanity *defense*. But without knowing how the plea portion of the process works, we can never create a clear picture of how the defense works. Therefore, in each of our four study states, we negotiated entry into the counties that produced the majority of insanity cases. We recruited, trained, and supervised field staff in the study states for nearly 4 years. We were supported by just over $1 million in research grants from the National Institute of Mental Health (1R01MH-38329). Through this level of long-term support and tremendous staff dedication and skill, we amassed plea data from our four study states that had never existed before, as well as acquittal and confinement information. While no one study can ever be definitive, we believe the reader will find the data brought to bear on these perplexing and challenging public policy questions in this book to be unmatched.

In Chapter 2 we provide an integrative framework for the investigation. Chapter 3 offers an overview of insanity defense reforms throughout the United States from Hinckley's acquittal in 1982 through 1990. Chapters 4 through 8 deal with the five types of legal reforms identified across the four study states. Chapter 9 summarizes the results of the analytic chapters and suggests implications that policymakers, the public, and other researchers might take away from our results. Appendix A offers an elaboration of our research procedures for readers who want the details of conducting far-flung, long-term research as we did (an overview of these procedures is found in the last section of Chapter 2). The data abstraction form used in the field is found in Appendix B, and Appendix C includes relevant sections of the Criminal Procedure Law from the four study states.

2

Insanity Defense Reform from a Systems Perspective

Our approach to studying insanity defense reform in the post-Hinckley era is premised on a systems perspective of the criminal justice and mental health systems. As Azumi and Hague (1972:11–12) point out, a "systems analysis means more than just the use of the word 'system,' and it is more than just a set of logical categories. It involves several rather critical assumptions." First, a system is composed of multiple parts that are interrelated in such a way that changes in one part affect changes in the others. Second, a system functions in an environment and the system has particular key components. Third, systems have regulatory processes that involve feedback of information. A variety of theories incorporating these assumptions have gained increasing prominence in the social and behavioral sciences in the last few decades (e.g., Buckley, 1967; Katz & Kahn, 1978; Miller, 1978; Scott, 1981).

Applied to insanity defense reform, a systemic perspective calls attention to the complex network of state and local agencies in the judicial, mental health, and corrections fields that have been established to serve the functions of social control and service provision for persons involved in insanity proceedings. It focuses heavily on the processing of a criminal case. The major points involve a defendant's movement through the adjudication, verdict, and postverdict disposition stages of the insanity defense process, ultimately to release in the community or confinement in either a criminal justice or mental health facility. The periodic pushes for reforms in this system come from an environment composed of the media, public opinion leaders, legislative bodies, professional associations, and other interest groups. While the target of reform often centers on modifications of the decision criteria at one or another stage of system processing, interventions have the potential for changes (both anticipated and unanticipated) at other stages of the system as well. Over time, as reforms or deliberate adjustments effect the volume, flow, and disposition of offenders, feedback processes are initiated whereby both the system decision makers and outside interest groups assess the impact of reform, alter their behavior or expectations, or deal with unanticipated consequences.

Consistent with the specific aims of the research reported here, we used this systems perspective to assess the impact of insanity defense reforms in several states. Although this type of perspective has been used in other criminal justice–mental health settings such as the movement of offenders through the juvenile courts (e.g., Cicourel, 1968; Cohen & Kluegel, 1978), of mental patients through the hospitalization and discharge process (e.g., Mishler & Waxler, 1963; Morrissey & Tessler, 1982), and of incompetent defendants (Steadman, 1979; Roesch & Golding, 1980), this approach has not been applied to insanity defense processes.

TYPES OF INSANITY DEFENSE REFORM

At the outset of this discussion of types of insanity defense reforms, we want to explain why we have chosen to refer to these statutory changes as "reforms." In fact, the term "reform" has not been commonly accepted for research or policy purposes. In general, it usually seems to be associated with some type of radical or substantial reaction to documented abuses. Our use of it to characterize this research was questioned at different points over the course of our project because some colleagues felt the changes we were studying were not terribly radical and, in given states, were not so much reactions to documented abuses as required legislative responses to emergent case law. While understanding these concerns, we have continued to feel that the term "reform" best captures what was taking place with the insanity defense in the years following John Hinckley's 1982 insanity acquittal. Indeed, the public clearly perceived Hinckley's acquittal as an abuse of justice. Even in less visible cases in individual states, quite often the impetus for statutory change was a notorious defendant. Reform is certainly what legislators most often had in mind. They wanted to fix the system, to close the perceived loopholes. Their proposals may not always have been terribly radical, but they were true attempts to reform the law and the systems of detention and treatment to which these laws applied.

The specific strategies of insanity defense reform have varied widely depending on which stage of the insanity defense process they targeted.

The ultimate goals of most recent reforms have been to make the insanity plea less attractive as a defense, thereby lowering the volume of pleas and acquittals, and to prevent early release of acquittees from mental hospitals by increasing the likelihood of commitment and expanding the length of confinement. There are three main stages in the insanity defense that serve as a key interface between the criminal justice and mental health systems: (1) adjudication, (2) verdict, and (3) postverdict disposition. These stages illustrate the decision points, statuses, and pathways through which will pass any cohort of defendants for whom an insanity plea is raised.

The *adjudication* stage encompasses the submission of an insanity or guilty but mentally ill plea and the initial processing of the charges. The *verdict* stage, the finding of the criminal court, may take one of four forms: not guilty, not guilty by reason of insanity (NGRI), guilty but mentally ill (GBMI), or guilty. The next stage, *postverdict disposition*, deals with where the court places the defendant after its verdict. The disposition may mandate hospitalization (or outpatient care) under mental health system auspices for successful insanity pleas or incarceration (or probation) under correctional system auspices for guilty verdicts.

Since John Hinckley's 1982 acquittal, a number of distinct insanity defense reforms have been enacted or proposed in various jurisdictions primarily as *disincentives* for using the insanity defense. These are intended to serve as procedural barriers that reduce the number of "inappropriate" insanity acquittals and/or to increase both the length and restrictiveness of confinements. These reforms can be grouped into three broad types: adjudication reforms, disposition reforms, or a combined form.

- *Adjudication reforms* focus exclusively on the "front-end" or plea stage of insanity proceedings. Specific changes may include modifications in one or more of the following: (1) substantive standard tests of mental illness (i.e., cognitive versus control or McNaughtan vs. ALI); (2) standard of proof (i.e., preponderance, clear and convincing, or evidence beyond a reasonable doubt); (3) burden of proof (i.e., defendant vs. state); and (4) role of experts (i.e., findings of fact vs. conclusory testimony on the ultimate issues). We will examine California's change of the insanity test in Chapter 4 and Georgia and New York's reform of their burden and standard of proof in Chapter 5.
- *Disposition reforms* focus exclusively on the "back-end" or postadjudication stage of insanity proceedings. Specific changes may include modifications in one or more of the following: (1) requirements for postacquittal evaluation; (2) type of evaluation; (3) location of detention (i.e., mental health vs. corrections auspices, maximum security vs. regular civil facility); (4) burden of proof of mental illness and dangerousness for continued detention; (5) rights to release

hearings; (6) burden of proof for release; and (7) final release authority (i.e., hospital superintendent vs. committing criminal court). We
will consider this type of reform in Chapter 6 by studying New
York's 1980 reforms.

- *Combination reforms* focus on both "front-end" and "back-end"
  stages of insanity proceedings and involve various combinations of
  the adjudication and disposition reforms identified above. This type
  of reform would include the GBMI plea/verdict. That is, the introduction of the GBMI option leads to changes in the adjudicatory
  process as well as changes in postverdict dispositions and institutional outcomes. We will probe two types of combination reforms,
  Montana's 1978 abolition of the NGRI verdict and Georgia's implementation of a GBMI statute in 1982.

Nearly all recent reforms were designed primarily to "narrow the
window" for insanity defense proceedings by making the law more restrictive. Consequently, all of the reforms we studied were efforts to restrict
use of the insanity defense. New York's reform restricted release procedures but also incorporated procedural protections for individuals acquitted NGRI. For most reforms we studied, the anticipated results included
reductions in the number of insanity pleas, the number of acquittals, and
the number of defendants who are hospitalized, and an increase in the
average length of hospitalization/incarceration.

With regard to *adjudicatory reforms*, for example, the statement by
the American Psychiatric Association Insanity Defense Work Group (1983)
indicated that a change in the *legal test* of insanity from ALI to McNaughtan
would represent a shift from a less-restrictive to a more-restrictive test.
Similarly, a shift in the *burden of proof* from the state to the defendant
represented an attempt to make the defense more restrictive. Furthermore,
if the *standard of proof* requires the defendant to provide evidence "beyond
a reasonable doubt," this standard would be more restrictive than one based
on a "preponderance of the evidence." Changes in the nature of psychiatric testimony are also thought to lead to more restrictive procedures. If
psychiatrists are limited to giving testimony only on medical and diagnos-
tic issues, this would be more restrictive than allowing them to address
legal and moral issues about sanity versus insanity. In each instance the
APA Work Group implied that, by shifting to more restrictive criteria,
insanity defense reformers hoped to achieve a reduction in the number of
pleas and acquittals.

The APA Work Group also viewed the introduction of a GBMI statute as a conservative procedure for reducing the volume of insanity acquittals and for shoring up posttrial mechanisms for containing the mentally
disordered offender. The person found GBMI is typically remanded to the
correctional system and thereafter is subject to different criteria in deci-

sions regarding parole and release. In general, this verdict is presumed to lead to longer periods of confinement, and thereby to increased public protection.

Even without changes at the "front-end" or adjudicatory stage of insanity proceedings, it is widely assumed that reforms in the *postverdict dispositional stage* can lead to a significant curtailment of premature releases from hospitals or prisons. In general, those changes that facilitate the commitment of insanity acquittees or that place the burden of proof for restoration of sanity on the patient/defendant rather than the state, or that introduce more stringent procedural reviews for release decisions, are seen as more conservative than procedures that leave these issues entirely in the hands of mental health professionals. The anticipated result is that by "closing the back door" of insanity proceedings (either by tightening mental hospital release criteria for NGRI acquittals or by diverting defendants from mental hospitals to prisons via GBMI statutes), both the number of premature releases and the volume of pleas will be sharply reduced. The plea reduction outcome is presumed to result from the increased reluctance of attorneys to introduce insanity pleas given their knowledge that acquittal may well lead to periods of hospitalization for their clients that are much longer than the criminal sentences following routine guilty verdicts.

For those states that introduced reforms, either prior to or following John Hinckley's acquittal, little empirical research was ever conducted on the extent to which anticipated reductions in pleas/acquittals/releases actually occur following these changes, or on whether any particular type of change (adjudicatory, dispositional, or combination) is more successful than another as a rate reduction strategy.

THE RESEARCH FRAMEWORK

We believe the work we are reporting is particularly useful to policymaking, and also makes a significant contribution to both scientific and practical knowledge about the uses and abuses of the insanity defense because it incorporates several important design considerations. It is: (1) multistate in scope; (2) adopts a systemic focus; (3) assesses the impact of all types of insanity defense reforms; (4) allows for a comprehensive assessment of each reform from the plea stage through postverdict disposition and release from custody; and (5) generates a longitudinal data base so that relevant information pre- and postreform can be contrasted and analyzed.

When simple description—the logical first step in new research areas —is the goal, the limitations of single-site studies are not overly problematic. However, as we move toward policy questions or more sophisticated substantive inquiries about the insanity defense, comparative research designs are needed. Unless longitudinal data bases are developed across jurisdictions, we will be unable to reach the level of generalization required both for middle range theorizing and for making informed public policy choices.

There are clear tradeoffs between single-state and multistate studies. Certainly, as the number of states in any one study increases, the possibilities for logistical problems in data collection and interpretive difficulties also increase. Moreover, the availability and reliability of comparable data varies greatly from state to state. As a result, almost inevitably some precision in measurement is lost as each additional state is added. Nonetheless, the severe limitations on generalizability and the slow cumulation of findings from single-state studies override any multistate research methods problems. Moreover, there are clear and pressing needs for research projects that can determine the extent to which any given insanity defense reform succeeds in altering the flow of NGRI cases, and whether one type of reform is more successful than others. These issues can be adequately addressed only in multistate studies that use the same sampling, data collection, measurement, and analysis procedures.

This is not to discount totally the utility of intensive, single-state studies for certain types of research questions. Such designs might be particularly appropriate to issues surrounding the dynamics of the legislative process in drafting, moving, and enacting insanity defense reforms. The complexities of the political process and the number and often low visibility of key actors and interest groups almost precludes multistate studies, unless these are done prospectively. The work of Bardach (1977) on California's Lanterman-Petris-Short Act exemplifies the complexity of an in-depth analysis, especially when done retrospectively. So, to the extent that research on insanity defense reform focuses on the politics of the legislation, single-state studies may be useful. However, at this point in time, such efforts are of secondary utility in addressing the major policy questions that require empirical data on the range of actual effects of legislative reform.

In moving forward with more comprehensive research designs, it also seems advisable to recognize the need for a systemic conceptualization of insanity defense reforms. Legislators are not interested in changing the insanity test simply on jurisprudential grounds. Law professors may be, but legislators are not; nor are the public or the media. Their dominant concerns are to tighten the system: to make it harder to avoid confinement and harder to get out once confined. The courts are seen as the entry point into a system of detention. They often are faulted for allowing the insanity defense to make them little more than a conduit to the community for dangerous people who are hospitalized for only a short time following insanity acquittal. Pragmatic questions revolve around how the judicial, mental health, and correctional systems can be adjusted to more effectively keep in confinement those who are seen as dangerous people. Statutory reforms concerning the insanity defense really reflect attempts at system-level change. Unless the discrete stages in this processing system (i.e., plea, adjudication, disposition, and outcome) are studied simultaneously, significant changes, whether intended or unintended, may go unrecognized.

Viewing the insanity defense processes as a "system" does not necessarily imply that the components are smoothly coordinated. Rather, it acknowledges that a number of sequential processes are set in motion with an insanity plea, and that a change in any one of these processes may have potential ramifications for the other components. For example, if a more restrictive review procedure for release from postacquittal hospitalization is introduced, the anticipated outcome is an increased length of hospitalization. However, as judges and juries become more comfortable with NGRI verdicts that assure prolonged confinement, this change may also increase the proportion of NGRI acquittals. Concurrently, as dispositional outcomes associated with the verdict (i.e., prolonged detention) make it less attractive from the perspective of defense counselors, this may decrease the number of insanity pleas. Thus, a reform at the "back end" of the system may have substantial impact at the "front end" too.

An emphasis on system-level studies further highlights the need for multistate designs to attain any level of generalization. Any given state, at any one time, is likely to implement only one or two of the potential reforms in the insanity defense, for example, a change in the insanity test or the burden of proof, the introduction of a GBMI statute, or the introduction of more restrictive postverdict disposition arrangements. No single-state study can address the impact of the full range of reforms; for a given type of reform, its results can be little more than a case study. The latter situation, of course, makes generalization extremely hazardous. Yet this is precisely the situation we are in regarding the insanity defense research conducted over the past decade. Further, when multiple reforms occur simultaneously or in close proximity, it becomes difficult, if not impossible, to separate out the effects of the individual reforms. Such occurrences make research on statutory reform difficult to conduct.

The work reported here is more than a simple accounting of whether the volume of insanity acquittals and modes of confinement are altered by various types of reform. The insanity defense is a lightning rod for a number of mental health policy issues. Under what circumstances may a person be detained as dangerous because of his or her mental illness? What factors are associated with longer confinements when dangerousness is the retention rationale? What type of detention is appropriate? When can/must release occur? What type of follow-up monitoring is appropriate? All these questions represent a mix of clinical, legal, social policy, and scientific issues. These issues are faced by state legislators and mental health administrators who must deal with the entire gamut of mental health treatment issues on an ongoing basis.

Unfortunately, most analyses of these issues, be they for theoretical or policy reasons, are thwarted by the negligible amount of relevant empirical data that are now available. This is why the National Commission on the Insanity Defense (National Mental Health Association, 1983:44) recommended "that federal and state governments initiate and appropriate funds for research on the insanity defense . . . in the following areas: the frequency of use of the plea, the frequency of the success of the pleas, the length of institutionalization of acquittees . . . and the availability of mental health treatment for acquittees." Our book will not only provide a multistate data base relevant to all these areas of insanity defense reform, but it will also address the broader issues of the rights of society versus the rights of the individual when mental illness and dangerousness are at issue. Thus, the findings of this study are not limited to the specific realm of insanity defense reforms; they will also contribute more generally to an understanding of mental health issues in the criminal justice system.

RESEARCH ON THE IMPACT OF CASE LAW

Before proceeding to an overview of how the data were generated for this research, we wish to remind our readers of the paucity of prior work studying the impact of legal reform in the mental health system. Indeed, what research on legal reform there is in the mental health arena has tended to overlook the type of reform sparked by the infamous cases often associated with state statutory reforms (for example, the Wayne Hightower case in Idaho, the Adam Berwid case in New York, or the Charles Meech case in Alaska). Rather, there is some research on the impact of important case law on the mental health system and its interfaces with the criminal justice system. A brief overview will demonstrate how these studies provide the context for the follow-up on statutory reform reported in this book. These prior studies examined the effects of some landmark mental health cases of the late 1960s and early 1970s on clients and on the systems of care. Their focus was on the core question, did "stunning paper victories . . . actually result in constitutionally and professionally adequate care and treatment for their intended beneficiaries?" (Lottman, 1976:69).

The earliest research of this type came from the first mental health case in the United States decided on constitutional grounds, *Baxstrom v. Herold* (383 U.S. 107). That 1966 landmark decision concluded that unequal protection had been given to a class of mentally disordered inmates and resulted in the mass transfer of 967 allegedly dangerous mental patients from two New York State maximum security correctional mental hospitals to 27 regular security hospitals between March and August, 1966. A 4-year follow-up study examined the impact of this decision on the patients and the mental hospitals to which they were transferred (Steadman & Cocozza,

1974). In 1971 a remarkably similar decision in Pennsylvania (*Dixon v. Attorney General of the Commonwealth of Pennsylvania*, 1971) produced another mass patient transfer and another follow-up research project to assess the impact of that decision (Thornberry & Jacoby, 1980). Both these studies suggested that the impact of the court decision was mainly positive, giving freedom to many individuals who could safely be confined in less secure institutions or be released into the community.

These two court decisions were part of a burgeoning mental health advocacy movement that was marked by class action suits and follow-up research in the early 1970s on civil mental health issues. No legal decision in the mental health arena was more important than *Wyatt v. Stickney* (1971) which appointed a court monitor to run the Alabama state mental health system. In its breadth and through its insertion of the judiciary into the direct, day-to-day operation of state mental hospitals, this decision has had few rivals. Following *Wyatt*, numerous attempts were made to assess its impact (see Jones & Parlous, 1981). These analyses tended to concentrate on the extent to which the decision produced real change in the Alabama state hospital system. Likewise, the major mental health liability case of the 1970s and 1980s, *Tarasoff v. The Regents of the University of California* in 1976, which required therapists in California to warn prospective victims of their clients' threats, led to some important impact research (Bowers, Givelber, & Blitch, 1986).

This body of research on the major legal cases in civil mental health law produced evidence that is mixed, at best (Lottman, 1976). As the editors of the *Harvard Law Review* (Comment, 1977:222) noted, "Despite the doctrinal advances, the implementation record [of key mental health case law] in mental health legislation has not been impressive. . . . The difficulty of enforcing far-reaching remedial decrees has raised serious doubts about the utility and desirability of litigation as a means of systemic reform in the mental health field."

RESEARCH ON THE IMPACT OF STATUTORY REFORM

In fact, some work on the impact of major mental health statutory revisions has occurred. Important studies in California and Massachusetts support the idea that legislative changes have more impact than case law. Urmer (1972) reported that, as intended by its sponsors, the Lanterman-Petris-Short Act of 1969, which revised California's civil mental health code, had measurable impacts on the census and average lengths of stay in state mental hospitals and shifted some responsibility for the care and management of the mentally ill to the police and correctional facilities. McGarry and his colleagues (McGarry, Schwitzgebel, Lipsitt, & Lelos, 1981) found that the Massachusetts Mental Health Act of 1970 did lead to a number of the changes sought by the legislature: due process protections were expanded, effective periodic review of involuntary commitments was initiated, and the use of mental hospitals by criminal courts was diminished. On the basis of their research, they concluded that "despite various imperfections in implementation, in large measure the drafters of the statute appear to have substantially accomplished their objectives" (McGarry et al., 1981: 146). These two studies that focus directly on mental health legislation seem to offer a basis for optimism about the prospects of producing real change from legislative reform.

The other area of mental health statutory reform that has received considerable attention in regard to the impact of its reforms is involuntary civil commitment. That literature was thoroughly reviewed by Bagby (1987) prior to his presentation of some of the most sophisticated statistical analyses of the issues. Major studies on the effects of revisions of involuntary civil commitment statutes on court processes and expert testimony have been done in North Carolina (Hiday, 1983), Oregon (Falkner, Bloom, McFarland, & Stern, 1985), Florida (Peters, Miller, Schmidt, & Packer, 1987), and Ontario (Page, 1980). Each of these studies tended to examine different questions so they lead to few summary conclusions.

More cumulative are the studies of involuntary civil commitment reforms that examined their impacts on admission rates to state mental hospitals. Bagby (1987) reviewed empirical studies from 12 states and the province of Ontario. He concludes that the results are inconsistent, partly as a function of limiting their data to public sector hospitals and having insufficient lengths of time for study. His own data from 9 years before and 5 years after Ontario's 1978 involuntary commitment revisions found an initial decline in involuntary hospital admission rates followed by an increase that approached the original level. Overall, these results seem to suggest that statutory reform in the area of involuntary civil commitment may produce different outcomes in different states, in part because of what the intended effects may be and what sorts of potential results are studied. They do suggest that the types of changes desired and expected through reforms of the insanity defense are not nearly as likely to happen or to occur in as straightforward a manner as the proponents of those measures may assume.

THE DATA SOURCES

With this context of prior research, we set off in the initial stage of our research to identify all criminal defendants who entered the insanity plea *at any time* during their defense in selected counties in the four study states. Since no statewide data existed on the frequency of insanity pleas in these jurisdictions, we selected our study counties based on their number of insanity acquittals. We aimed to select sufficient counties to obtain about two-thirds of all insanity acquittals in each state. We achieved this goal in all but one state. In Georgia, we settled for 60% of the acquittals which 12 counties produced, since obtaining 66% would have required us to collect data in 15 counties, a task for which we did not have the resources.

Once our selection of study counties was complete, we began our search to locate the necessary data sources. Our first task was to identify all criminal defendants who raised the insanity plea at any time during the court process in each of the 31 study counties in the four study states. In general, these plea data were obtained from county courts. The state data sources were the department of mental health for data on persons acquitted NGRI and the department of corrections for persons found guilty and sent to prison. Most of the discussion below deals with the procedures for the county data collection, which presented the major challenge for project staff.

The major lesson learned at this initial stage was how each county substantially differed from the others. This continued to be true throughout the data collection. We had assumed when the project began that there would be some uniformity across a given state in terms of who needed to be contacted, what the records would look like, and what procedures were used for accessing those records. But we found that there was little consistency across counties in the same state; indeed, it was almost as if each county maintained its own system. It was necessary to be very resourceful in locating and gaining access to the data. It was also necessary to be flexible enough to adapt our data collection procedures to fit the situation in each county. In some states this meant a different procedure for virtually every county, while still trying to maintain comparable and reliable data collection across sites.

The typical scenario for locating and gaining access to data sources involved several steps. The first step was to contact the office of court administration, a statewide agency, to explain the project and ask for assistance in finding out how county court data were organized. It was rare that we found the information we needed on the first phone call. Often, the spokesperson could give us only a general idea of the organizational structure of the county courts; occasionally he or she also provided us with the names of the clerks or judges we would need to contact in our study counties. In one state no one from the individual courts would talk to us until we received approval for the study from one individual in their office of court administration. But usually this initial contact was just the start of what turned out to be some serious detective work.

Almost without exception, the next step was to call court officers in the individual counties. These were "cold calls" to try and identify the name of the clerk of the criminal court and any other individuals we might have to approach for approval to access the records. A brief description of the study over the phone was usually not sufficient. A letter was requested to describe the project and the information we required, and a copy of the data collection instrument was also required. The next step was for our project director to arrange a time to meet with the clerk of criminal court to discuss the project and look at how the records were kept. It proved very helpful to mention the other counties we were scheduled to visit and any prior contact we had with the office of court administration. This seemed to increase the likelihood of cooperation in setting up these initial meetings. The key was to get our foot in the door.

These initial meetings to gain entry and to locate the data sources were crucial in accessing the records. These procedures placed a heavy demand on our project director. However, there was no substitute for meeting face to face and seeing the records at firsthand. The terminology used by the clerks and others in their office was often so specific to the individual site that it was hard to ascertain over the phone whether the data we required were truly available. For instance, records of individual indictments might be kept in books (open and closed), in lists, in files, or on microfilm. They might be called "indictments," or "filings," or "cases," or by various other terms. Unless we knew the correct term, we could make little progress with the clerks toward gaining access to the proper files. Further, while many county court officials told us over the phone that there was no way to locate NGRI pleas from the records they maintained, once on site we often discovered differently. In fact, the travel costs for these scouting expeditions were a major consideration that led us to reduce the number of study states from ten to eight. These meetings were indispensable, however, for without them we would not have secured the necessary cooperation or obtained the data we needed.

The staff at the county courts were generally most cooperative. The two major reservations they expressed repeatedly were fear that we were creating extra work for them, and anxiety that we would somehow upset or misfile the records. After reassuring them that we would be providing our own staff to do the research and that we would be very conscientious and careful with the records, they were usually very willing to cooperate as long we worked around their schedules as best we could. Despite the fact that court records are "public documents" theoretically available to anyone who requests them, we realized that court staff cooperation was absolutely necessary when we were requesting the hundreds of cases we reviewed day after day.

Sometimes these scouting expeditions lead us to alter our research design for a given state. In California, for example, our original list of study counties had included San Mateo, but after visiting that county and reviewing court records it became clear that there was no way for us to identify NGRI pleas and that another county would have to be substituted. In Los Angeles County we discovered that the court records were not kept in one location. Instead there were 11 districts for the county, each with its own separate records and procedures. We selected a representative sample of 6 districts (including Central District which handled over 50% of the indictments), and the jury administrator for the Central District was able to provide us with information on indictments in each district.

In each state, and more rarely in individual counties, there was one person who was the key to our gaining access to and obtaining the cooperation of the court staff. After numerous phone calls, letters, and scouting expeditions to each county, we became pretty adept at identifying the key actor(s) in each study state. This key person could be a bureaucrat in the office of court administration, a regional court administrator, a judge, or a clerk. Often we kept the data collection rolling by dropping his or her name, or by turning to this person for help when court personnel put roadblocks in our way.

As part of the initial scouting expedition, the project director conducted interviews with the key persons we identified in each state as being knowledgeable about the insanity defense. These people were identified through a snowball sampling technique. The number and types of persons interviewed varied by state, but always included lawmakers, public defenders, prosecutors, and hospital administrators. These interviews provided some significant insights. For example, during one of these interviews with a person at Warm Springs Hospital in Montana, we learned of the importance of looking at persons found incompetent to stand trial (IST) in order to interpret the impact of the abolition of the insanity defense in Montana. As a result of that input, we expanded our sample in Montana to include all defendants who had had a mental health evaluation.

Access to state-level data from the departments of mental health and corrections involved submitting the request for data to that agency's Institutional Review Board (IRB). These requests for approval for the research often took months, so the process was initiated as soon as we began our contacts with county officials. In cases where the information was not centralized, it was sometimes necessary to request approval from multiple IRBs and even from individual mental health facility directors. The confinement data on persons found guilty and sent to prison was always available at the central office of the department of corrections either through computer printouts, card files, or individual records. In California, New York, and Georgia, it was necessary to collect a second round of data for both the prison and hospital confinement information because our first data collection pass took place prior to the end of the follow-up period. We requested another printout or checked the card files a second time to record whether the person had been discharged during follow-up. In contrast to county-level data collection, access to the state-level data sources was straightforward.

When the data sources for insanity pleas were identified, we used a standardized data collection instrument to abstract information from each criminal case record. We did not attempt to follow any defendants who were released into the community after trial. Our total sample of insanity pleas from the four study states was 5,302. Most of the data collection was completed by local researchers who were supervised by research coordinators located in each state. To assure consistency in data collection, these researchers and supervisors were trained on site by the project director and the assistant project director. Continual contact was maintained throughout the data collection process. For those who are interested, more detailed information regarding all these procedures can be found in Appendix A.

Insanity Pleas

As the information presented in Table 2.1 suggests, the process of gathering information about insanity pleas is extremely complicated. We examined nearly 600,000 indictments to find the 5,302 insanity pleas.

The most common method of identifying cases was to hand-search the individual criminal dockets maintained in county clerks' offices. This entailed reviewing every docket page of every indictment for the study years, searching for any reference to an insanity defense. Often this procedure led to oversampling, for we initially instructed the field researchers to include any cases with a reference to the mental health of the defendant (e.g., "NGRI," "expert," "mental illness," "psychiatrist," "state hospital," "exam," "IST"). In those counties where the dockets were not available, we relied upon other techniques for identifying insanity cases.

In some counties the researchers pulled every case file during the study years from the shelves or file drawers and reviewed each one to determine whether an insanity plea was ever raised. Of course, this is a much more time-consuming task than reviewing docket pages. Another time-consuming procedure for identifying insanity pleas was used in some New York counties where the dockets contained none of the information we needed. This task required the researchers to review all cases where a fitness to proceed (i.e., competency to stand trial or IST) exam was ordered. From these cases, we anticipated that we would capture most cases where an insanity plea was used, for an IST exam is often the first step to an NGRI plea in New York. We were able to rely on a computerized search in only one county. Finally, in one county we were given the indictment number of all defendants who were evaluated for insanity.

Once a case was selected by one of the above procedures, the file was pulled. The initial review of these files was made to determine if an insanity plea was, in fact, ever entered. If documentation of a plea existed, the case then became a study case. Documentation of an insanity plea ranged from a formal notice or motion to rely on the defense to a notation of the plea in the case minutes. A data collection form was then completed by

TABLE 2.1. Information Sources for Insanity Pleas and Acquittal by Study State

State	No. of study counties	Study years	Plea information obtained from: (No. of counties)				Statewide acquittal information obtained from:		
			Court dockets	Computer	Case records	Other	Computer	No. of state hospitals visited	Central records
California	7	7/78–6/87	4	1	2		1		
Georgia	12	1/76–12/85	11		1			1	
Montana	7	1/76–12/85	7					1	
New York	5	10/77–9/87	0			5			1
Total	31		22	1	3	5	1	2	1

the field researchers. The form included sections on sociodemographics, target crimes, criminal justice processing, diagnoses, known prior criminal justice and mental health histories, target confinement, and release information. As much data as possible were collected at the county level. The data were then completed at the facility or facilities where the defendant was confined and/or at the centralized information center.

Insanity Acquittals

Case records on NGRIs committed to state mental health systems are not necessarily maintained in one location. As Table 2.1 indicates, we relied on a number of procedures to obtain the necessary follow-up information. In California we were able to obtain most of our information through a number of customized computer reports from the state's Department of Mental Health. In New York we used centralized computer records and paper files. The most common procedure for collecting follow-up mental health data was to go to the actual facilities. Fortunately, in both Montana and Georgia this involved going to only one facility.

Unsuccessful Insanity Pleas

The data collection procedures for unsuccessful insanity pleas were relatively simple because most state departments of corrections maintain centralized paper or computerized records. Generally, we were able to request information on all of our cases and receive the data directly from state officials. However, in some states we relied on centralized paper records as well as case records in the prisons. In Montana, for example, we collected data on-site at the state's one prison.

It is important to emphasize that not all persons who unsuccessfully pleaded NGRI were convicted. Further, even those who were found guilty did not necessarily go to prison. We found that approximately 28% of persons who initially pleaded NGRI, but were found guilty, were released following conviction.

General Remarks on Data Collection

The data collection phase of our project was uninterrupted between October 1985 and June 1990. Cooperation from court officials was essential to conducting this type of research, and the project director personally visited the study sites to establish a cooperative working environment, to gain access to the records, to interview key officials, and to interview potential field researchers.

Identifying the study cases was fraught with frustrations that were often compounded by missing files. Aside from misplaced criminal records, some of "these types" of cases were kept in judges' chambers for a number of reasons including mandated periodic court hearings, the notoriety of the defendant and/or victim, and the unpopularity of the outcome. Within case files, key documents were sometimes missing. Because the clerks' records are the official case records, there was no other place to search for missing court data. At some sites the clerks allowed the researchers to pull their own records. In other counties the researchers were required to fill out a request form for *every* file they wanted to review, and were often limited to reviewing only a few files at one time.

Our research on the insanity defense has underscored the fact that to understand the use of the insanity defense, researchers must start as near to the beginning of the criminal justice process as possible—at the original plea stage. As with all areas of criminal justice research, once an insanity plea is entered, negotiation starts and the composition and outcome of the case changes. Limiting study only to successful insanity pleas underestimates the frequency of the plea: we found that only about one-quarter of original NGRI pleas result in an NGRI acquittal. Furthermore, generalizations based upon successful pleas need to be limited to those cases only, and even such conclusions need to be carefully interpreted. Studying all insanity pleas is essential to building a knowledge base adequate to inform the debates about the insanity defense that erupt after the notorious cases that rarely, but inevitably, occur.

AN OVERVIEW OF THE STUDY STATES

The frequency and rate (per 100 felony indictments) of insanity pleas are presented in Table 2.2. Also included in Table 2.2 are the frequency and rate of insanity acquittals and the success rate of insanity pleas.

Across the four study states, the insanity defense was raised in only about 1% (0.90%) *of all felony cases.* Of additional importance is the wide variation in the proportion of defendants who rely on an insanity defense. It is interesting to note that Montana had the highest proportion of defendants pleading insanity or raising the issue of mental illness in their defense even though they abolished the affirmative insanity defense in 1979 (Steadman, Callahan, Robbins, & Morrissey, 1989). The insanity plea rate was lowest in New York, but this is probably due to the fact that in New York City less information is recorded early in the defense process, making it nearly impossible to identify those cases where an NGRI plea was entered and later withdrawn. Our multijurisdictional findings on the plea rate are consistent with Janofsky, Vanderwalle, and Rappeport's (1989) recent data in which they found a 1-year plea rate of 1.2% of all felony indictments in Baltimore City.

As Table 2.2 demonstrates, the acquittal rates showed less variability than the plea rates. *Acquittal rates ranged from 0.12 to 0.41 per 100 felony indictments.* The success rates (NGRI acquittals/NGRI pleas) of insanity

TABLE 2.2. Volume of Insanity Cases by Study State

States	Felony indictments (No.)	Insanity pleas (No.)	NGRI[a] acquittals (No.)	Plea[b] rate	Acquittal[c] rate	Success[d] rate
California	225,152	1,300	665	0.58	0.30	45.52
Georgia	151,669	2,630	426	1.73	0.28	13.11
Montana	14,227	816	58	5.74	0.41	7.31
New York	195,015	556	226	0.30	0.12	39.78
Total	586,063	5,302	1,375	0.90	0.23	22.71

[a]NGRI acquittals includes all acquittals identified through county records as well as acquittals (in study counties) identified via state-level records (state hospitals).
[b,c]Plea and Acquittal rates are per 100 felony indictments.
[d]Success rate is the percentage of NGRI pleas that result in acquittal. It is based *only* on data obtained through county-level records (see Note a). We did not include acquittals identified through state records in the success rate because we could not identify comparable insanity pleas from such records.

pleas showed wide variation from a high of 46% in California to a low of 7% in Montana. Montana's low success rate is due to the fact that in 1979 it abolished the insanity defense after which the success rate was virtually zero (see Chapter 8). *Overall, the success rate of insanity pleas across the four study states was 23%.*

McGinley and Pasewark (1989) called for a determination of the success rate for all cases entering NGRI pleas as well as for those where the final plea was NGRI. While it was our intention to collect and report all these data as well, we found that the insanity defense process is not as rational as we originally assumed. Our a priori assumptions were that some defendants would plead NGRI, but withdraw the plea for a plea bargain or as the result of a disadvantageous psychiatric report. However, we did not expect that defendants would be found NGRI without entering an NGRI plea. In fact, approximately 15% of all insanity acquittees never actually plead NGRI; of these, most plead not guilty. So it is misleading to assume that an NGRI acquittal is always preceded by an NGRI plea.

Janofsky, Vandewalle, and Rappeport (1989) illustrate the processes involved in pleading NGRI and subsequent outcomes in their study of Baltimore City. Their research tracked all criminal defendants who initially entered an insanity defense through to their final disposition, demonstrating the proportion of original pleas that result in guilty verdicts (26%), withdrawn NGRI plea (53%), dropped charges (11%), and final NGRI acquittal (10%). What may be missing from their study, however, are those defendants who were found NGRI without a final NGRI plea. Given the fact that we identified such defendants in every state in our study, this illustrates the necessity of studying actual judicial processing rather than statutes only to understand the interaction of the mental health and legal systems.

PROFILING THE INSANITY DEFENSE

This book is about system changes in particular states. It is about what happens to the state systems that deal with persons who plead that they are not responsible for criminal conduct due to mental disorder. These systems include the courts and the mental health systems. More specifically, what we examine here to assess the impacts of major statutory reforms are the flows of people through these systems, both the volume of the flow and the characteristics of the flow. The information on how the volume and characteristics of defendants pleading insanity and found not responsible because of insanity varied before and after the statutory reforms of interest were studied for each state and are presented in Chapters 4 through 8 for each state being analyzed.

When the data from the four states under consideration are combined, they provide a unique and comprehensive profile of who pleads not guilty by reason of insanity in the United States and who is successful with the plea, that is, who is found not responsible for criminal conduct as a result of mental disorder. These summary profile data are presented in this section, before moving to the main analyses of the questions of the impact of reforms, to provide a fuller context for those system-level analyses.

To develop a profile of insanity acquittees, we combined all cases identified at the county level in the four study states, California, Georgia, Montana, and New York (N = 4,140). In addition, we wanted a relevant comparison group of persons from the criminal justice system who had received the more usual processing in the courts. Based on relevancy and availability we obtained information on convicted felony offenders in state courts for 1986 (U.S. Department of Justice, 1988). Convicted felony offenders seemed to be the most appropriate comparison group because they were a group that had gone through the entire court system, just as the insanity acquittees had, and because they had been charged with felony offenses. This information is presented in Table 2.3. Surprisingly, we found the sociodemographic characteristics of insanity acquittees to be quite similar to those of the larger cohort of convicted felons. Insanity acquittals tended to be somewhat older and were more likely to be members of a racial minority than the larger cohort of convicted felons, yet there were no major differences in their gender.

They differed substantially, however, in terms of criminal charges. Overall, persons acquitted NGRI were more likely to be charged with either

TABLE 2.3. Comparison of Characteristics of Convicted Felons in U.S. State Courts with Insanity Defendants Convicted and Acquitted in Four Study States

	Convicted Felons[a] (N = 582,764)	Insanity Pleas	
		Convicted (N = 3,041)	Acquitted (N = 1,099)
Age:			
<20	10	15.2	5.5
20–29	50	49.2	46.1
30–39	28	22.6	32.3
40 or more	12	13.0	16.0
Gender:			
Male	87	91.9	86.4
Female	13	8.1	13.6
Ethnicity:			
White	57	48.9	47.0
Nonwhite	43	51.1	53.0
Diagnosis:			
Schizophrenia	N/A	26.9	67.4
Other major M.I.	N/A	9.9	14.9
Personality disorder	N/A	19.1	2.9
Substance abuse	N/A	10.6	2.7
Other M.I./M.R.	N/A	12.0	11.4
Not mentally ill	N/A	21.4	.6
Charges:[b]			
Murder	1.7	14.9	22.5
Rape	3.4	6.5	4.6
Robbery	7.3	11.7	7.4
Aggravated assault	6.6	15.3	29.5
Burglary	17.6	14.3	6.5
Larceny	15.6	9.2	5.4
Drugs	13.1	2.4	.5
Other	34.7	25.6	23.2
Mean sentence (in months):			
Violent offenses	35.7	33.2	N/A
Property offenses	18.5	19.3	N/A
Drug offenses	16.7	16.2	N/A
Public order offenses	13.2	27.4	N/A
Other offenses	17.8	11.9	N/A
Total	23.4	27.1	
Mean × length of confinement (in months):			
Violent offenses	92.2	83.2	34.1
Property offenses	53.2	47.2	19.6
Drug offenses	55.2	36.3	5.3
Public order offenses	35.4	70.4	25.2
Other offenses	51.4	52.6	18.4
Total	64.7	68.3	28.7

[a]Convictions in U.S. State Courts (U.S. Department of Justice, 1988).
[b]Charges for convicted felons represent charges at conviction whereas charges for insanity pleas are at arrest. Arrest charges were used to facilitate comparisons in our analysis since most acquittees are not involved in plea bargaining negotiations.

murder (23%) or physical assault (30%) as compared to smaller percentages of felony offenders convicted of murder (2%) and aggravated assault (7%). Conversely, fewer persons acquitted NGRI were charged with burglary and larceny (12%) than the larger group of convicted offenders (33%). Further, persons acquitted by reason of insanity were more likely to have been related to their victim (35%) than the larger cohort of offenders (17%).

Further, we found that the sentences given to convicted felons and to our cohort of defendants pleading insanity who were convicted were very similar. Moreover, the lengths of confinements for all these groups—convicted felons, convicted insanity pleas, and NGRI acquittals—were nearly identical.

These comparisons are not ideal, in that we are comparing arrest charges for persons acquitted NGRI with conviction charges for the larger group. Undoubtedly, conviction charges would be less serious than arrest charges. Moreover, all felony assaults, simple and aggravated, were included for insanity acquittees, but they were compared only to aggravated assault for the larger offender cohort. Despite these discrepancies, it is clear that persons raising the insanity defense had been charged with more personally violent offenses than the larger group of felons.

A comparison of persons who rasied the insanity defense and were ultimately convicted with those acquitted NGRI indicated that women were more likely to be acquitted than men. However, *the decision to acquit was most strongly influenced by clinical factors.* While 82% of those acquitted were diagnosed with a major mental illness—schizophrenia, another psychosis, or a major affective disorder—only 37% of the insanity cohort found guilty were diagnosed with a major mental illness. There was also evidence that those acquitted were more likely to have had a prior hospitalization and less likely to have had a prior arrest than those convicted.

With this background and overview, we can now proceed. The next chapter reports on how many states made changes in response to John Hinckley's insanity acquittal. It also includes a discussion of how federal regulations were overhauled in 1984 as a result of a series of congressional hearings precipitated by Hinckley's acquittal. Following that review of the evolving law, we will turn to the data collected in each state to see just what all these reforms actually accomplished.

3

The Course of Insanity
Defense Reform: 1978–1990

Periodically, the acquittal due to insanity of a notorious defendant results in an outpouring of public concern and outrage about perceived abuses of the criminal justice system. These concerns are usually accompanied by calls to reform both the tests by which a defendant is found insane and the procedures for handling the defendants, particularly those procedures that specify how long acquittees will be detained and who decides on whether they get out. The national outrage that followed John Hinckley's acquittal was unprecedented in recent history, as was the amount of statutory reform that occurred in its aftermath.

As noted by Appelbaum (1982), public concern regarding the insanity defense is a relatively new phenomenon. In the 165 years between the enactment of the Criminal Lunatics Act of 1800, which allowed the state to automatically and indefinitely confine anyone acquitted on the grounds of insanity (Moran, 1985), and the mental health advocacy movement of the 1960s and 1970s, during which procedural protections were extended to all classes of mentally ill persons by the courts, there was little cause for public concern about the insanity defense. During this period, most people acquitted by reason of insanity were confined for long periods of time, if not for the rest of their lives, in high security institutions. As a result, the public had little to fear from the defendants who were found NGRI; moreover, the conditions of their confinements were largely invisible to the public.

Although there was little public concern about legal insanity during these years, the period was marked by two major debates. One centered on efforts to integrate the growing body of knowledge in the psychiatric field with legal principles to define appropriate tests or standards of insanity to use in the defense. The McNaughtan standard was the common test used throughout the United States from the mid-1800s until the introduction of the American Law Institute (ALI) test in 1962. McNaughtan held that a person was not criminally responsible if, at the time of the crime, he or she did not know the nature of the act or that it was wrong. The ALI test, adopted by a majority of the states during the 1960s, was seen as a broader test than McNaughtan. It expanded the insanity test by lowering the standard from an *absolute* knowledge of right from wrong to a *substantial incapacity* to appreciate the difference between right and wrong and broadened it to include a volitional or irresistible impulse component (see Chapter 4). The Durham test, which was adopted by the Federal Circuit Court of Appeals for the District of Columbia in 1954, stated an accused was not responsible if his or her unlawful act was the product of mental disease or defect. In later years, there was also a flurry of legal debate regarding the morality and viability of the insanity defense in light of the fact that successful acquittals were confined indefinitely (Goldstein & Katz, 1963; Szasz, 1963; Halleck, 1967; Goldstein, 1967; Morris, 1968).

Beginning in the late 1960s and 1970s, the use of the insanity defense in criminal court proceedings underwent a major transition (LaFond & Durham, 1992). In addition to "liberalizing" the test of criminal responsibility, a number of state courts ruled against procedures that resulted in the automatic and indefinite commitment of insanity acquittees. In 1968 the Court of Appeals for the District of Columbia ruled in *Bolton v. Harris* (395 F.2d. 642) that equal protection required that insanity acquittees receive procedural protections roughly equal to those afforded civil commitment patients. In 1974 the Michigan Supreme Court found that state's policy of automatic and indefinite commitment unconstitutional (*People v. McQuillan*). Other states followed suit in prohibiting the automatic and indefinite commitment of insanity acquittees, among them Indiana (*Wilson v. State*, 1972), New Jersey (*State v. Krol*, 1975; *State v. Field*, 1978), and Georgia (*Benham v. Edwards*, 1980). The courts held that the due process and equal protection concerns raised in these cases required a psychiatric evaluation and hearing following acquittal to determine the acquittee's "present" mental status and the periodic review of insanity acquittees under mental illness and dangerousness criteria to determine justification for continued confinement. Following these court decisions, states began to revise their criminal codes to incorporate these procedural changes into their statutes. By the early 1980s, only 10 states still allowed the automatic commitment of insanity acquittees without a hearing (Hermann, 1983).

As a result of these court rulings some insanity acquittees were released to the community in relatively short periods of time. Their releases fostered grave, if misguided, public concerns for safety. Within a brief span of time highly publicized cases in a number of states resulted in legislative efforts to restrict use of the defense and to prevent the premature release of insanity acquittees. Major legislative reforms in Michigan (introduction of GBMI verdict), Georgia (introduction of GBMI plea and verdict), Ohio (change in the court of jurisdiction), and New York (change in commitment procedures) were the result of such notorious cases in the late 1970s. With Hinckley's acquittal in 1982, there was a virtual flood of reforms: 34 states revised their insanity codes in the 3 years immediately following his acquittal (Callahan, Mayer, & Steadman, 1987).

This chapter presents an overview of the current status of insanity defense laws in the United States and documents recent reforms that have occurred since our earlier review (Callahan, Mayer, & Steadman, 1987). We have been able to document these statutory changes for the 13-year period from 1978 through 1990. These years can be divided into four distinct phases: (1) Pre-Hinckley (January 1978 through March 1981), (2) During Hinckley (April 1981 through June 1982), (3) Post-Hinckley (July 1982 through December 1985), and (4) Recent reforms (January 1986 through December 1990).

We conducted an extensive analysis of statutes and case law for all 51 U.S. jurisdictions. We looked at changes in laws for the 3 years prior to Hinckley's acquittal to get a baseline or reference point for later phases. We included all reforms that directly affected the insanity defense, although we realize that changes in other parts of the mental health and criminal justice systems, for example, the civil mental health system or laws relating to incompetency to stand trial (Wexler, 1985), might also have had an impact on the insanity defense. We categorized the reforms into six major types: abolition, test of insanity, burden and standard of proof for acquittal, the addition of a guilty but mentally ill verdict, trial procedures, and commitment and release procedures. We did not include such minor changes as expanding the expert witness list.

A brief description of each type of reform follows. More detailed accounts of the five reforms we examined in our case studies are presented in Chapters 4 through 8.

Abolition of the insanity defense occurs when the special defense of insanity is eliminated. In abolition states the issue of mental illness can still be raised by the defense for the purpose of negating the criminal intent (*mens rea*) prong of the state's case against the defendant.

The *test of insanity* is the legal definition of mental disorder used in determining whether someone is criminally responsible. The two most common tests used in the United States are the McNaughtan standard and the ALI standard.

The *burden of proof* indicates who (the prosecution or the defense) has the responsibility for affirmatively proving a particular fact. The *standard of proof* refers to the specified degree of certainty to which a fact, such as insanity, must be proven. The standards of proof, in descending order, are beyond a reasonable doubt, clear and convincing evidence, or preponderance of the evidence.

Guilty but mentally ill (GBMI) is both a plea and a verdict in which a mentally ill defendant can be found criminally responsible for an act despite mental impairment; in other words, impairment is recognized but judged not severe enough to make the defendant legally insane.

Trial issues refer to reforms involving the structure of the trial, such as a bifurcated trial or a unitary trial; the way in which the insanity defense is raised, such as a separate plea or as part of a "not guilty" or "guilty" plea; and the role of psychiatric testimony during the trial.

Commitment and release procedures relate to the disposition of an insanity acquittee after the court verdict. Dispositions vary widely across jurisdictions. Some states require the automatic commitment of insanity acquittees, while others require an evaluation and hearing prior to commitment. Some use civil commitment standards and others have special criminal procedures for insanity acquittees. Release procedures also vary; the authority for the release decision may rest with the court, with mental health professionals, or with a specially appointed board. The burden and standard of proof varies at both commitment and release. Some states have instituted conditional release and others have not.

THE RUSH TO REFORM FOLLOWING HINCKLEY'S ACQUITTAL

Figure 3.1 presents a graphic representation of the number of reforms occurring in each of the four time periods between 1978 and 1990. Although the four periods are not of equal length—they range from 15 to 48 months—it is nonetheless obvious that in the period immediately following the Hinckley acquittal there were many more reforms than in any of the other periods. A total of 124 different reforms occurred in 34 jurisdictions from 1978 to 1990, with 80% of them occurring after Hinckley's acquittal. Few of these reforms could be construed as liberalizing the defense; nearly all were aimed at making the insanity defense a less attractive option for the defendant.

We have enumerated the various types of reform and the period in which they were enacted in the 51 U.S. jurisdictions in Table 3.1. The most common type of reform was in the area of commitment and release procedures. A total of 34 states revised their commitment and release procedures, enacting a total of 47 reforms from 1978 to 1990. Eighty-five percent of the states that made such revisions did so after the Hinckley deci-

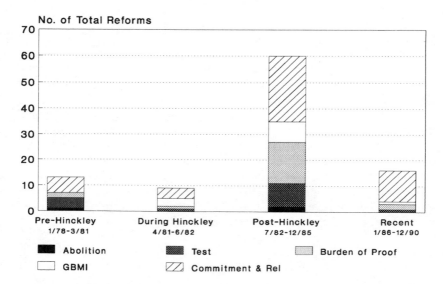

FIGURE 3.1. Number of insanity defense reforms in 51 jurisdictions from 1978 through 1990.

sion. In most states where changes in the procedures for committing insanity acquittees were enacted, the reforms were designed to require a period of commitment for evaluation following acquittal, to establish procedures depending upon the crime, to change the court of jurisdiction, or to change the burden of proof for commitment. Many of the reforms in the release area were enacted to establish new law regarding conditional release or to revise such laws.

The second most common type of insanity defense reform concerned the burden of proof; 20 states made changes in the burden of proof from 1978 to 1990, with 17 states acting after Hinckley's acquittal. Most often, states shifted the burden of proof from the state to the defense. As of 1990, 36 states and the District of Columbia (73% of all jurisdictions) required the defense to bear the burden of proof to establish grounds for acquittal. The frequency of reform in the standard of proof closely correlated with the burden of proof; 18 states made such changes. The highest standard, beyond a reasonable doubt, is only required in states where the burden of proof rests with the state. In no instance is this standard of proof required of defendants who bear the burden of proof. They are held to the lower standards of clear and convincing evidence or a preponderance of the evidence.

Changes in the test of insanity, the definition of mental illness required to exculpate a defendant, took place in 13 states, 10 (77%) of which occurred after the Hinckley trial. In most instances, these reforms marked a return to the McNaughtan test of insanity, generally regarded as more restrictive

TABLE 3.1. The Status of the Insanity Defense (as of 12/31/90)

State	Test Used	Locus of Burden of Proof	Standard of Proof	GBMI	No Reforms
Alabama	ALI	D	Prep.		x
Alaska	M'Nm	D	Prep.	x	
Arizona	M'N	D	C&C		
Arkansas	ALI	D	Prep.		
California	M'N	D	Prep.		
Colorado	M'N	S	BYRD		
Connecticut	ALIm	D	Prep.		
Delaware	M'N	D	Prep.	x	
District of Columbia	ALI	D	Prep.		x
Florida	M'N	S	BYRD		
Georgia	M'N	D	Prep.	x	
Hawaii	ALI	D	Prep.		
Idaho	n/a°	S	BYRD		
Illinois	ALI	D	Prep.	x	
Indiana	M'N	D	Prep.	x	
Iowa	M'N	D	Prep.		
Kansas	M'N	S	BYRD		x
Kentucky	ALI	D	Prep.	x	
Louisiana	M'N	D	Prep.		
Maine	ALI	D	Prep.		
Maryland	ALI	D	Prep.		
Massachusetts	ALI	S	BYRD		x
Michigan	ALI	S	BYRD	x	x
Minnesota	M'N	D	Prep.		
Mississippi	M'N	S	BYRD		x
Missouri	ALIm	D	Prep.		
Montana	n/a°	S	BYRD		
Nebraska	M'N	D	Prep.		
Nevada	M'N	D	Prep.		
New Hampshire	Dur.	D	C&C		
New Jersey	M'N	D	Prep.		x
New Mexico	M'Nm	S	BYRD	x	
New York	M'Nm	D	Prep.		
North Carolina	M'N	D	Prep.		
North Dakota	ALIm	S	BYRD		
Ohio	ALI	D	Prep.		
Oklahoma	M'N	S	BYRD		
Oregon	ALI	D	Prep.		
Pennsylvania	M'N	D	Prep.	x	
Rhode Island	ALI	D	Prep.		
South Carolina	M'N	D	Prep.	x	
South Dakota	M'N	D	C&C	x	
Tennessee	ALI	S	BYRD		
Texas	M'N	D	Prep.		
Utah	n/a°	S	BYRD	x	
Vermont	ALI	D	Prep.		
Virginia	M'Nm	D	Prep.		x
Washington	M'N	D	Prep.		
West Virginia	ALI	S	BYRD		
Wisconsin	ALI	D	Other		
Wyoming	ALI	D	Prep		

° Question of sanity relates to mens rea at the time of the crime.

KEY

ALI = American Law Institute
Dur. = Durham
M'N = M'Naughtan
m = modified
Prep = preponderance of the evidence

D = defense
S = state
BYRD = beyond a reasonable doubt
C&C = clear and convincing evidence

than the ALI test. These reforms resulted in a slight majority of jurisdictions (25 states and the District of Columbia) using the McNaughtan or modified McNaughtan test. Twenty-one states use the ALI standard; New Hampshire continues to use a standard similar to Durham; and three states—Montana, Idaho, and Utah—that have abolished the insanity defense have no test.

A popular reform with the public and many legislators is the "guilty but mentally ill" (GBMI) verdict. It was first enacted in Michigan in 1975 and currently exists in 12 states. Three states adopted the GBMI verdict during the period of the Hinckley case, and eight adopted it shortly after his June 1982 acquittal. The GBMI verdict does not eliminate the insanity defense. It simply offers an alternative verdict for mentally ill offenders. Those raising the insanity defense can be found guilty, not guilty, not guilty by reason of insanity, or guilty but mentally ill. Defendants found GBMI are sentenced in the same manner as others who have been convicted. GBMI laws vary as to requirements for the provision of mental health care during incarceration.

When states have adopted a bifurcated (two-stage) insanity trial, the first stage is concerned with the occurrence of the alleged acts and the second stage deals with the insanity issue. It is possible under these procedures for a defendant to be found guilty or to plead guilty during the first stage of the trial and then to raise insanity as a defense in the second stage. These cases are sometimes referred to as "guilty *but* insane." Occasionally this structure is misidentified as GBMI, for the defendant is factually guilty but asserts a defense of mental illness. Such was the case with Jeffrey Dahmer in Wisconsin. Many media stories referred to his case as a guilty but mentally ill plea when in fact Wisconsin does not have a GBMI law. His trial was simply a bifurcated procedure.

Another situation, which actually resembles a GBMI verdict, can occur in states that have abolished the insanity defense, but allow defendants who are found guilty or the court itself to raise the issue of mental illness at sentencing. In Montana the court can actually sentence a mentally ill defendant to the state hospital to serve his or her sentence. In this book we refer to this situation as "guilty *and* mentally ill" in order to distinguish it from GBMI laws.

Reforms in trial procedures occurred in only seven states during the study period, with nearly an even split before and after the Hinckley decision. The majority of these changes were intended to establish a bifurcated trial procedure. Oklahoma allowed access to psychiatric experts for indigent persons in order to support an insanity plea (*Ake v. Oklahoma*, 1985).

Over this entire study period, only three states abolished the special defense of insanity. Montana and Idaho passed legislation to this effect prior to the Hinckley verdict, and Utah abolished the insanity defense shortly after Hinckley was acquitted.

The current status of insanity defense laws in the 51 jurisdictions in the United States is shown in Table 3.2. The table displays the current test used, the locus of the burden of proof for acquittal, the standard of proof, states with GBMI statutes, and those that have made no changes in their laws. Only eight jurisdictions made no changes in their insanity defense throughout the 13 years of our legal review: Alabama, District of Columbia, Kansas, Massachusetts, Michigan, Mississippi, New Jersey, and Virginia. The statutory and case law citations for each jurisdiction are shown in Table 3.3.

INSANITY DEFENSE ATTAINS A NEW BALANCE

The wave of reform following John Hinckley's acquittal in 1982 represented legislative efforts to restore a balance in the operation of the insanity defense between individual rights and public protection, a balance that the public would deem acceptable. The old balance, which was based on the long-term confinement of those successfully raising the insanity defense, had been shaken when the automatic and indefinite confinement of insanity acquittees was called into question and declared unconstitutional (*Bolton v. Harris*, 1968).

The resulting advocacy movement to assure that insanity acquittees were afforded the procedural protections given to civilly committed patients dramatically increased public fears that those acquitted would be released too quickly. Before long states began to alter their insanity laws to restrict use of the insanity defense and to make it less attractive for defendants. With Hinckley's acquittal, the reform movement exploded. People were outraged with the insanity defense. The Supreme Court's decision in *Jones v. United States* (1983) reflected the public's consternation: it ruled that insanity acquittees could be treated differently than civil committees. In this case, Michael Jones was arrested for attempting to steal a jacket from a department store on September 9, 1975; 6 months later he was found NGRI. In accordance with the law, a hearing was held 50 days later to determine whether commitment should be continued. Michael Jones did not provide evidence that he was no longer dangerous, and his commitment was continued. A second release hearing was held 1 year later, at which time the defense raised the argument that confinement beyond the maximum sentence that would have been given to someone convicted of a similar offense was unconstitutional. This argument continued in the courts until November 1983, when the Supreme Court ruled that an insanity acquittal is adequate justification for automatic commitment when the defense had the burden of proof. The court also held that the maximum sentence has no bearing on the decision to release. The ruling gave support to the automatic and indefinite confinement of insanity acquittees who

TABLE 3.2. Insanity Defense Reforms

State	Abolition	Test Used	Locus of Burden of Proof	Standard of Proof	GBMI	Trial Procedure	Release/Committed
Alabama							
Alaska		4			3		4
Arizona			3	3			3,4
Arkansas							3,4
California		1,2,3					1
Colorado		3	3				3
Connecticut		3	3	3			3
Delaware					3	3	3
Dist. of Columbia							
Florida							1,3,4
Georgia			1	1	3		3
Hawaii			2,3	2		1	3
Idaho	3	3					3
Illinois			3	3	2		3
Indiana		3			2		2,3
Iowa			3	3			3
Kansas							
Kentucky					3		
Louisiana							4
Maine		3					
Maryland			3	3		3,4	3
Massachusetts							
Michigan							
Minnesota			3				3
Mississippi							
Missouri							3
Montana	1	1					3
Nebraska			3	3			1,2
Nevada							4
New Hampshire			1	1,4			2,3,4
New Jersey							
New Mexico					2		
New York			3	3			1
North Carolina						1	2,3,4
North Dakota		3	3	3		3	3
Ohio							1
Oklahoma						3	3
Oregon		3					1,4
Pennsylvania			3	3	3		
Rhode Island		1					
South Carolina			4	4	3,4		
South Dakota			3	3	3		
Tennessee							3
Texas		3					3,4
Utah	3		3	3	3		3,4
Vermont			3	3			
Virginia							
Washington							3
West Virginia		1	4	4			
Wisconsin						1	4
Wyoming			3	3			
Total No. Reforms	3	15	21	19	12	8	47
Total No. States	3	13	20	18	11	7	34

KEY

1 = Pre-Hinckley (1/78–3/81)
2 = During Hinckley (4/81–6/82)
3 = Post-Hinckley (7/82–12/85)
4 = Recent Reforms (1/86–12/90)

had established their insanity during their trial. Further, it granted substantial latitude to the states in defining commitment procedures (LaFond & Durham, 1992; Ellis, 1986). Many of the states that shifted the burden of proof to the defense after the Jones decision may have done so in order to make use of automatic commitment.

The Insanity Defense Reform Act of 1984, passed by Congress to govern federal law regarding the insanity defense, represents an archetype of the new balance being sought in the operation of the insanity defense in the post-Hinckley era. The Act defined, for the first time, a federal code for use in insanity cases (Simon & Aaronson, 1988). The act included the following provisions:

1. A test that eliminated the volitional prong of the ALI version and modified the cognitive prong to "unable to appreciate," resulting in a standard similar to McNaughtan. It further specified that the mental disease or disorder must be severe.
2. The burden of proof was shifted from the prosecution to prove the defendant was sane beyond a reasonable doubt, to the defense to establish the defendant's insanity with a standard of clear and convincing evidence.
3. The diminished capacity defense, which had previously been used to show that the defendant, due to mental disease or disorder, lacked the capacity to have the required mental state associated with a specific crime, was eliminated.
4. Commitment was to the custody of the U.S. Attorney General for treatment at a suitable facility with a provisional sentence for the maximum term authorized for the offense for those convicted. If the defendant recovers before the term expires, the court can revise the provisional sentence.

In sum, the 1983 *Jones* decision and the Insanity Defense Reform Act of 1984 marked the end of the most turbulent period of insanity defense reform in the 20th century. This period began in the 1960s with attempts to extend the procedural rights guaranteed under due process and equal protection and ended in the early 1980s with a decision that indicated those rights were not necessarily applicable to insanity acquittees. What was left in the wake of this major reform movement was a markedly different insanity defense. A new balance had been struck between public protection and individual rights, although the scales were still tipped in the direction of public protection.

Prior to this period of transition the balance strongly favored the state at the expense of individual rights. It was fairly easy, though still uncommon, to raise the insanity defense and be acquitted with the ALI test and the state bearing the burden of proof. However, successful defendants were likely to be confined for long periods of time. Defendants most likely to

TABLE 3.3. Statutory and Case Law Citations

State	Statutory Compilation	NGRI Citation	GBMI Citation	Commitment
Alabama	Ala. Code	§15-16-2		§15-16-41; 22-52-33
Alaska	Alas. Stat.	§12.47.010	§12.47.030	§12-47, et seq.
Arizona	Ariz. Rev. Stat. Ann.	§13-502A; §13-502B		§13-3994
Arkansas	Ark. Stat. Ann.	§5-2-312		§5-2-314
California[1]	Cal. Evidence Code	§522 Penal Code §25(b)		Penal Code §1026, et seq.
Colorado	Colo. Rev. Stat	§16-8-101(1); §16-8-104; §16-8-105(2)		§16-8-115, et seq.
Connecticut	Conn. Gen. Stat.	§53a-12; §53a-13		§17-257a to §17-257w
Delaware	Del. Code Ann.	11 §304a; 11 §401	11 §401(b)	11 §403
Dist. of Columbia	D.C. Code Ann.	§24-301		
Florida	Fla. R.Cr. Proc.	§3.216		§3.216; §3.217; §3.218
Georgia	Ga. Code Ann.	§16-3-2; §16-3-3	§16-3-3	
Hawaii	Hawaii Rev. Stat.	§704-402; §704-408		§704-411, et seq.
Idaho	Idaho Code	§18-207		
Illinois	Ill. Ann. Stat.	§6-2; §6-2(e)	§6-2(c)(d)	Chap. 91½ Sect. 1-100 et seq.
Indiana	Ind. Code Ann.	§35-41-3-6; §35-41-4-1(b)	§35-36-2-3(4)	§35-36-2-4; §16-4-9.1-10, et seq.
Iowa	Iowa Code Ann.	§701-4		§813.2
Kansas[2]	Kan. Stat. Ann			§22-3428, 22-3428a
Kentucky	Ky. Rev. Stat. Ann.	§504.020; §500.070; §504.060	§504.130	
Louisiana	La. Rev. Stat. Ann.	R.S. 14:14; Art. 652		R.S. 28:59; COGP Act 655 et seq.
Maine	Me. Rev. Stat. Ann.	17-A §39		§15 5104-A
Maryland	Md. Ann. Code	§12-108; §12-109		H6 §12-111 to §12-111
Massachusetts[3]				123 §16
Michigan[4]	Mich. Comp. Laws Ann.	§768.21(a)	§768.36	§330.2050
Minnesota	Minn. Stat. Ann.	§611.026		§253B.01, et seq.
Mississippi[5]				§99-13-7, §41-21-61 et seq.
Missouri	Mo. Ann. Stat.	§552.030		§552.040
Montana[6]	Mont. Code Ann.	§46-14-201		§46-15-331; §46-14-301 et seq.
Nebraska[7]	Neb. Rev. Stat.	§29-2203		§29-3701 et seq.
Nevada[8]	Nev. Rev. Stat.			§175.521
New Hampshire[9]	N.H. Rev. Stat. Ann.	§628.2(II)		§651.8-6 et seq.
New Jersey	N.J. Stat. Ann.	§2C:4-1		§2C:4-8, et seq.
New Mexico[10]	N.M. Uniform Jury Instructions	§14-5102	§31-9-3	Crim. Pro. 5-602
New York	N.Y. Penal Law	§40.15		CPL §330.20
North Carolina[11]				§15A-132

State	Code			
North Dakota	N.D. Cent. Code	§12.1-04-01; §12.1-04-02		§12.1-04.1-21 to §12.1-04.1-25
Ohio[12]	Ohio Rev. Code Ann.	§2943.03; §2901.05		§2945.40
Oklahoma[13]	Okla. Stat. Ann.	21 §152		22 1161; 22 §924
Oregon	Or. Rev. Stat.	§161.305; §161.055; §161.295		§161.341 et seq.
Pennsylvania	Pa. C.S.A. (Purdon)	18 §315; 18 §315(b)	18 §314	§50 PS 4413 §50 PS 4406
Rhode Island[14]				§40.1-5.3-4
South Carolina	S.C. Code	§17-24-10	§17-24-20	§44-23-610; §44-17-570-600
South Dakota[15]	S.D. Codified Laws Ann.	§22-5-10, §22-1-2(20)	§23A-26-11	§23A-26-12; §23A-26-12.5
Tennessee[16]		§39-11-501		§33-7-303
Texas	Tex. Code Ann. Penal	§2.04; §8.01		Texas Code C. Cr. P. Act §46.03
Utah[17]	Utah Code Ann.	§76-2-305	§77-35-21.5	§77-38-1 to §77-38-8
Vermont	Vt. Stat. Ann.	13 §4801		T13 §4820, et seq.
Virginia[18]				§19.2-1.81
Washington	Wash. Rev. Code Ann.	§10.77.030(2)		§10.77.110
West Virginia[19]				§27-6A-3; §27-6A-4
Wisconsin	Wis. Stat. Ann.	§971.15; §971.175		§971.17
Wyoming	Wyo. Stat.	§7-11-305		§7-11-302

1. People v. Drew, 149 Cal. Rep. 275; 583 P.2d 1318 (Cal. 1978).
2. State v. Granerholz, 654 P.2d 395 (Kan. 1982); State v. Roaderbaugh, 673 P.2d 1166 (Kan. 1982); State v. Lawton 734 P.2d 1138 (1987).
3. Commonwealth v. Brown, 434 N.E.2d 1286 (Mass. 1980); Commonwealth v. Brennan, 504 N.E.2d 612 (1987).
4. NGRI, People v. Savoie, 349 N.W.2d 139 (Mich. 1984); GBMI, Michigan v. John, 341 N.W.2d 861 (Mich. Ct. App. 1983).
5. Herron v. State, 287 So.2d 759 (Miss. 1974); Davis v. State, 551 So.2d 165 (1989).
6. State v. Doney, 636 P.2d 1384 (Mont. 1981); State v. Koreu, 690 P.2d 992 (1984).
7. State v. Lamb, 330 N.W.2d 462 (Neb. 1983).
8. Poole v. State, 625 P.2d 1163 (Nev. 1981); State v. Behiter, 29 P.2d 100 (Nev. 1934); Clark v. State, 588 P.2d 1027 (1979).
9. State v. Plummer, 374 A.2d 431 (N.H. 1977).
10. State v. Wilson, 514 P.2d 603 (N.M. 1973).
11. State v. Vickers, 291 S.E.2d 599 (N.C. 1982).
12. State v. Staten, 267 N.E.2d 122 (Ohio, 1971).
13. Munn v. State, 658 P.2d 482 (Okla. 1983).
14. State v. Johnson, 399 A.2d 469 (R.I. 1979); State v. Munn, 432 Ad 1773 (1984).
15. State v. Kost, 290 N.W.2d 482 (S.D. 1980).
16. State v. Clayton, 656 S.W.2d 344 (Tenn. 1983); Stacy v. Love, 679 F.2d 1209 (6th Cir. 1982).
17. State v. Baer, 638 P.2d 517 (Utah 1981).
18. Davis v. Commonwealth, 204 S.E.2d 272 (Va. 1974); Price v. Commonwealth, 323 S.E.2d 106 (Va. 1984).
19. State v. Rhodes, 274 S.E.2d 920 (W.Va. 1981); State v. Bias, 301 S.E.2d 776 (W.Va. 1983); State v. Mikim, 260 S.E.2d 295 (1979).

raise the defense under this scenario were those charged with capital offenses. When laws were changed in the 1970s to incorporate due process rights, the old balance was shaken and the scales tilted in favor of defendants, who no longer had to face indefinite confinement. Improved treatment offered the chance of regaining their sanity in relatively short periods of time, at which point they could be released. The insanity defense was extended and more people raised the defense, especially in less serious cases.

The possibility of quick release for defendants perceived to be dangerous alarmed the public, especially because such defendants appeared to have escaped punishment. So the outraged public demanded reform. Efforts at reform included changes in the test of insanity, the burden of proof, commitment and release procedures, as well as abolition of the insanity defense and the addition of GBMI laws. The massive amount of reform resulted in considerable variation in the actual operation of the insanity defense; current procedures vary widely across the 50 states. However, the majority of jurisdictions now use the more restrictive McNaughtan standard, place the burden of proof on the defendant to establish his or her insanity, and require some period of commitment, if only for evaluation. Mayer (1987:28) captures the central thrust of these changes when she notes that "the public's overwhelming fear of the future acts of acquittees produced reforms that clearly reflect the overriding interest in public safety to the near exclusion of concern for the due process rights of acquittees."

What did all this furor accomplish? Laws were changed, but what impact did the reforms have on use of the insanity defense? Were these symbolic changes designed to soothe public outrage, or did they have real effects on who uses the defense, who succeeds and who does not, and what happens to both groups of defendants? These questions guided our research in several states over the past 9 years. Our answers and their implications are presented in the remainder of this book.

4

Effects of Changing
the Insanity Test
in California

Changing the test of insanity is the archetypal adjudication stage reform. It is the core element in law that determines who will be found not responsible by reason of insanity for their criminal conduct. California's 1982 change in the test of insanity from the American Law Institue (ALI) test to a McNaughtan standard was the reform we picked to study. It met our criteria as a clear change in statute, and California has a high volume of insanity cases compared to most states. Its change of the insanity test was an effort to restrict use of the defense to a more limited group of mentally ill offenders. Our research hypothesis was that changing the test would have no significant effect on the number of insanity pleas or acquittals, the rate of use, or the composition of those using the defense. This expectation was based on a study of Wyoming's revisions of its insanity test over six years that found no measurable effects from their reforms (Pasewark, Randolph, & Bieber, 1984). Also, Simon's (1967) jury simulation work found that the test of insanity was less important to jurors' decisions on insanity acquittals than the judge's instructions to the jury.

OVERVIEW OF THE HISTORICAL DEVELOPMENT
OF INSANITY TESTS

Several insanity tests have been adopted and used in the United States during the last 150 years. The McNaughtan standard, commonly known as the "cognitive" or "right-wrong" test, was widely adopted in most U.S. courts by the mid-1800s. It states that a person is not criminally responsible if, "at the time of the committing of the act, the party accused was laboring under such a defect of reason, from disease of the mind, as not to know the nature and quality of the act he/she was doing; or if he/she did know it, that he/she did not know he/she was doing what was wrong" (Moran, 1985). By the early 1900s a number of states had broadened the insanity test by adding to the McNaughtan standard a "volitional" or "irresistible impulse" standard, which generally states that an accused is not criminally responsible if he or she could not exercise control over his/her unlawful actions.

In 1954, the Federal Circuit Court of Appeals for the District of Columbia adopted the Durham test, a modern version of a standard known as the product standard adopted in New Hampshire in 1870. This formulation of legal insanity states simply that an accused is not criminally responsible if his/her unlawful act was the product of mental disease or mental defect (*Durham v. United States*). The Durham test was seen as reflecting growing advances in the field of psychiatry and as broadening the range of persons able to use the insanity defense. Although it was acclaimed in the psychiatric community, it did not win acceptance in the state courts and ultimately was replaced in Washington, D.C., the only jurisdiction that implemented the Durham rule, in 1972 with a standard developed by the ALI.

The ALI standard, which was drafted in 1962, combined the cognitive aspect of McNaughtan and the volitional emphasis of an irresistible impulse test. It states that "a person is not responsible for criminal conduct if at the time of such conduct as a result of mental disease or defect he/she lacks substantial capacity either to appreciate the criminality (wrongfulness) of his/her conduct or to conform his/her conduct to the requirements of the law" (American Law Institute, 1962). The cognitive aspect of the ALI standard was broader than that contained in McNaughtan in that it included those who lacked "substantial capacity," rather than only those with total impairment due to mental disease or defect. Unlike the Durham standard, the ALI standard was widely accepted in state courts and remains a commonly used test throughout the United States today.

THE REEXAMINATION OF INSANITY TESTS AFTER HINCKLEY'S ACQUITTAL

The 1982 insanity acquittal of John Hinckley, Jr., for his assassination attempt on then-President Ronald Reagan prompted many calls to reform the insanity defense, including the reexamination of insanity tests. Both the American Bar Association (ABA) (American Bar Association Standing

Committee on Association Standards for Criminal Justice, 1984) and the American Psychiatric Association (APA) (American Psychiatric Association Insanity Defense Work Group, 1983) proposed new, more restrictive standards. The ABA endorsed a standard based solely on cognitive impairment, rejecting the volitional aspect as too encompassing. Similarly, the APA recommended the removal of the volitional prong and endorsed more restrictive wording that included only those "unable to appreciate" the wrongfulness of their conduct. In 1984 the U.S. Congress passed the Insanity Defense Reform Act (IDRA) that contained a standard like those proposed by the ABA and the APA. It stated that the insanity defense was an affirmative defense that at the time of the acts the defendant, as a result of severe mental disease or disorder, was unable to appreciate the nature and quality or the wrongfulness of his/her acts. It is interesting that this new standard, endorsed by the ABA and the APA and used in the IDRA, is similar to the McNaughtan standard which earlier had been revised or rejected as too narrow in both the federal jurisdiction and many states (see Melton, Petrila, Poythress, & Slobogin, 1987:115–135).

California's experience with the insanity test very much reflected the national trend. The McNaughtan standard was used there from the early 1900s until September 1978 when it was replaced by the ALI test. Then, in 1982, as part of Proposition 8, the voters of California endorsed another change in the insanity test. With the passage of Proposition 8, the ALI standard was replaced with a modified, more restrictive version of the McNaughtan test which held that a person was not criminally responsible if he/she did not know the nature and quality of the act *and* did not know the action was wrong. The key difference in the version endorsed by the California voters was that a conjunctive "and" had replaced the disjunctive "or" used in the traditional McNaughtan standard. This reform was an attempt to restrict use of the insanity defense. In 1984 the California Supreme Court (*California v. Horn*) ruled that the standard adopted in 1982 should be viewed as a return to the traditional McNaughtan test, rather than as the creation of a new standard.

NO SIGNIFICANT IMPACT EXPECTED

As we indicated briefly in the introduction to this chapter, our expectation was that this reform of California's insanity test would not produce any significant change in the volume, rates, or composition of insanity pleas or acquittals. This expectation was based largely on the work of Pasewark and colleagues who had conducted a 6-year study of changes in the insanity test and trial procedures in Wyoming (Pasewark, Randolph, & Bieber, 1984). Utilizing data on all persons raising the insanity plea, he and his colleagues examined the effects of changing the insanity test from a modified McNaughtan to an ALI standard as well as changes in the trial procedure (from single-faceted to bifurcated and back to single-faceted). They concluded that neither change affected the plea rate, success rate, or the characteristics of defendants using the defense in Wyoming.

Although we based our expectations primarily on the work of Pasewark and his colleagues, data from five other states that made the opposite change in their insanity test, from the McNaughtan standard to a seemingly more liberal ALI or Durham standard, suggested a different hypothesis. Since these studies found an increased number of acquittals after test revision, they suggested we would find a decrease in the number of insanity acquittals when the test was made more restrictive. A study of insanity acquittals in the District of Columbia following the 1954 change from a modified McNaughtan standard (with an irresistible impulse) to the less restrictive Durham test found an increase in the percentage of cases that were acquitted by reason of insanity over a 6-year period from 0.5% in 1954 to 2.5% in 1959 (Arens, 1967; Keilitz, 1987; Krash, 1961; Matthews, 1970). Similarly, data from Maryland and Oregon and findings from earlier work in California suggest that the volume of insanity acquittals rose after these states changed from the McNaughtan to the ALI standard. In Maryland, the percentage of male felons evaluated for mental illness who were determined to be not responsible was 8% in 1966 and 19% in 1973, 6 years after the change to the ALI test in 1967 (Sales & Hafemeister, 1984). In the 6 years prior to Oregon's change from McNaughtan to ALI (1966–71), 44 cases were acquitted NGRI compared with 734 cases during the years 1972–82 (Reynolds, 1984). And in California, the number of insanity acquittals rose sharply in the year following the switch to ALI, from 187 acquittals in 1978 to 270 in 1979 (Slobogin, 1985).

Beyond these studies, a review of forensic evaluations in a large midwestern city during a 2-year period supported the idea that the insanity test did affect the number and composition of those using the insanity defense (Wettstein, Mulvey, & Rogers, 1991). Evaluating psychiatrists were asked to indicate which criterion—ALI cognitive, ALI volitional, APA cognitive, or McNaughtan cognitive—were met by defendants evaluated as nonresponsible. The investigators found high correlations between the three cognitive standards. More importantly, they found that nearly one-quarter (24.4%) of those evaluated as nonresponsible met only the volitional criterion. Their data implied that a test incorporating both a cognitive and a volitional prong would be broader than one with only a cognitive aspect, regardless of which cognitive definition was used.

Research on mock jurors' decisions in insanity defense cases is inconsistent. In a mock jury trial involving incest, Simon (1967) found that juries rendered more insanity acquittals when instructed according to the Durham test or when given no instructions than when they were instructed according to the McNaughtan test. Other studies have not duplicated these results, however. Finkel and Handel (1989) found no significant differences in the verdicts of mock juries instructed according to six different tests.

All of these prior studies on the effects of changing the test of insanity have serious limitations. With the exception of Pasewark and colleagues' research, all of the studies that found an increase in insanity acquittals following a switch from the McNaughtan test to either Durham or ALI looked only at the number of insanity *acquittals*. Change in the number of insanity acquittals does not represent a very comprehensive examination of use of the defense. Such studies ignore trends across time, the volume of insanity *pleas*, and the characteristics of both those pleading and those acquitted by reason of insanity. Also, while forensic evaluation has been found to be a strong predictor of insanity adjudication (Steadman, Keitner, Braff, & Arvanites, 1983), one cannot generalize from a psychiatrist's ratings on the forensic evaluation to the overall use of the insanity defense.

Studies based on the verdicts of mock juries are also limited in that the vast majority of insanity cases do not go to a jury. Rather, as the data reported in this book will amply demonstrate, most insanity pleas are settled by a plea bargain or with a bench trial. Finally, Pasewark and colleagues' work, which was a direct study of the effect of changing the test of insanity, found that the changes had no significant effect on use of the insanity defense. The statutory changes they studied took place in a state in which the insanity defense was rarely used, however. It also can be argued that changing the insanity test from the McNaughtan with an irresistible impulse clause to an ALI standard is a relatively minor change in that both contain a cognitive and a volitional aspect. The major difference in the two standards used in Wyoming was simply in the level of cognitive impairment required for acquittal.

This chapter will examine the effects of changing the insanity standard in California in 1982 from the ALI test, which is commonly seen as broad because it includes both a cognitive and a volitional aspect, to a modified McNaughtan standard, which was reworded to make it even more restrictive than the traditional McNaughtan test. This chapter will focus on whether California's revision of its insanity test affected the number of insanity pleas and acquittals, the characteristics of persons using the defense, and the length of stay of defendants found NGRI.

OBTAINING THE DATA

In order to assess the effects of the reform, we collected information on all persons who raised an insanity plea in seven California counties during a 6-year period, 3 years prior to the July 1982 reform and 3 years after the reform (July 1979–June 1985). (Insanity cases identified during the last 6 months of the study period, January to June, 1985, included only those cases that were found in the county court records and did not include cases identified through the records maintained by the state mental health department. The number of cases was substantially lower than in other observation periods, and since we were not confident that all the cases raising an insanity plea during this time period had been identified, these data were excluded from the analyses. As a result, the period after the reform actually includes only 2½ years of data rather than 3 years.) The counties included in the study were Alameda, Los Angeles, Orange, Sacramento, San Diego, San Francisco, and Santa Clara. We obtained information on 1,272 persons who pleaded insanity and 659 persons who were successfully acquitted NGRI from a search of more than 200,000 felony indictments in the court records of the study counties.

VOLUME OF CASES RAISING THE INSANITY DEFENSE IN CALIFORNIA

The number of cases using the insanity defense rose briefly during the first 1½ years of our study period and then began a steady decline. Figure 4.1 presents the number of insanity pleas, insanity acquittals, and felony indictments in the study counties of California during our study period. The information is presented in 6-month intervals. Insanity pleas rose during the first year of the study and reached a high of 173 in the second half of 1980. The number of pleas then started a sharp, steady decline to a low of 57 in the last half of 1984. Insanity acquittals followed a similar pattern, with small increases until January 1981 when they reached a high of 90. Then a sharp drop began, reaching a low of 32 in the last half of 1984. In contrast, felony indictments showed a gradual increase throughout the study period, from a low of 15,000 in the last half of 1979 to a high of more than 21,000 in the last half of 1984. So, while nearly 50% more felony cases were being processed in the California courts over these 6 years, the number of insanity pleas decreased by nearly two-thirds.

DECLINING USE OF INSANITY DEFENSE AND DETERMINATE SENTENCING

The plea rate, the number of insanity pleas per 1,000 indictments, for each 6-month period in California is presented in Figure 4.2. The plea rates for the first six observation periods preceded the 1982 reform while the

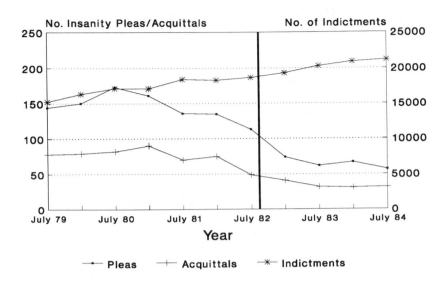

FIGURE 4.1. Number of insanity pleas, insanity acquittals, and felony indictments (right axis) in study counties of California before and after the 1982 insanity test reform.

plea rates for the remaining five periods followed the reform. The plea rate dropped from a high of 10 per 1,000 felony indictments in the second half of 1980 to a low of 3 per 1,000 in the second half of 1984. The plea rates for the time periods subsequent to the test reform were obviously lower than those for the time periods before the reform. There was, however, a general decline in the plea rate over the complete study period, and there was no change in the plea rate associated with the enactment of the new insanity test ($p < .174$).

Over the course of the study period the plea rate (per 1,000 indictments) was declining by 0.8 pleas per 6-month period, or roughly 1.5 per year. We had no reason to expect such a steady and steep decline. What the data suggested, however, was that the decline in the volume and rate of insanity pleas began well before the reform in July 1982 and continued after the reform. The fact that our information on insanity pleas was limited to just 3 years prior to the reform made it difficult to ascertain exactly what the longer term pattern might have been. Based on the data we have, it would seem that there was a downturn in insanity pleas in late 1980 and early 1981.

One potential explanation for the observed downturn was a "get tough" attitude in California that fostered changes in sentencing practices and the

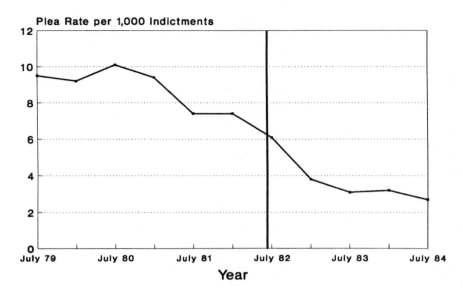

FIGURE 4.2. Insanity defense plea rate (number of insanity pleas per 1,000 felony indictments) in study counties of California before and after the 1982 insanity test reform.

Each time period denoted by July represents the second 6 months of the year, and the period in between, which is not labeled, represents the first 6 months of the following year.

determinate commitment of insanity acquittals. In 1977, California adopted determinate sentencing for convicted defendants. In 1978, the California Supreme Court found that equal protection precluded persons committed to state institutions following acquittal for criminal offenses on grounds of insanity from being retained in institutional confinement indefinitely or beyond the maximum term of punishment for the underlying offense (*In re Moye*). In September 1979, the California legislature responded to the 1978 court decision by mandating a maximum term of commitment for those acquitted NGRI that equaled the longest term of imprisonment that could have been imposed for the offense *disregarding* any "good-time" credit applicable to those convicted. Since good-time credit, which can accumulate up to 50% of the sentence, was not included in the maximum term of confinement, persons acquitted NGRI were given commitment terms that were longer than if they had been found guilty.

David Guthman, a Los Angeles district attorney specializing in insanity cases, indicated in a telephone interview that the determinate sentences associated with most offenses were subsequently increased by the legislature, which in turn increased the maximum term of confinement for insanity acquittees. The increasing terms of confinement, plus hospitals' tendency to routinely keep patients to their maximum term (Turner & Ornstein, 1983), made defense attorneys increasingly reluctant to use the insanity defense with their clients (J. Monahan, personal communication, April 23, 1991). Thus it appears that the 1982 reform of the insanity test had less to do with producing a lower rate of insanity pleas and acquittals than changes in sentencing guidelines and criminal commitment laws; in other words, the latter produced a long-range trend that was much more significant than the insanity test reform.

THE SUCCESS RATE OF INSANITY PLEAS DID NOT CHANGE

Figure 4.3 presents the success rate, or the percentage of successful insanity pleas raised by the defense, for each 6-month period in the study. The percentage of successful cases was fairly stable throughout the study period. It was highest (52%) in the first half of 1981 and lowest (38%) in the second half of 1982. The success rate, like the plea rate, did not change significantly with the enactment of the 1982 reform ($p < .155$). Unlike the plea rate, which showed a steady decline, the percentage of successful cases remained fairly stable, fluctuating between 40% and 50% of those who raised the insanity plea.

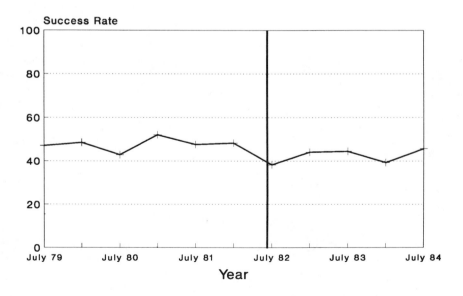

FIGURE 4.3. Percentage of insanity pleas acquitted NGRI in study counties of California before and after the 1982 insanity test reform.

To determine whether these results were different for various types of crimes, we broke crimes into two categories, violent and nonviolent. Violent crimes included murder, physical assault, rape, arson, and kidnapping. Nonviolent crimes included robbery and other nonviolent felonies. Figure 4.4 displays the percentage of successful cases for both types of offenses. Neither success rate changed significantly with the enactment of the new standard (violent crimes, $p < .507$; nonviolent crimes, $p < .364$). It is clear that the likelihood of a successful insanity defense was higher for cases involving a violent crime than for cases involving a nonviolent crime; between 47% and 62% of defendants charged with a violent crime were successful, while only 13% to 48% of those charged with nonviolent offenses were successful.

The success rates for nonviolent crimes were much more variable than those for violent crimes. Moreover, the success rates for nonviolent crimes appeared to be lower after the reform than before the reform, although the difference was not significant. Although this result was somewhat counterintuitive, since one would expect reforms to impact more on violent crimes than on nonviolent ones, we found a similar phenomenon in both New York and Georgia where the success rate for insanity pleas for nonviolent crimes dropped after a reform of the insanity defense.

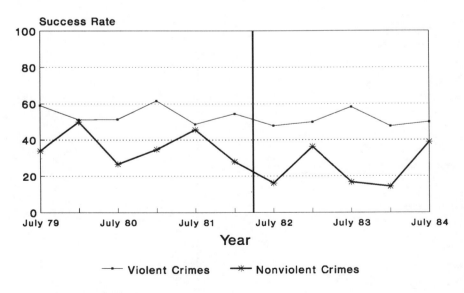

FIGURE 4.4. Percentage of insanity pleas acquitted NGRI by violent and nonviolent crimes in study counties of California before and after the 1982 insanity test reform.

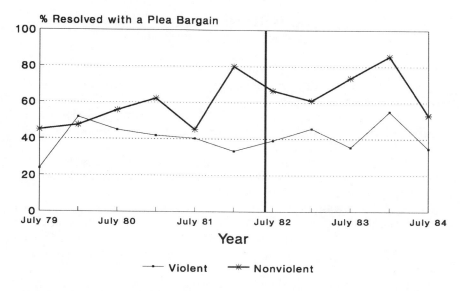

FIGURE 4.5. Percentage of insanity pleas resolved with a plea bargain by violent and nonviolent crimes, in study counties of California before and after the 1982 insanity test reform.

To examine this issue further, we looked at the method of adjudications: judge, jury, or plea bargain. We thought that perhaps those charged with nonviolent offenses were continuing to plead insanity but, once they learned of the potential consequences of an acquittal, they plea bargained to a lesser guilty charge. As illustrated in Figure 4.5, the percentage of all nonviolent insanity defense cases who had their case resolved with a plea bargain increased dramatically in 1982. Before that time, 51% of defendants charged with nonviolent crimes used a plea bargain. After the reform, 70% were resolved with a plea bargain. Further, over 80% of the defendants plea bargained to a guilty verdict, rather than to an NGRI verdict. The dramatic increase in insanity cases agreeing to accept a guilty plea occurred at the beginning of 1982, 2 years after the enactment of the maximum term of commitment legislation and 6 months before the target reform. Because of the lag in time, it is hard to know whether the observed increase in the percentage of cases resolved by plea bargain was the indirect result of instituting a maximum term of commitment or anticipatory of the reform. The fact that the legislature subsequently increased the term of commitment associated with various crimes may have accentuated the initial effect and produced the lag we observed.

THE CHARACTERISTICS OF PERSONS USING
THE DEFENSE WERE UNCHANGED

Having found no strong evidence that the 1982 change in the insanity test affected the overall rate of use or the success of an insanity defense, we examined whether there were any changes in who used the insanity defense and/or who was successful. We found no systematic changes in the composition of either the plea or the acquittal group associated with the enactment of the 1982 reform.

Defendants entering the insanity plea were in their early 30s, male (91%), and diagnosed with a major mental illness (69%). We defined major mental illness as a diagnosis of schizophrenia, of another psychosis, or of a major affective disorder. Approximately half (46%) of those raising the insanity defense were nonwhite. The demographic characteristics remained generally stable over the study period, as did diagnoses. The average age increased slightly, from 31 years before the reform to 33 years after the reform.

The characteristics of the acquittal group also remained stable across our study period. The average age for acquittals prior to the reform was 32 years and after the reform was 34 years. The composition of the acquittal group generally mirrored that of the plea group. In terms of diagnosis, however, the difference between those acquitted NGRI and those pleading insanity was striking. A much larger proportion of the NGRI acquittals were diagnosed with a major mental illness (84%) as compared to those defendants raising the plea (69%). As expected, defendants pleading insanity who were diagnosed with a major mental illness were more likely to be acquitted than those with less-serious diagnoses.

Figure 4.6 shows the percentage of defendants charged with violent offenses. Across the study period about 66% of defendants who pleaded insanity and roughly 74% of all those who were acquitted by reason of insanity were involved in violent crimes. While there was some fluctuation, the overall percentage was fairly stable. These data show, as did the disaggregated success rates discussed earlier, that defendants pleading insanity for cases involving a violent crime are more likely to be acquitted.

We also examined the victims of the crimes associated with an insanity plea in which there was a victim. Two measures of victim type were included: the gender of the victim and the existence of a familial relationship between the defendant and the victim. Over the study period, approximately 52% of the cases involved a female victim, and 20% involved a victim who was related to the defendant. The patterns were similar for both the pleas and acquittals on both measures. Type of victim seemed to have little to do with the success of an insanity plea, and the distribution of victim types did not change with the reform of the insanity test.

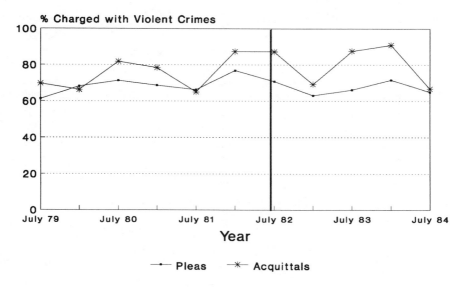

FIGURE 4.6. Percentage of defendants pleading insanity and those acquitted NGRI charged with violent crimes in study counties of California before and after the 1982 insanity test reform.

We found no change in the method of disposition for those using the insanity defense as a result of the reform. The method of disposition was fairly stable throughout the study period, although some change was observed in the first part of the study period. Insanity pleas were more likely to be successful when the cases were disposed of by a judge and less likely to lead to an NGRI acquittal when tried before a jury or settled by a plea bargain. Other studies (Smith & Hall, 1982; McGraw, Farthing-Capowich, & Keilitz, 1985) have found similarly high percentages of NGRI acquittals occurring before a judge. Smith and Hall found that the majority of NGRI bench trials in Michigan were cases in which both the defense and the prosecution tacitly agreed that an NGRI acquittal was appropriate. It is likely that only those cases in which there is significant disagreement between the defense and the prosecution regarding insanity actually go to a jury trial, a logical supposition that would explain why such a small percentage of the cases that do go to a jury are actually acquitted NGRI.

The characteristics of the defendants, the types of offenses for which an insanity plea was entered, the disposition of those persons raising the insanity defense, and the profile of those who were successful with the defense remained stable over time. There were no significant changes in these composition variables, either for the plea or acquittal groups, associated with the introduction of the 1982 change in the insanity test. Nor did we find any change in these composition variables that corresponded to the observed decline in the plea rate, with the possible exception of the increase in plea bargaining among nonviolent offenders. Whatever factors might have contributed to the decline in the use of the insanity plea, including the introduction of determinate sentencing, did not affect who was using the defense or who was successful. Similar types of people charged with similar crimes were using the insanity defense and being acquitted throughout the study period.

HOW LONG WERE INSANITY ACQUITTEES CONFINED?

We were also interested in changes in the length of time those acquitted NGRI were confined for psychiatric treatment before and after the reform. There was no significant change in the length of confinement of NGRI acquittals in any of three major crime categories—murder, other violent crimes, and nonviolent crimes—due to the reform. These findings were consistent with all the prior analyses presented in this chapter: California's 1982 change in the insanity defense test had no major impact on the practices associated with the insanity defense.

The analyses associated with the length of confinement information revealed a number of important facts. The results of our analysis contradicted popular belief that NGRI acquittals are allowed to go free (Hans, 1986). Over the complete study period, only 1% of all NGRI acquittees were actually released after their NGRI verdict without follow-up, 4% were placed on conditional release or were treated as outpatients, and 95% were hospitalized.

The NGRI acquittees' lengths of confinement varied considerably by crime. Over 50% of NGRI acquittees charged with murder were still hospitalized 6 years (2,196 days) after they were admitted to the hospital. Similarly, half of the NGRI acquittees charged with other violent offenses were still hospitalized after 3.5 years (median = 1,278 days), while the other half had been released. For those charged with nonviolent offenses, 50% were still hospitalized after nearly 3 years (938 days). Further, approximately 25% of all persons acquitted NGRI were still hospitalized after nearly 10 years. These data confirm that the vast majority of persons acquitted NGRI in California are hospitalized and that they are hospitalized for relatively long periods of time.

We also found a steady increase in the average sentence of those pleading insanity and found guilty and in the "maximum term of commitment" (the "sentence") for those defendants acquitted NGRI throughout the study period. The maximum term of commitment, for all insanity acquittees, is shown in Figure 4.7. It showed a steady increase from an average of 4.9

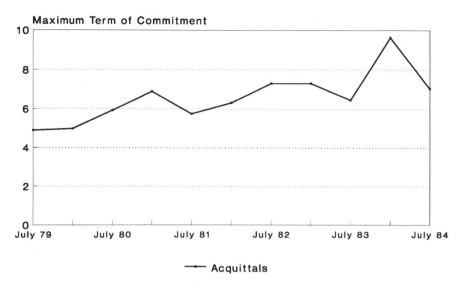

— Acquittals

FIGURE 4.7. Maximum term of commitment for persons acquitted NGRI in study counties of California before and after the 1982 insanity test reform.

years in 1979 to an average of 7.4 years by 1984. There was a significant negative correlation ($-.69$, $p < .001$) between the "sentence or maximum term of commitment" and the plea rate. For every 1-year increase in the average term of commitment, there was a decrease of 1.4 pleas (per 1,000 indictments) in the plea rate.

Although not related to the target reform, we found significant differences in the lengths of confinements of insanity acquittees when compared with length of incarceration of defendants who pleaded NGRI and were found guilty for the same types of crimes. Figures 4.8, 4.9, and 4.10 show the patterns of confinement for insanity acquittees and those convicted of murder, of other violent offenses, and of nonviolent offenses. For murder, the length of confinement for insanity acquittees was less than for those convicted ($p < .001$). However, this was *not* the case for other violent or nonviolent offenses. For other violent offenses, insanity acquittees were more likely to be confined and they stayed longer than those convicted (median length of stay was 1,238 days vs. 603 days). Similar patterns were observed for nonviolent offenses: the median length of stay for insanity acquittees was nearly ten times as long as those convicted (938 days vs. 99 days). These data strongly suggest that mentally ill offenders charged with nonviolent offenses would be better off not by pleading insanity, but by pleading guilty and serving their terms of incarceration.

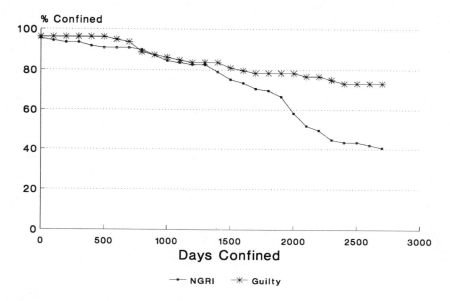

FIGURE 4.8. Confinement patterns of insanity defendants acquitted NGRI and convicted for murder in study counties of California: 1978–1984.

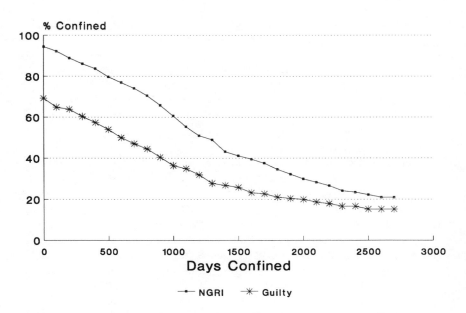

FIGURE 4.9. Confinement patterns of insanity defendants acquitted NGRI and convicted for other violent offenses in study counties of California: 1978–1984.

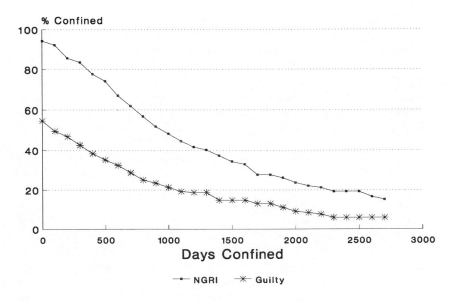

FIGURE 4.10. Confinement patterns of insanity defendants acquitted NGRI and convicted for nonviolent offenses in study counties of California: 1978–1984.

CHANGING THE INSANITY TEST DID NOT AFFECT USE OF THE INSANITY DEFENSE

Changing the insanity test is one of the most visible ways any jurisdiction can express its attitude toward defendants judged not to be responsible for their criminal behavior. California's 1982 reform of its insanity test was even more expressive of public sentiment than other changes: it was done by voter referendum, as part of Proposition 8. Our data indicate that California's reform accompanied a downturn in the volume and rate of insanity pleas and acquittals in California that was already well underway. The reform was not the cause of the decline. The sharp decline in California began in 1980, well before the insanity test was changed.

Due to the decreasing number and rate of insanity pleas in California at the time of the reform, the expectation of its proponents that it would reduce the volume of insanity acquittals appeared to be met, but in fact the reform had little impact. A decline in insanity pleas and acquittals had begun prior to the reform, and this decline simply continued. It was not accentuated in any way by changing the insanity test. The apparent decline linked to the reform is illusory.

The reform was nothing more than an expression of the public's growing concern about crime and its desire for greater punishment for the perpetrators. The late 1970s saw an increasingly less tolerant attitude toward criminal defendants throughout the nation (LaFond & Durham, 1992; Rackmill, 1991). There was increasing dissatisfaction with the rehabilitative ideology and repeated calls for new approaches, including deterrence and punishment-oriented philosophies, to deal with criminal defendants. This change in philosophy, coupled with a growing awareness of severe disparities in sentencing (Von Hirsch, 1976), due to judicial discretion in the sentencing process, brought about the advent of determinate or mandatory sentencing in many jurisdictions across the country. In 1982, 37 states had mandatory sentencing laws (Rackmill, 1991), but by 1983, 49 states had such laws for select crimes (LaFond & Durham, 1992).

The move to mandatory sentences resulted in increased sentences for many offenders and contributed to an increase in prison populations. The United States Bureau of Prisons noted that the average time served for robbery following implementation of determinate sentencing increased from 46 months to 64 months and for drug offenses it increased from 18 to 57 months (Rackmill, 1991). Further, a report to Congress by the General Accounting Office (1987) indicated the potential effect of determinate sentencing on the federal criminal justice system; the report predicted a dramatic increase in federal prison populations due to enhanced prosecution, mandatory sentences for drug offenders, and the repeat felon laws.

Perhaps this "get-tough" attitude brought about the decline in the use of the insanity defense in California. California cracked down on criminals earlier than many states. It adopted mandatory or determinate sentencing in 1977 and funded the construction of new prisons in the 1980s to meet the needs of its growing prison population, which more than doubled (an increase of 148%) following the advent of mandatory sentencing. It is likely that linking the confinement of insanity acquittals to the determinate sentence associated with those convicted of similar offenses, as California did with the In re Moye (1978) decision, will result in a similar increase in the population of persons detained in hospitals following acquittal by reason of insanity. In fact, our data suggest this has already occurred. The fact that insanity acquittees charged with nonviolent offenses were more likely to be confined and stayed for longer terms than those convicted suggests a major buildup of acquittees has already begun.

5

Changing the Burden and Standard of Proof: Georgia and New York

Shifting the burden of proof from the prosecution to the defense—a reform in the adjudication stage of the criminal process—is commonly believed to have a powerful influence on diminishing the use of the insanity defense. To date, however, no empirical study exists of its actual effects. This reform involves a fundamental change in the process of establishing the basic facts in insanity cases. At the beginning of our research we believed that changing the burden of proof would lead to a reduction in the volume and rate of insanity pleas and would affect the composition of those raising the plea by reducing the percentage of cases with less serious charges that would not make it "worth" the defense's efforts to meet the increased burden. We looked at this reform in two states, Georgia and New York. Georgia shifted the burden of proof to the defendant in January 1978; New York made the same change in November 1984.

LEGAL DEBATES REGARDING BURDEN AND STANDARD OF PROOF

One of the most controversial aspects of John Hinckley's 1982 acquittal was the fact that the burden of proof in his trial rested on the prosecution

to prove Hinckley was sane beyond a reasonable doubt when he attempted
to assassinate President Reagan. Critics of Hinckley's acquittal argued that
it is virtually impossible to prove that *anyone* is sane "beyond a reasonable
doubt" (Caplan, 1984). They argued that while it was traditional in criminal cases to place the burden of proof on the state, based on the assumption of the defendant's innocence, such a demand was unfair in insanity
cases because of the complexity of psychiatric testimony and the ease of
raising a reasonable doubt about sanity.

At the time of Hinckley's 1982 acquittal, federal courts, along with a
majority of state courts, required the prosecution to bear the burden of
proof in insanity cases. That is, once the defense introduced evidence in
support of an insanity plea, the prosecution was required to prove the
defendant's sanity beyond a reasonable doubt. Following Hinckley's acquittal, between 1982 and 1990, 16 states made changes in their burden and
standard of proof for insanity cases. After these reforms, a large majority
of state courts (75%) and the federal courts required the defense to prove
the defendant was insane either by a preponderance of the evidence or by
clear and convincing evidence.

The question of who should bear the burden of proof in an insanity
defense case has been the subject of some debate among legal scholars
(Simon & Aaronson, 1988; Hermann, 1983). Common law requires not only
the commission of an act, but also *mens rea*—a guilty mind. Under the
due process clause, the state is required to prove each "element" of a criminal offense beyond a reasonable doubt (*In re Winship*, 1970). Proponents
of placing the burden of proof on the state argue that sanity is an element
of the crime. They maintain that legal insanity negates the ability to form
intent, and therefore to present its case successfully the state must prove
that a defendant was sane at the time the criminal act was committed.

Those who advocate placing the burden on the defense contend that
sanity is not an "element" of the offense that must be proven by the prosecution. Instead, they argue, the insanity defense recognizes that a defendant who cannot know or appreciate the wrongfulness of the act may not
be criminally culpable even if he or she had the "intent" required for conviction. These scholars distinguish between evidence that would negate
"intent" and evidence that would relate to a defendant's sanity (Hermann,
1983). Hence, the state must still bear the burden of proof of all the requisite elements of the crime, but the defense must bear the burden of proof
of insanity.

The Supreme Court first considered the constitutionality of placing
the burden of proof on the defense in *Davis v. United States* (1895). In its
decision, the Court ruled that *in federal courts* sanity was an element in
the crime of murder and that the burden of proof rested on the state to
prove all elements of the crime beyond a reasonable doubt. In *Leland v.
Oregon* (1952), the Court upheld the constitutional right of states to place

the burden of proof on the defendant, arguing that it did not violate due process rights. The court indicated that insanity could be a special or "affirmative" defense with the burden of proof on the defendant as long as the state met its burden of proving all elements of the crime beyond a reasonable doubt.

Since *Leland* the Court has continued to affirm and uphold the constitutionality of placing the burden of proof on the defense, arguing that insanity, like the other special defenses of self-defense or extreme emotional duress, is an affirmative defense in which the defense bears the burden of proof (*Rivera v. Delaware*, 1976; *Patterson v. New York*, 1977).

In addition to these constitutional issues, the locus of the burden of proof for insanity proceedings has become a controversial public policy issue. The debate, fueled by Hinckley's acquittal, centers on the impact the burden of proof has on the outcome of all insanity cases. It has been argued that the location of the burden of proof can be *a*, if not *the*, critical factor in the determination of outcome (Hermann, 1983). Legal scholars have argued that placing the burden of proof on the defense will decrease the likelihood of a successful insanity defense. In theory, when the burden of proof is on the state to prove a defendant's sanity, the defendant has only to raise a reasonable doubt as to his or her sanity in order to be acquitted. Shifting the burden to the defendant *may* make acquittal much more difficult for the defense, as they must now establish insanity by either a preponderance of the evidence or by clear and convincing evidence.

In practice, placing the burden of proof on the defense might lead to the conviction of a number of defendants who, in actuality, are mentally ill, but unable to legally establish their insanity (Hermann, 1983). By contrast, in states where the burden of proof for insanity is on the prosecution, it is possible that some defendants who are not truly insane may be found insane and acquitted because they are able to establish a reasonable doubt regarding their sanity. Morse (1985:145) stated that placing the burden of proof on the defense "would minimize the risk of an insanity defense in questionable cases, and at the same time permit the defense to succeed in the few cases in which it is morally proper." Morse also posited that placing the burden of proof on the prosecution would increase the number of insanity cases because the burden of proof would be so difficult.

Professional organizations vary in their positions about who should bear the burden of proof in insanity cases. The American Bar Association (1984) recommended that the burden of proof be on the state when the McNaughtan test for insanity is the law, and that the burden be on the defense when the ALI test is applied. Concurrently, the United States Department of Justice proposed that the burden be placed on the defendant with a standard of a preponderance of the evidence for states using either the McNaughtan or the ALI test. While the American Psychiatric Association did not take a position on who should have the burden of proof, it recognized the assumptions underlying burden and standard reforms when it stated that "[i]t is commonly believed that the likely effect of assigning the burden of proof to defendants rather than to the state in insanity trials will be to decrease the number of such successful defenses" (Mental Disability Law Reporter, 1983:146).

Likewise, there is considerable diversity among individual professionals on the issues of the burden of proof in insanity cases. Simon and Aaronson (1988) reported results from a July 1982 (post-Hinckley) survey of professionals including judges, prosecutors, defense attorneys, and forensic experts. Respondents were asked which party should shoulder the burden of proof. Not surprisingly, public defenders and private attorneys were the only groups of legal experts who believed the state should have the responsibility. Also not surprisingly, judges and prosecutors believed the defense should bear the burden of proof. But more "neutral" professionals, including forensic psychiatrists, forensic psychologists, and mental health directors, also believed that the defense should have the burden of proof.

Not everyone has agreed that changes in the burden and standard would have an impact on the insanity defense. While considering a reform in the insanity defense in New York State, Melvin Miller, then-chairman of the New York State Assembly's Codes Committee, argued (*New York Times*, May 17, 1984:A26) that the reform "won't make much practical difference in the few insanity pleas in New York courts each year." William French Smith, U.S. Attorney General under President Ronald Reagan, believed that the defense should bear the burden of proof because of symbolic reasons, but he also stated (Smith, 1982:613) that shifting the burden of proof to the defendant "would probably make little practical difference."

While many states have enacted burden and standard of proof reforms, to date no empirical investigations have been conducted regarding the effects of these reforms on insanity proceedings. We included Georgia and New York in our research to address these issues. The same changes in burden and standard of proof were made in both states. The burden was shifted from the prosecution to the defense and the standard of insanity was lowered from "beyond reasonable doubt" to "by a preponderance of the evidence."

The timing and context of the reforms differed. The Georgia reform (1978) predated the insanity trial of John Hinckley, and also predated a major revision of Georgia's insanity defense laws in 1982 that included the enactment of the guilty but mentally ill plea and verdict (see Chapter 7). The New York reform in 1984 occurred after the Hinckley verdict; it also followed upon an earlier reform in 1980 of the commitment and release procedures for insanity acquittees (see Chapter 6). New York was one of 16 states that shifted the burden of proof to the defendant after Hinckley's acquittal. These reforms provided two distinct cases in which the impact of burden and standard reforms could be assessed. We will present each case separately and then compare the findings to highlight similarities and differences between the two states' experiences.

GEORGIA

In January 1978, Georgia shifted the burden of proof in insanity cases to the defense by a preponderance of the evidence (see Appendix C, Georgia Criminal Procedure Law, Section 27-1503). To determine the impact of this reform we collected data for 2 years before and 3 years after the reform in 12 counties in Georgia: Bibb, Chatham, Cherokee, Clarke, Cobb, DeKalb, Dougherty, Floyd, Fulton, Newton, Richmond, and Thomas. We obtained information on 1,072 insanity pleas and 246 acquittals from 69,093 indictments reviewed.

The Use of the Insanity Defense Decreased

Figure 5.1 depicts the number of insanity pleas, insanity acquittals, and felony indictments from January 1976 to December 1980 by 6-month inter-

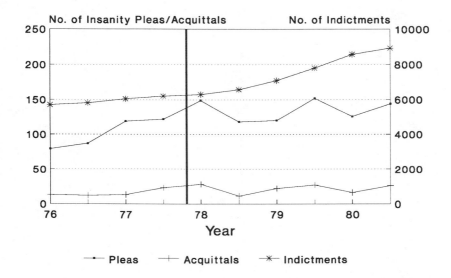

FIGURE 5.1. Number of insanity pleas, insanity acquittals, and felony indictments (right axis) in study counties of Georgia before and after the 1978 burden and standard reform.

vals. The first four time periods include cases that occurred prior to the reform, and the last six time periods include cases that occurred after the burden and standard changes. In general, the volume of insanity pleas was increasing prior to the reform, at which point it became more level despite continued fluctuation. The number of acquittals remained relatively constant, with periods of fluctuation across the study years.

The plea rate—the number of insanity pleas per 1,000 felony indictments—is shown in Figure 5.2 for each 6-month period. Prior to the reform, the plea rate was increasing by approximately 2.2 insanity pleas per 1,000 felony indictments every 6 months. The increase continued into the first half of 1978, after which time it reversed. The actual number of pleas then leveled off, while the number of felony indictments continued to increase. Thus, the plea rate began to decline by approximately 1.3 pleas per 1,000 indictments every 6 months. This represents a significant ($p <$ .05) decline in the plea rate due to the reform.

These data indicate that shifting the burden of proof to the defense did indeed reduce the rate of use of the insanity defense. This finding supports the contention of people who have maintained that placing the burden of proof on the defendant will decrease use of the insanity defense. In Georgia, we found that the insanity plea was used less often when the burden of proof fell on the defense to establish insanity than when it rested with the state.

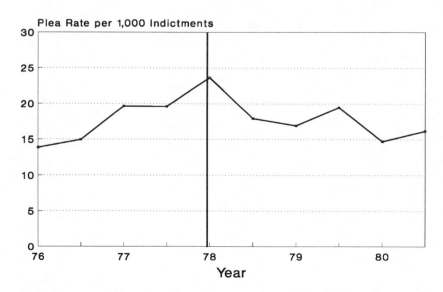

FIGURE 5.2. Insanity defense plea rate (number of insanity pleas per 1,000 felony indictments) in study counties of Georgia before and after the 1978 burden and standard reform.

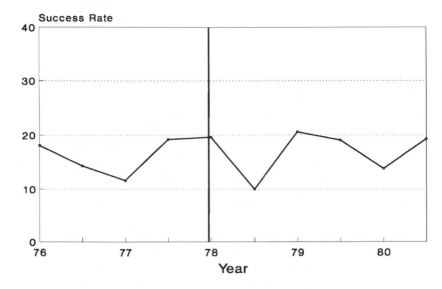

FIGURE 5.3. Percentage of insanity pleas acquitted NGRI in study counties of Georgia before and after the 1978 burden and standard reform.

Likelihood of a Successful Insanity Plea: No Change

The success rate, or percentage of insanity pleas acquitted NGRI, is shown in Figure 5.3 by 6-month periods. There was no change in the success rates associated with the reform. On average, 17% of all persons raising the insanity defense were acquitted NGRI over the entire study period. Shifting the burden of proof to the defense did not lead to a change in the overall probability that defendants would be acquitted by reason of insanity once they had introduced an insanity plea. These results are somewhat surprising. Most arguments regarding the burden and standard of proof suggest that fewer pleas will be successful when the burden is placed on the defense, leading ultimately to a decrease in the use of the insanity defense. In Georgia, we found that changing the burden and standard of proof did not impact on the overall success rate for insanity pleas, even though we did see a decline in the plea rate.

Obviously, a rate may remain constant while the number and characteristics of the people included in the rate may vary widely. In the case of defendants pleading insanity, perhaps shifting the burden to the defense could have altered not only how often the plea was raised, but also the type of person who raised the plea and the type of person who was acquitted. In order to better understand what was happening, we next analyzed the characteristics of all persons employing the insanity defense and of all persons acquitted not guilty by reason of insanity both before and after Georgia shifted its burden and standard of proof in insanity cases in 1978.

Defendant Characteristics: The Imperative of Diagnosis

The percentage of insanity defendants, both pleading and acquitted NGRI, that were diagnosed with a major mental illness (schizophrenia, another psychosis, or a major affective disorder) is displayed in Figure 5.4. Although a slightly larger percentage of defendants raising the insanity plea were diagnosed with a major mental illness after the reform than before, the pattern for those acquitted was very striking. While roughly 60% of those acquitted prior to the reform were diagnosed with a major mental illness, nearly 90% of those acquitted subsequent to the reform were so diagnosed. This finding suggests that the relationship between diagnosis and verdict changed dramatically with the enactment of the reform.

Prior to the reform, a defendant diagnosed with a major mental illness was 1.4 times more likely to be acquitted by reason of insanity than a defendant without such a diagnosis. Following the reform, defendants with a major mental illness were 8.4 times as likely to be acquitted by reason of insanity than defendants not diagnosed with a major mental illness. In other

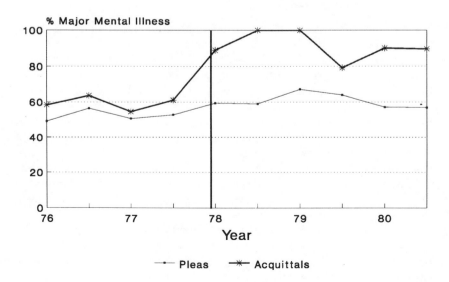

FIGURE 5.4. Percentage of insanity pleas and insanity acquittals diagnosed with a major mental illness in study counties of Georgia before and after the 1978 burden and standard reform.

words, after the reform a defendant with a major mental illness was 6 times more likely to be acquitted than a defendant with a major mental illness before the reform. This finding strongly suggests that placing the burden on the defense will have an impact on who is acquitted even though it had little, if any, effect on the volume of insanity acquittals or the rate of success. It is not surprising that acquittees who must prove their insanity are more likely to be seriously mentally ill than those who have only to raise a reasonable doubt about their sanity.

There were no significant changes in the demographic characteristics of either those pleading insanity or those acquitted NGRI associated with the 1978 burden and standard reform. The average age of defendants raising the plea was 28 years and 31 years for those acquitted. Almost all were males (92%). Roughly 60% of defendants raising the insanity defense and acquitted NGRI were nonwhite. While there was a general increase over time in the proportion of nonwhite defendants using the plea, there was no change associated with the reform.

The proportion of defendants pleading insanity who were charged with violent crimes did change as a result of the reform. For both those defendants raising the plea and those acquitted, the proportion charged with a violent offense was increasing prior to the reform, but leveled off at the time of the reform. As Figure 5.5 indicates, the average percentage of acquittees charged with violent crimes (50%) exceeded that of those pleading (36%). The probability of being acquitted by reason of insanity was greater throughout the study period for cases involving violent offenses than for cases involving nonviolent crimes.

We also examined our data to determine whether there was an interaction effect for diagnosis and violent crimes, that is, to discover if there were any special combinations of crimes and diagnoses that had higher or lower probabilities of success. We found that defendants charged with violent offenses who had a diagnosis of a major mental illness were significantly ($p < .05$) more likely to be acquitted after the reform than before it. In contrast, those defendants who were diagnosed with mental problems other than a major mental illness were less likely to be acquitted after the reform, regardless of whether they were charged with a violent or a nonviolent offense. There was no change in the success rate for those defendants diagnosed with a major mental illness who were charged with a nonviolent offense: they were acquitted at the same rate after the reform as before. These findings demonstrate the importance of a diagnosis of major mental illness for a successful insanity plea when the burden of proof is on the defense.

There were no changes in the method by which insanity cases were adjudicated. As we discussed with regard to other states, most cases in which the defendant pleaded insanity were resolved by plea bargains (60%) both before and after the burden and standard reform. However, the major-

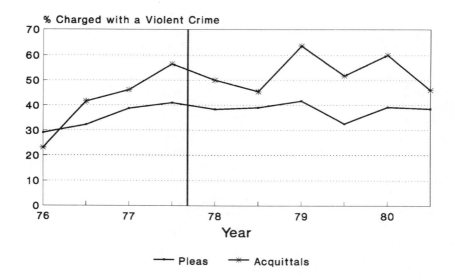

FIGURE 5.5. Percentage of insanity pleas and insanity acquittals charged with a violent crime in study counties of Georgia before and after the 1978 burden and standard reform.

ity of cases (62%) in which a defendant was acquitted NGRI were bench trials. Only a small percentage of successful insanity pleas were resolved by either a plea bargain (10%) or a jury trial (28%). These patterns were fairly stable over time.

For crimes involving a victim, we found no changes in the victim characteristics after the reform. We did discover notable differences in the crime victim characteristics associated with those pleading insanity and those who were acquitted. For defendants raising the plea, 31% of the cases involved a victim who was related to the defendant and 56% of the victims were female. For defendants acquitted, 61% of the victims were related to the defendant and 46% were female. Clearly, in Georgia, defendants who victimize relatives are more likely to be acquitted than those who offend against strangers. To a lesser extent, insanity acquittees were more likely to have offended against males than against females.

Our results indicate that the Georgia burden and standard reform affected the characteristics of both those who pleaded insanity and those who were acquitted. The reform appeared to halt an increasing use of the insanity defense by defendants charged with violent offenses. The clearest impact of the reform, however, was on the relationship between diagnosis and chance of acquittal. After the 1978 reform, virtually all defendants who proved that they were insane at the time of the crime had been diagnosed as having a major mental illness such as schizophrenia or a major affective disorder. While it was possible to succeed without such a diagnosis, it was highly unlikely (10%).

No Change in Length of Confinement

We next examined the disposition and confinement patterns of insanity defendants who were either found guilty or who were acquitted as not guilty by reason of insanity. There were no significant changes in the disposition of insanity acquittees. Both before and after the reform all were hospitalized.

The length of confinement of insanity acquittees before and after the reform is displayed in Figure 5.6. To best test for possible changes, we disaggregated this information by three major crime categories: murder, other violent crimes (physical assault, rape, arson, and kidnapping), and nonviolent crimes (robbery, burglary, and other minor felonies). We found no significant change associated with the reform in any category. This was not surprising since the reform did not in any way effect the commitment or release procedures of those acquitted. The median length of confine-

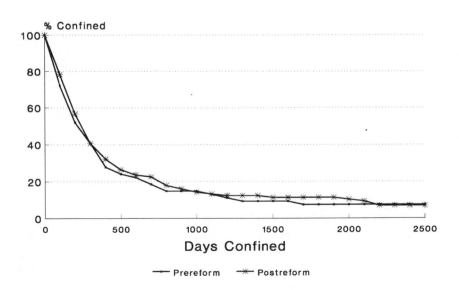

FIGURE 5.6. Confinement patterns of insanity defendants acquitted NGRI for all crimes in study counties of Georgia before and after the 1978 burden and standard reform.

ment for NGRIs—the number of days at which half of the defendants were released and half were still confined—for those charged with murder was virtually the same (1,097 days vs. 1,095 days) before and after the reform. Likewise, there was little change in the median length of confinement for those NGRIs with other violent offenses (202 days vs. 247 days) or non-violent offenses (188 days vs. 232 days).

The Net Results in Georgia

The Georgia data revealed that changing the burden and standard of proof was associated with a reduced rate of use of the insanity defense, as well as with changes in who raised the defense and who was acquitted. The reform had no impact on the length of confinement for insanity defendants. The Georgia data allowed us to investigate the impact of a burden and standard reform that was enacted prior to the Hinckley case. In the next section we present the results of New York's burden and standard reform, enacted eight years later, soon after John Hinckley's acquittal.

NEW YORK

In November 1984, New York revised its insanity defense laws to make insanity an affirmative defense. Prior to enactment, the state had to prove beyond a reasonable doubt that the defendant was sane at the time of the crime in order to convict the defendant. Subsequent to enactment, insanity defendants had to prove by a preponderance of the evidence that they were insane at the time of the crime in order to be acquitted by reason of insanity.

To determine the effect of this reform, we gathered data on all persons raising the insanity defense from January 1982 through October 1987 in five counties: Bronx, Kings (Brooklyn), Queens, Nassau, and Erie (Buffalo). We obtained information on 294 insanity pleas and 114 acquittals from over 135,000 felony indictments.

Use of the Insanity Defense: An Accelerated Decline

Figure 5.7 presents the number of felony indictments, insanity pleas, and insanity acquittals from 1982 to 1987. The first six observations occurred prior to New York's burden and standard reform; the last six occurred after the reform. The numbers in the last observation period (second half of 1987) are very low because we only obtained information for 4 of the 6 months in the period. Prior to the reform, the number of insanity pleas had been declining. It continued to decline after the reform, with an abrupt drop in the number of pleas immediately after the reform. Acquittals also showed

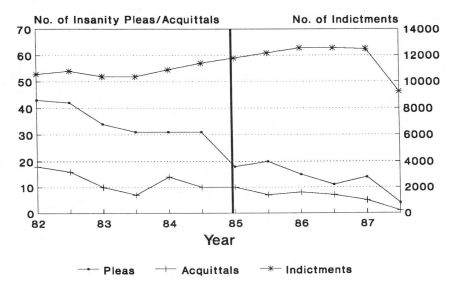

FIGURE 5.7. Number of insanity pleas, insanity acquittals, and felony indictments (right axis) in study counties of New York before and after the 1984 burden and standard reform.

a general decline. Although there was a sudden increase at the beginning of 1984, it was followed by a continued decline. In contrast to the declines seen in the volume of insanity pleas and acquittals, the number of felony indictments was increasing over time.

To determine the effect of the change in burden and standard on the use of the insanity defense, we also analyzed the plea rate—the number of insanity pleas per 1,000 felony indictments. Figure 5.8 displays the plea rate for each 6-month period. Use of the insanity defense in the study counties was infrequent and was steadily declining throughout the study period. At its peak, there were only 4.1 insanity pleas per 1,000 felony indictments. Across the entire study period, there was an average of only 2.2 insanity pleas per 1,000 felony indictments.

Even with the overall decline in the insanity plea rate across the study period, there was a significant change ($p < .05$) in the rate of use associated with the reform. This result was due to the large decline in the plea rate immediately following the shift in burden and standard. After this sharp drop, it continued to decline at about the same rate (0.21 pleas per 6-month period) as it had prior to the reform (0.29 per 6-month period). These findings suggest that shifting the burden of proof to the defense accelerated an already declining use of the insanity defense. The insanity defense was

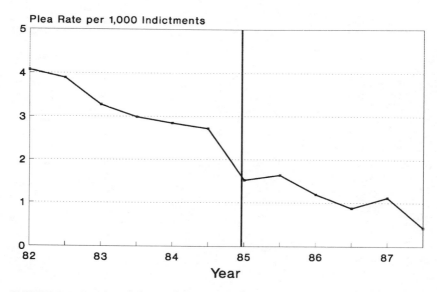

FIGURE 5.8. Insanity defense plea rate (number of insanity pleas per 1,000 felony indictments) in study counties of New York before and after the 1984 burden and standard reform.

rarely used in New York in the early 1980s, and our analyses suggest it became even rarer after the 1984 reform. For example, out of the 21,730 felony indictments in the first 10 months of 1987 in the five study counties, we found only 18 cases (0.08%) that involved an insanity defense.

We conclude that the infrequency with which the insanity defense is used in New York reflects both the effects of the change in the burden of proof that occurred in 1984 as well as changes in the commitment and release procedures that occurred in 1980 (discussed in Chapter 6). The combination of strict release procedures and the requirement that the defense bear the burden of proving a defendant's insanity greatly reduced use of the insanity defense in New York during the 1980s.

Likelihood of a Successful Insanity Plea

We next examined the success rate, the percentage of insanity pleas resulting in acquittal by reason of insanity. The total number of insanity pleas entered and resolved during the study period was small ($N = 285$). This sample size prohibited analysis of success rates for 6-month intervals. Figure 5.9 displays the success rate by year, but with so few observations it was impossible to analyze trends in the success rates. Thus, our statistical analysis relied on a pre-post design. The success rates were generally higher after the reform (48.1%) than they were prior to the reform (36.4%), and the difference was significant ($p < .10$).

These results are surprising, given many experts' belief that placing the burden on the defense would reduce the proportion of successful insanity defenses. One possible explanation for these findings is that shifting the burden to the defense detracted from the attractiveness of the insanity defense for those with "questionable" cases. Under these circumstances, a greater proportion of those who pleaded not guilty by reason of insanity after the reform consisted of those who were most likely to succeed. To investigate this possibility, we next checked whether there were reform-associated changes in the characteristics of those who used the insanity defense and those who were most likely to be acquitted.

Defendant Characteristics: Diagnosis, Violence, and Gender

Because of the small sample sizes, we used a pre-post design to examine defendant characteristics. Figure 5.10 displays the proportion of defendants

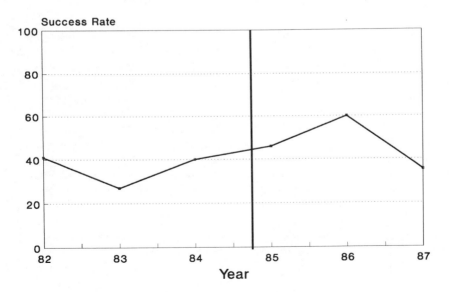

FIGURE 5.9. Percentage of insanity pleas who were successfully acquitted NGRI in study counties of New York before and after the 1984 burden and standard reform.

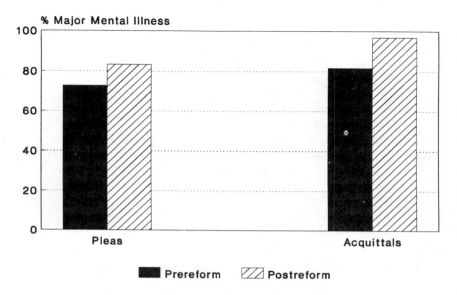

FIGURE 5.10. Percentage of insanity pleas and insanity acquittals diagnosed with a major mental illness in study counties of New York before and after the 1984 burden and standard reform.

who were diagnosed as having a major mental illness, for all defendants raising the insanity defense, and for all defendants who were acquitted by reason of insanity. Both before and after the reform, the majority of defendants raising the insanity defense were diagnosed with a major mental illness. The percentage of defendants pleading insanity who were diagnosed with a major mental illness rose slightly from 73% before the reform to 83% after the reform. The magnitude of the increase for acquittees was much larger: the percentage with a major mental illness increased from 82% to 97% ($p < .05$).

The chances of an NGRI acquittal were always higher for defendants diagnosed with a major mental illness than for defendants without such a diagnosis, but the discrepancy was even greater after the reform. Prior to the reform, a defendant diagnosed with a major mental illness was 6 times more likely to be acquitted by reason of insanity as a defendant without this diagnosis. Following the reform, defendants with a major mental illness were 47 times as likely to be acquitted by reason of insanity as were defendants without this diagnosis. As in Georgia after its 1978 reform, when the burden of proof was placed on the defense, a diagnosis of a major mental illness became almost essential for an insanity acquittal. When the state bore the burden of proof there was a much greater chance for a defendant without a major mental illness diagnosis to successfully plead insanity. This is strong evidence that shifting the burden of proof to the defense will tighten the use of the insanity defense by allowing a narrower range of diagnoses to warrant an NGRI acquittal.

Figure 5.11 shows the proportion of insanity cases in which the defendant was female. There was a small increase in the proportion of female defendants pleading insanity, with 11% before and 15% after the reform. However, the proportion of female acquittals actually doubled, increasing from 12% before to 24% after the reform. Likewise, the success rates for insanity pleas for women nearly doubled after the reform, increasing from 43% to 82%. Of the 11 women who raised the insanity defense after the reform, 9 were acquitted by reason of insanity. Both before and after New York's 1984 reform, women were more likely to be acquitted by reason of insanity than men were, but their success rate was substantially increased when the burden of proof was placed on the defense.

We also found that the proportion of insanity cases in which the defendant was charged with a violent crime increased significantly due to the reform. The percentage of insanity cases involving a violent crime increased from 65% to 78% ($p < .07$). Similarly, the percentage of acquittees charged with violent offenses increased from 73% to 92% ($p < .05$). As with defen-

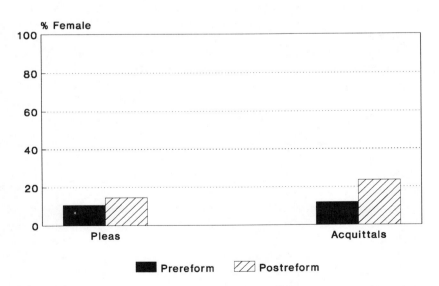

FIGURE 5.11. Percentage of defendants pleading insanity and acquitted NGRI who were female in study counties of New York before and after the 1984 burden and standard reform.

dant diagnosis and gender, the magnitude of the change for acquittals exceeded that for pleas. The success rate for cases involving a violent crime increased significantly from 42% to 56% ($p < .06$). In contrast, the success rate for cases involving nonviolent crimes decreased from 27% to 18%.

We found no significant interaction effect of diagnosis and crime in New York as we did in Georgia. This was probably due to the fact that the number of cases in the postreform period was so small.

Although it seems counterintuitive that the reform would result in the acquittal of a larger proportion of violent defendants, this finding is consistent with data from other states. Although much of the publicity associated with the insanity defense centers on violent crimes, and although one would assume that reforms are aimed primarily at the restriction of successful insanity pleas for violent crimes, in New York we found the opposite relationship. The success rate for insanity pleas related to violent crimes actually increased after the reform, and the success rate for nonviolent crimes decreased. Clearly, tightening the insanity defense makes it less attractive for those charged with less serious crimes. Apparently, defendants are not willing to risk the long period of confinement that accompanies an NGRI acquittal. Such restrictions apparently make the insanity defense worthwhile only for those charged with serious offenses.

When we investigated this further, we found that women who raised the insanity defense were more likely to have been involved in a violent crime than men who raised this defense. Likewise, defendants who pleaded insanity and who were diagnosed with a major mental illness were more likely to be charged with a violent crime than defendants who pleaded insanity without such a diagnosis. As already discussed, defendants' chances of an acquittal by reason of insanity were much higher for women than for men and for persons with a major mental illness than for those without a major mental illness. Furthermore, the percentage of insanity pleas that involved defendants with a major mental illness was slightly higher after the reform than it had been prior to the reform. Therefore, the increase in the success rate for violent crimes is probably associated with these patterns in defendant characteristics. That is, those persons who still wanted to raise the defense, females and defendants with major mental illness, were most likely to be charged with violent crimes, and they were also the defendants most likely to be found NGRI.

None of the other defendant and victim characteristics showed any significant changes due to the reform. The average age of persons pleading insanity was 30 years before the reform and 32 years after the reform. There was a similar increase for acquittees from 31 years to 33 years. The majority (roughly 62%) of defendants pleading insanity were nonwhite both before and after the reform.

We found no significant changes in victim characteristics either. The percentage of crimes with a female victim increased slightly for both the insanity plea group (from 48% to 54%) and the acquittal group (from 45%

to 50%). The percentage of cases involving a victim related to the defendant decreased for both pleas (from 34% to 31%) and acquittals (from 38% to 31%).

There were no significant changes in the method of adjudication for insanity pleas or acquittals. Across the study period, the vast majority of pleas were resolved by plea bargain (78%); very few cases were resolved by a bench trial (10%) or by a jury trial (12%). Plea bargain was also used in the preponderance of acquittals (85%). Contrary to common assumptions, only 5% of insanity acquittals were determined by a jury trial.

To sum up the results for New York, a number of changes in who used the defense and who succeeded occurred after the 1984 reform that shifted the burden and standard of proof in insanity cases to the defense. The proportion of defendants diagnosed with a major mental illness increased. Likewise, the proportion of insanity pleas involving violent crimes increased. Further, these types of defendants were more likely to be acquitted by reason of insanity.

Women were more likely to be acquitted than men, and the disparity in their relative success with the defense was greater when the burden was on the defense than when it had been on the state. As a result, the increase in the overall success rate was partially due to an increase in the number of cases involving women, defendants with a major mental illness, and violent offenses. Put another way, much of New York's increase in the overall success rate was due to the fact that more cases in which the insanity plea was raised involved defendants and crimes that were more likely to result in an NGRI acquittal.

In addition to changes in the pool of people pleading insanity, the success rates associated with certain characteristics changed. After the change in burden and standard, the chances of female defendants being found NGRI increased dramatically as did those of defendants with a major mental illness and those of defendants charged with a violent crime.

These results indicate that shifting the burden of proof to the defense in New York, as in Georgia, altered both who used the insanity defense and who was likely to be acquitted by reason of insanity. The increase in the overall success rate of insanity pleas was due to the reduction in its use by defendants who were generally unlikely to succeed with the defense. Furthermore, even though use of the insanity defense in New York was declining, the change in the burden of proof further reduced insanity acquittals, and of those defendants who were acquitted, more were seriously mentally ill.

Length of Confinement: A Change for Cases Involving Murder

The final set of issues we examined to discover the impact of New York's 1984 reform were the disposition and confinement patterns of insanity defendants who were either convicted of their charges or who were acquitted by reason of insanity. There was no change in the proportion of insanity acquittees who were hospitalized. Approximately 86% were hospitalized and 14% were placed on conditional release or in outpatient treatment both before and after the reform. Convicted defendants were less likely to be placed on probation after the reform (11%) than they had been prior to the reform (25%). This change may have been due to the fact that a larger percentage of insanity cases raised after the reform were for violent offenses.

Figure 5.12 displays the confinement patterns before and after the reform for persons acquitted by reason of insanity for murder. The figure illustrates the proportion of defendants still confined at a given number of days. Persons found NGRI for murder were released significantly sooner after the reform than those acquitted prior to the reform ($p < .05$). The median length of confinement was 2,463 days (6.7 years) for cases raised prior to the reform and 1,331 days (3.6 years) for cases after the reform.

Although this difference startled us at first, we found that much of it was due to three defendants acquitted after the reform who were placed on conditional release following the 30-day evaluation period. One of the defendants was a man in his 70s who had murdered his wife. A second

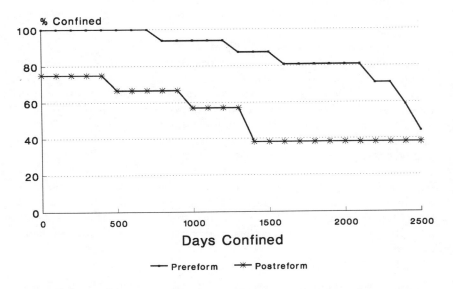

FIGURE 5.12. Confinement patterns of insanity defendants acquitted NGRI of murder in study counties of New York before and after the 1984 burden and standard reform.

was an elderly man in his 60s. The third defendant was a 20-year-old man who had murdered his mother. In each case, the postacquittal psychiatric evaluation found that these defendants were no longer dangerous nor actively mentally ill.

The remaining difference in length of confinement may be attributable to systematic differences in the composition of the two groups. For example, of the 16 acquittees prior to the reform, only 1 was female. Of the 12 persons acquitted subsequent to the reform, 5 were female. Two of the defendants who raised the defense after the reform and were released within 3 years were female; both of them had murdered their children. With such small sample sizes, we could not disentangle the effects of the defendants' characteristics on the length of confinement, but women were more apt to be successful in their insanity pleas than men, and to be released from confinement earlier than men.

We found no change in the confinement patterns for insanity acquittees charged with other violent crimes or with nonviolent crimes due to the reform. Only two persons were acquitted by reason of insanity for nonviolent crimes after the reform. One of these acquittees was released immediately after examination; the other had not been released at the end of the study.

We also analyzed the length of confinement patterns for insanity defendants who pleaded insanity but were found guilty. For murder, we found no significant difference in the patterns of confinement between insanity defendants who were convicted and those who were acquitted by reason of insanity either before or after the reform. Both groups were institutionalized for most of our study period.

For the other two categories, other violent crimes and nonviolent crimes, defendants who had been convicted were released sooner than defendants who had been acquitted by reason of insanity ($p < .01$ and $p < .10$, respectively). This difference in confinement, with insanity acquittees being held longer than those convicted, was also found when we studied the earlier reform in New York (see Chapter 6). Clearly, in New York insanity acquittees are not being released quickly. They are staying for long periods of time. For nonmurder cases, NGRIs stay hospitalized longer than their peers who are found guilty and placed in prison.

Overall, the New York data revealed that the reform of the burden and standard of proof reduced the use of the insanity defense, affected who used the defense, and altered patterns concerning who was acquitted. After the shift in the burden of proof, defendants raising the plea were more likely to have been seriously mentally ill and to have committed a violent offense. Defendants who were more likely to be acquitted included women, those with a diagnosis of major mental illness, and those charged with a violent offense. The reform had little impact on the length of confinement. We did find, however, that insanity acquittees were likely to be confined as long or longer than insanity defendants who had been convicted.

CONCLUSIONS

The results from our analyses of Georgia's and New York's insanity defense reforms showed consistent outcomes. There was a reduction in the use of the insanity defense in both states. In Georgia, use of the insanity defense had been increasing prior to the reform, but when the burden was shifted to the defense the plea rate began to decline. In New York, use of the insanity defense was declining prior to the reform, but when the burden was placed on the defense the decline accelerated, resulting in a sudden and abrupt drop.

In both Georgia and New York, when the burden of proof was shifted to the defense, a diagnosis of a major mental illness, such as schizophrenia or a major affective disorder, became an imperative for an insanity acquittal. In Georgia, after the reform, there was a sixfold increase in the relative likelihood of an insanity acquittal for those with a major mental illness when compared to defendants without such a diagnosis; in New York the reform resulted in an eightfold increase.

The consistency of the pattern of decreased use of the insanity defense and the increasing importance of psychiatric diagnosis was particularly significant given differences across the two states. Georgia enacted its reform in the late 1970s while use of the insanity defense was on the rise. The decision to shift the burden of proof to the defendant closely followed the wave of court decisions addressing the due process reforms of insanity acquittees in which they were granted many of the rights given to civil commitments. Georgia's 1978 reform was among the nation's first aimed at restricting use of the insanity defense. A few years later (1982), Georgia attempted to further restrict the use of the insanity defense by enacting a guilty but mentally ill plea and verdict. The impact of that reform is examined in Chapter 7.

In contrast, New York's 1984 reform was one of the many reforms that followed Hinckley's acquittal, when many states were tightening the use of the insanity defense. Furthermore, New York's change in the burden and standard of proof followed another major insanity defense reform in 1980 that had altered the commitment and release procedures for insanity defendants.

Georgia and New York also differed in the general frequency of use and in confinement patterns for insanity defendants. A much higher proportion of defendants in Georgia raised the insanity defense than did defendants in New York. There were approximately 18 insanity pleas per 1,000 cases in Georgia versus 2 per 1,000 in New York. In fact, the numbers were so low in New York that the reform's impact on use was particularly striking. In terms of confinement patterns, insanity acquittees were typically released sooner than other insanity defendants who were convicted in Georgia. This was not the case in New York, where insanity acquittees stayed as long if not longer than convicted insanity defendants. Despite these major differences in the two states studied, the fundamental changes in use and in who was acquitted associated with the change in the burden and standard of proof were the same.

The results suggest that who shoulders the burden and standard of proof in insanity cases does have a major impact on how the insanity defense is used and by whom. Fewer defendants appear willing to assert this defense when they themselves are required to prove their *insanity* than when the state must prove their *sanity*. When the defense does attempt to prove insanity, a diagnosis of schizophrenia, another major psychosis, or a major affective disorder almost becomes a prerequisite for success. It also helps to be female.

6

Changing the Conditions
of Confinement and Release
in New York

The most common type of reform introduced following John Hinckley's acquittal was dispositional reform—changes in commitment and release procedures for insanity acquittees. New York revised its commitment and release procedures for insanity acquittees in September 1980 when the legislature passed the Insanity Defense Reform Act (IDRA). Although the reform occurred before the Hinckley trial, the newly defined procedures were very similar to those proposed by the American Bar Association in August 1984 (Ellis, 1986). Our hypothesis was that dispositional reforms would have the greatest impact on all our dependent measures of possible impacts. We expected a large impact because these types of changes most directly increase the lengths and restrictiveness of confinements. If length of confinement were to increase, we anticipated declines in the volume and rate of insanity pleas as they became less-attractive alternatives to defendants and their lawyers.

A BRIEF HISTORICAL REVIEW OF
CONFINEMENT PROCEDURES AND CASE LAW

The 1970s brought a heightened awareness of issues related to the insanity defense to state courts and legislatures across the United States due to two landmark decisions, *Bolton v. Harris* (1968) and *People v. McQuillan*

(1974), that required the procedures for commitment and release of insanity acquittees to be substantially the same as those for civil patients. As states modified their laws and procedures governing the commitment and release of insanity acquittees to comply with these rulings, public concern about the perceived, and sometimes actual, possibility that dangerous people might be released into the community after only brief periods of hospitalization began to grow. In many states public concern turned into outrage as the result of locally notorious cases involving insanity acquittees. In New York State, for example, two highly celebrated cases greatly heightened the public's and legislators' concerns about these issues.

New York's insanity defense procedures were revised in 1971 as part of the mental health advocacy movement. By the late 1970s it was clear that they would need to be amended again in order to incorporate changes into the law mandated by subsequent court decisions regarding the commitment and release of insanity acquittees (Weyant, 1981). Then a highly publicized case (*In re Torsney*, 1979) started the process in which use of the insanity defense in New York would undergo major reevaluation.

On Thanksgiving Day, 1976, Robert Torsney, a white New York City police officer, shot and killed a 15-year-old black youth on a Brooklyn street. Tried for murder, he was acquitted based on one doctor's testimony that he had a rare form of epilepsy that no other medical examiner could find. He was released just 1 year after his automatic commitment when he was no longer judged to be a danger to self or others. The psychiatrists in the state mental hospital to which Torsney was committed were never able to find the disease that had secured his acquittal. Accordingly, after 1 year they applied for his release from confinement. It was granted and Torsney was placed on conditional release. Torsney's quick release caused an outrage among both professionals and the public. The appellate court overturned the lower court decision to release Torsney, who was then returned to the hospital. But then the court of appeals reversed the appellate ruling and reinstated Torsney's conditional release, which mandated that he could not carry a gun, no longer work as a police officer, and must continue receiving treatment. The case received major coverage in the press and was the subject of many editorial comments (Weyant, 1981).

Shortly following the Torsney case another highly publicized case increased public anger. Adam Berwid, who was being held as incompetent to stand trial for charges of aggravated harrassment against his wife for continued harrassment and death threats, escaped from the custody of the Mental Hygiene Department. The department did not act quickly to notify his wife of the escape, even though the District Attorney had advised the department of his dangerousness. Berwid killed his wife before she was notified of his escape.

Following Torsney's release in 1979, Governor Hugh Carey requested the New York State Law Revision Commission to undertake an in-depth examination of the insanity defense to determine whether it was the best way to safeguard the public, while protecting individual rights. The Insanity Defense Reform Act (IDRA) of 1980 reflected the results of the Commission's report to the governor.

Prior to the enactment of the IDRA, a defendant acquitted by reason of insanity was automatically committed to the custody of the Commissioner of Mental Health for placement in an appropriate state mental hospital. The term of commitment had no upper limit; release was contingent on demonstrating the acquittee was no longer mentally ill nor dangerous. Under the old law, there were few regulations governing the handling of insanity acquittees by the New York State Office of Mental Health (OMH). Transfers and furloughs were the result of administrative decisions made solely by mental health staff at the hospital and central office levels. A court review was required only when clients were released to the community under specified conditions or unconditionally discharged. The court of review was often the superior court in the county where the state mental hospital holding the acquittee was located. This meant that the original criminal court and the original prosecuting attorney had very little input into these decisions, although they were notified.

THE IDRA: BALANCE OF PATIENT RIGHTS AND PUBLIC SAFETY

The 1980 IDRA reform, which was precipitated by highly visible cases that caused public outrage, contained both liberal and conservative measures. It incorporated the due process and equal protection rights recently affirmed by New York state courts and the U.S. Supreme Court into the sections of the Criminal Procedural Law (CPL) governing the insanity defense, but it also tightened the procedures for release of defendants in an attempt to safeguard the public. The law specifies that a defendant found NGRI must immediately undergo a 30-day psychiatric evaluation period to determine *current* mental status. The focus of the evaluation is to determine whether the person has a dangerous mental disorder, is mentally ill but not dangerous, or is not mentally ill. If the defendant is in custody at the time of the acquittal, the examination is to be carried out in a secure setting. If the defendant is not in custody, for example, if he or she was released on his or her own recognizance or is out on bail, the court has the option of issuing an outpatient examination order. The examination, prepared by two qualified mental health examiners, is then submitted to the original criminal court, which then holds an initial hearing.

Defendants found to be dangerously mentally ill are committed to a secure forensic facility for a minimum of 6 months, and until such time as the court finds them no longer dangerous and approves their transfer to a civil facility. Retention hearings are scheduled at regular intervals: after the first 6 months, 1 year later, and thereafter at 2-year intervals. At these hearings the OMH must prove that the defendant remains dangerously mentally ill and should be retained in a secure facility or, conversely, that the defendant is not dangerously mentally ill and can safely be transferred to a civil facility.

When it is determined that a defendant can be transferred to a civil facility, that facility retains jurisdiction over the client until the court approves of a release to the community and issues a release order with an order of conditions (OC). The OC mandates the OMH to monitor client compliance with specified conditions. It is valid for 5 years and can be extended for an additional 5 years with good cause. A provision also exists whereby the OMH can seek a court order to discharge a client who is no longer mentally ill after 3 years, if such a discharge is consistent with public safety.

Defendants found mentally ill, but not dangerous, at the initial hearing are placed in the custody of the OMH for civil commitment to a psychiatric center with an OC. The commitment is for a period not to exceed 6 months. After the expiration of this 6-month commitment, their stay at the civil facility is governed by the provisions of Mental Hygiene Law, which means that their release is handled administratively by hospital staff and does not require a criminal court hearing. Clients released into the community are subject to the OC issued at the time of civil commitment, with or without modifications.

Defendants found not mentally ill at the initial hearing are given a discharge order by the court and are released with or without an OC. The law provides for a recommitment order for clients on a conditional release (CR). An application for recommitment can be filed by the OMH or the District Attorney at any time during the period covered by the OC if it is felt the defendant is dangerous. The court is then required to hold a hearing wherein the applicant has to establish, to the satisfaction of the court, that the defendant has a dangerous mental disorder.

Other changes included in the 1980 IDRA law were that the District Attorney must be given notice of all hearings, including transfer, furlough, and release. Previously, such notice was required only for release hearings. In order to be procedurally consistent with civil law, the burden of proof at release and transfer hearings was shifted to the state. Previously, they had been on the acquittee to prove his/her recovery from insanity (Weyant, 1981). The IDRA also established procedures for a plea of not responsible by reason of mental disease or defect as an alternative to jury trials when the defense and prosecution agree that the defendant is NGRI. In effect, the procedures formalized a plea bargain process.

This effort by New York to ensure that the procedural safeguards required in civil proceedings were incorporated into the law for insanity acquittees also contained measures designed to protect public safety.

Measures to ensure public involvement in the release process, such as the notification of the District Attorney of all hearings and court approval for transfer and furlough in addition to release, made the law responsive to public concerns. The continuation of the conditional release program, where defendants could be released from inpatient care, but maintained under the supervision of the OMH, also worked to ensure the public safety. Conditional release allowed the court to comply with the constitutional mandate to release someone who was no longer considered dangerously mentally ill, while ensuring that they be supervised by the OMH for a period of 5 years or more.

The tripartite classification system defined in the IDRA distinguished, early on, which acquittees were dangerous and committed them to a secure facility. Any movement of these defendants, be it transfer, furlough, or release, was made subject to criminal court approval. In contrast, those who were not considered to be dangerous were transferred to the custody of OMH where they were treated and released in the manner of any other civil patient.

The results of two prior studies of the effects of the IDRA in New York (McClellan, 1986; Stokman & Heiber, 1984) both suggested that the reform increased protection for insanity acquittees' due process rights and increased public protection. McClellan (1986) found that the law increased the number of reviews, formalized procedures, and provided court review for everyone acquitted NGRI. Stokman and Heiber (1984) found that the average number of insanity acquittals increased after the reform, although the increase had already begun prior to the reform and appeared to be temporary. They found that only a small percentage (14%) of acquittees were classified as not mentally ill and released without hospitalization, while two-thirds were found dangerously mentally ill and confined in a secure facility. An increasingly large percentage of acquittees were found to be dangerously mentally ill from 1980 to 1983. The researchers concluded that increased length of hospitalization and court supervision of those found dangerously mentally ill would, over time, make the insanity defense less desirable for defendants.

In this chapter we will expand substantially on these earlier works by examining the effects of this dispositional reform by using, for the first time in New York, information on insanity pleas, as well as acquittals. Also, we have the benefit of a much longer follow-up period than either of the prior studies. We looked at use of the insanity defense in five counties: Bronx, Erie (Buffalo), Kings (Brooklyn), Nassau (Long Island), and Queens. We collected information on insanity pleas and acquittals from January 1, 1978, through December 31, 1983. This produced 412 insanity pleas and 164 acquittals drawn from the 101,904 felony indictments that we reviewed.

USE OF THE INSANITY DEFENSE

The number of insanity pleas, insanity acquittals, and felony indictments from January 1978 through December 1983 are shown in Figure 6.1 in 6-month intervals. Similar to the results obtained by Stokman and Heiber (1984), we found that insanity acquittals were increasing prior to the reform from an average of roughly 10 per period in 1978 and 1979 to 20 per period in 1980 at the time of the reform. This increase then leveled off shortly after the reform to 20 per 6-month period in 1981 and 1982, and then began to decrease. By 1983, the number of insanity acquittals had decreased to approximately the same level as in 1978. Insanity pleas showed a similar pattern. They increased steadily from less than 30 per 6-month period during 1978 and early 1979 to a high of about 40 pleas per 6-month period in 1981 and 1982, at which point they began to decline to just over 30 pleas per period in 1983.

Figure 6.2 presents data on the plea rate, the number of pleas per 1,000 felony indictments, during the study period. The IDRA legislation became effective in September 1980. Thus the last 6-month period of 1980

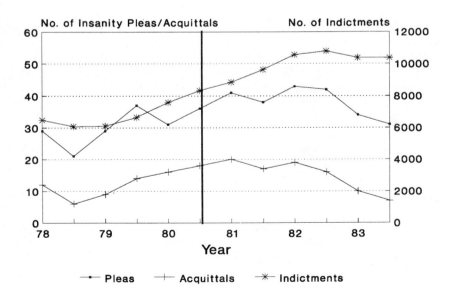

FIGURE 6.1. Number of insanity pleas, insanity acquittals, and felony indictments (right axis) in study counties of New York before and after the 1980 reform.

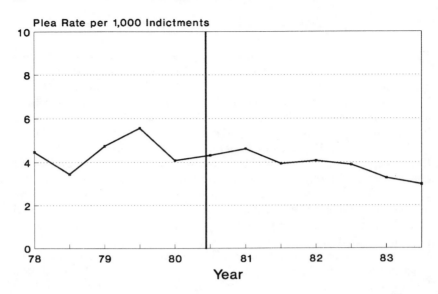

FIGURE 6.2. Insanity defense plea rate (number of insanity pleas per 1,000 felony indictments) in study counties of New York before and after the 1980 reform.

contained some cases indicted prior to the reform and some after the reform. Since a majority of the cases fell in the postreform period, for ease of presentation we placed the entire 6-month period after the reform. Thus the first five observations preceded the 1980 reform and the last seven periods followed the reform.

The plea rate remained relatively stable across the study period at approximately 4 pleas per 1,000 felony indictments. Although there was a gradual decline in the plea rate from 1981 to the end of the study period, three years of postreform data indicate no significant change in the rate due to the reform. The highest plea rate, 5.6 pleas per 1,000 indictments, occurred in the last half of 1979, while the lowest rate, 3.0 pleas, occurred in the last period of the study in 1983.

It may be recalled from the analysis presented in Chapter 5 that when New York's 1984 reform in the burden and standard of proof went into effect, the plea rate continued to decline and then dropped significantly after the 1984 reform. That result in no way alters our conclusion here that changes in the conditions of confinement in 1980 produced no significant change in the insanity plea rate. The significant decline occurred only with the subsequent reform.

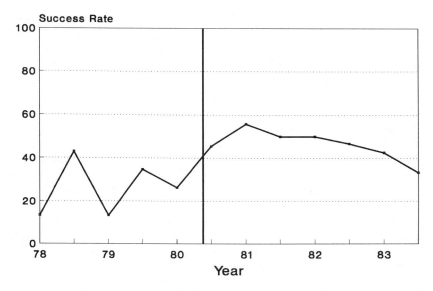

FIGURE 6.3. Percentage of insanity pleas acquitted NGRI in study counties of New York before and after the 1980 reform.

LIKELIHOOD OF A SUCCESSFUL INSANITY PLEA

The success rate, the percentage of defendants raising the insanity plea who were acquitted NGRI, is shown in Figure 6.3 in 6-month intervals. Prior to the reform, the success rate fluctuated around 30%. At the time of the reform it increased briefly to 56%, but then it began a gradual decline through the end of the study period to 34%. Overall, the success rate during the postreform period averaged 46% which was significantly higher than the average rate (26%) prior to the reform ($p < .07$).

To attempt to discover what might have caused the change in the success rate, we disaggregated the crimes with which the defendants were charged into violent (murder, physical assault, rape, and kidnapping) and nonviolent (robbery, burglary, other property offenses, and minor felonies) and found some interesting results. A larger percentage of insanity pleas were entered for nonviolent crimes in the postreform period (29%) than in the prereform period (19%). Given the tripartite system of classifying cases after acquittal, perhaps more defendants accused of nonviolent offenses were choosing to enter an insanity plea after the reform. They would not be committed automatically for indefinite periods of time as had been the case before the reform. In fact, if their evaluation found them to be *not dangerous*, they could either be committed to a civil facility for

6 months or be released outright. Thus the IDRA may have made it more appealing for those with less serious offenses to raise the insanity plea. This result, of course, is in sharp contrast to the California situation described in Chapter 4 where a determinate sentence associated with an NGRI acquittal turned out to be longer for insanity acquittees than for those convicted because it did not allow for "good time."

We also looked at the success rate by crime before and after the reform. This information is presented in Figure 6.4. Given the observed increase in the success rate demonstrated in Figure 6.3, we anticipated an increase in successful cases for both types of crimes. However, the increase occurred only for violent offenses (from 29% to 53%). For nonviolent offenses the percentage was practically identical in the pre- and postreform periods (from 21% to 25%).

Together, these results indicate that even though the proportion of cases entering an insanity plea for nonviolent crimes increased following the reform, the success rate for nonviolent crimes remained roughly the same. In contrast, the success rate for violent crimes increased substantially from 33% before the reform to 50% after the reform. This observed increase in the success rate for violent offenses may also have been a result of the tripartite system of classifying cases after acquittal. With the IDRA, the original criminal courts were assured that they would have nearly total

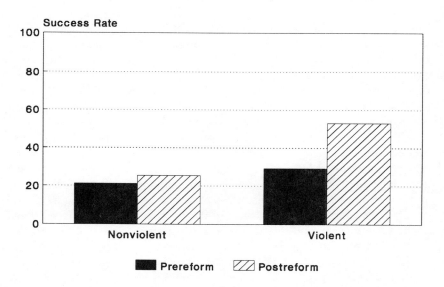

FIGURE 6.4. Percentage of insanity pleas successfully acquitted NGRI in study counties of New York by violent and nonviolent crimes before and after the 1980 reform.

control over the movement of defendants acquitted by reason of insanity who were judged to be dangerous. All movement, even within the mental health system for transfer or furlough, needed the approval of the court. Judges and prosecutors no longer needed to be concerned about psychiatrists and distant courts releasing insanity acquittees whom the local community felt were still dangerous. Of course, this did put in place the distinct possibility that the treating mental health professionals would find an acquittee fully treated and no longer dangerous, and thus warranting release, while judicial review mandated keeping the defendant hospitalized when no treatment was being provided. In other words, the IDRA increased the prospect of preventive detention for insanity acquittees in New York.

AFTER THE REFORM: INCREASE IN NONVIOLENT OFFENSES AND MORE PLEA BARGAINING

We next examined whether there were any changes in who used the insanity defense after the 1980 law in New York. This information is presented only as pre-post data because the number of acquittals is too small to break out by 6-month periods. These analyses use the actual date of the reform (September 1, 1980) to divide the pre- and postreform periods.

The characteristics of defendants raising the insanity plea did not change significantly due to the reform. Both before and after the reform, defendants were, on average, 31 years of age, mostly nonwhite (60%), males (90%), diagnosed with a major mental illness (75%).

As noted above, the proportion of cases entering the insanity plea for nonviolent crimes increased after the reform from 20% to 29%. This was the only significant change in the types of crimes associated with the insanity plea. For crimes with a victim, there was a slight decrease in the proportion involving a female victim (from 56% to 47%), but it was not statistically significant. The method by which insanity cases were disposed of changed significantly due to the reform (see Figure 6.5). The percentage resolved by a judge or bench trial was halved from 21% to 11%, while the percentage resolved with a plea bargain increased from 65% to 75%.

Overall, the pool of defendants pleading insanity changed very little due to the IDRA reform. There was a modest increase in the proportion of cases involving nonviolent crimes. But what about the characteristics of defendants who were actually found NGRI? We turn to that question next.

CHANGE IN PROCESSING OF ACQUITTALS

The profiles of insanity acquittees were very similar before and after the reform. In fact, the only significant change in the sociodemographic char-

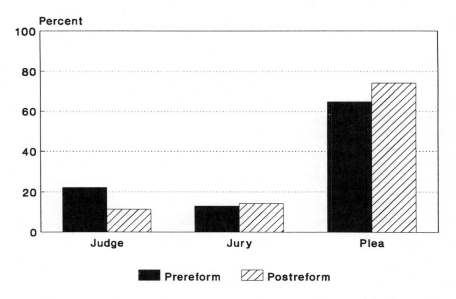

FIGURE 6.5. Percentage of defendants raising the insanity plea adjudicated by a judge, jury, or plea bargain in study counties of New York before and after the 1980 reform.

acteristics of NGRI acquittals was their age. It increased from 27 years prior to the reform to 33 years after the reform ($p < .01$). As Figure 6.6 makes clear, the major impact for insanity acquittees was in their court processing. Prior to the reform, the majority of insanity acquittals (84%) were adjudicated by a judge; after the reform, the large majority (85%) were resolved with a plea bargain. The reform formally established procedures for acceptance of a plea of not responsible by reason of mental disease or defect as an alternative to trials. It is clear that these procedures were so attractive that the vast majority of all insanity acquittals after the reform used these procedures.

SMALLER PERCENTAGES WERE HOSPITALIZED
AFTER THE REFORM

Since this reform was a dispositional reform, that is, it focused on changes in the postverdict commitment and subsequent release of insanity acquittees, we were interested in determining whether the reform had any impact on the confinement histories of those acquitted NGRI.

We first examined whether the reform had any impact on the percentage of insanity acquittees who were hospitalized after acquittal. It did.

Prior to the reform, *all* insanity acquittees were hospitalized following acquittal. After the reform, 12% received conditional release or were referred for outpatient services, thereby going directly into the community after their 30-day evaluation period. The rest (88%) were hospitalized for treatment. While 12% is a modest number, it represents a new category of cases for which the public will always have special concern. The possibility of an outright release must be attractive to defendants trying to decide whether to enter an insanity plea. A comparison of the characteristics of the 12% who were released with those hospitalized indicated a similar profile to other acquittees, with one major exception. A significantly larger percentage of those directly released after evaluation were women (43%) as compared to those hospitalized (13%). In all other regards—age, ethnicity, diagnosis, target offense, and method of adjudication—those directly released were similar to those hospitalized. In general, female NGRI acquittees appear to be less threatening to mental health professionals and the courts.

LENGTHS OF CONFINEMENT DID NOT CHANGE

Next, we looked at whether there were any changes in the lengths of confinement of insanity acquittees after the reform. We looked at length of

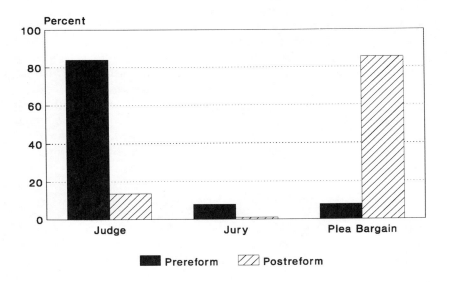

FIGURE 6.6. Percentage of insanity acquittees adjudicated by a judge, jury, or plea bargain in study counties of New York before and after the 1980 reform.

confinement by three major crime categories: murder, other violent crimes (physical assault, rape, and kidnapping), and nonviolent crimes (robbery, property offenses, and other minor offenses). We found that after the reform a small percentage (12%) of the NGRI acquittees were released directly after evaluation following their acquittals. This occurred in all three crime categories. Despite the fact that some people were released without being hospitalized, there were no significant changes in the length of stays associated with any crime category due to the reform. The median length of stay for acquittees charged with murder was 10 years before the reform and 6.4 years after the reform; for those charged with other violent offenses it was 6.9 years before and 5.2 years after; and for nonviolent crimes it was 2.6 years before and 2.8 years after.

INSANITY ACQUITTEES STAY LONGER THAN UNSUCCESSFUL DEFENDANTS FOUND GUILTY

We also compared the lengths of confinement of defendants pleading insanity who were found guilty with those acquitted NGRI. Contrary to popular belief, insanity acquittees in New York were confined as long or longer than those found guilty. Although there was no difference in the length of confinement of insanity acquittees and those found guilty of murder, there were significant differences for the other two crime categories, other violent crimes ($p < .02$) and nonviolent crimes ($p < .01$). For these crimes, insanity acquittees were confined for longer periods of time than those found guilty on similar charges (see Figures 6.7 and 6.8). The median length of stay for those found NGRI for other violent offenses was 5.25 years (1919 days) compared to 2.7 years (982 days) for those found guilty—nearly twice as long. Similarly, for nonviolent offenses, the median length of stay for NGRI acquittees was 2.8 *years* compared to 8.5 *months* for those found guilty—nearly four times as long. It is important to note that the long lengths of stay for insanity acquittees was not due to the reform; we found no changes in length of confinement due to the reform. Long confinement of insanity acquittees in New York predated this dispositional reform.

ULTIMATELY PROCEDURAL CHANGES, BUT LITTLE ELSE

Probably the most significant impact of New York's IDRA was that not all insanity acquittees were automatically committed to a state mental hospital after an evaluation following acquittal. When evaluated for their current mental status, a small proportion (12%) were determined to be not dangerous and not mentally ill and were therefore released to outpatient programs or given conditional release rather than being hospitalized.

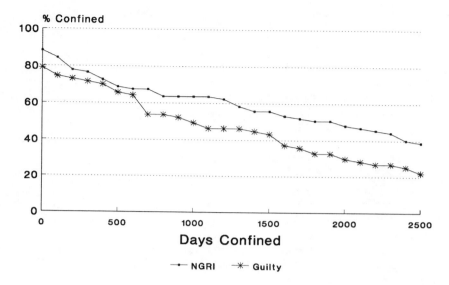

FIGURE 6.7. Confinement patterns of insanity defendants acquitted NGRI and convicted of other violent offenses in study counties of New York: 1978–1984.

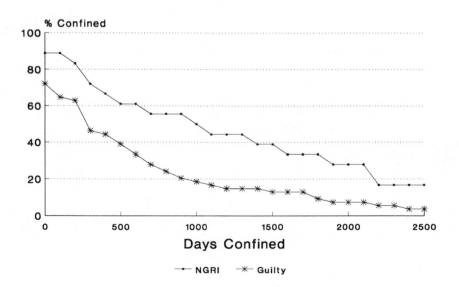

FIGURE 6.8. Confinement patterns of insanity defendants acquitted NGRI and convicted of nonviolent offenses in study counties of New York: 1978–1984.

The fact that outright release was possible may have produced the observed increase seen in the percentage of insanity pleas for nonviolent offenses after the reform. Defendants charged with these less-serious offenses may have been more willing to enter the insanity defense once the possibility of outright release existed. There was no change in the percentage of nonviolent cases that were successfully acquitted, however.

On the other hand, the success rate of insanity defenses for violent offenses increased significantly after the reform. Apparently after the reform the judicial system was more willing to acquit by reason of insanity defendants charged with violent crimes. This may have been due, in part, to the measures included in the law designed to protect the public from insanity acquittees determined to be dangerous. The law specified increased involvement by the District Attorney and the original criminal court in all transfer and release decisions involving insanity acquittees determined to be dangerous.

New York is unique among our study states with regard to the use of the plea bargain to resolve insanity cases. Prior to the reform, there was no formal procedure by which someone could be acquitted with a plea bargain, even though a few cases were the result of informal plea bargains. We found that after the reform 85% of insanity acquittals were resolved with a formal plea bargain. None of the other study states had such a high percentage of NGRI cases resolved in this way, although none had defined specific procedures for plea bargaining as in New York. In states without defined procedures for plea bargaining, a bench trial is probably, de facto, quite similar to a plea bargain negotiation. New York simply instituted a formal process for plea bargaining. This finding highlights the need to obtain process-oriented information in future research on the use of the insanity defense in order to understand how and with whom the insanity defense is used.

New York also stands out from the other states we studied in the rate at which the insanity defense was raised. It had the lowest plea rate of all the states we studied with 3 out of every 1,000 indicted felony defendants raising the plea. The other states varied between 6 and 57 insanity pleas per 1,000 defendants. This may be due in part to the relatively long periods of confinement associated with the insanity defense in New York. Although the length of confinement for insanity acquittees did not change as a result of the reform, NGRI acquittees were likely to stay as long, and in most cases longer, than people pleading insanity who were convicted. The fact that release decisions are made by the criminal court of jurisdiction may influence the long confinement periods. Judicial approval of release is required. This was the case in New York prior to the reform as well as after.

New York's revision of its insanity defense laws in 1980 was the result of a concerted effort by the governor and legal professionals to reform the insanity defense so that it both protected the public and safeguarded the due process rights of individuals. The resulting revisions in the commitment and release process accomplished what many states have sought to do with other types of reforms, namely, long confinement and tight supervision of acquittees who are potentially dangerous to the public. These goals were accomplished by defining different commitment and release procedures based on dangerousness and by ensuring the right to periodic review for those who are criminally confined.

New York's reform appeared to be well thought out, perhaps because it was the result of a special task force. The procedures defined for commitment and release are similar, in most ways, to those later defined by the American Bar Association (Ellis, 1986). The major component of the IDRA is the special, more restrictive, commitment procedures for those considered dangerous, with the alternate of using procedures similar to civil commitment for those judged not to be a danger to self or others. This distinction allows for more supervision and more restrictive release procedures for those who most concern the public while not subjecting everyone to such harsh terms of commitment. Ellis (1986) has suggested that the phase of the insanity defense that really is the focus of public concern is that wherein the NGRI acquittee is up for release. In his view, the public really does not care how many of what types of defendants are found NGRI as long as they get their just desserts (restrictive confinement) for a long time. The types of reform reflected by New York's 1980 IDRA are intended to be responsive to these public opinions. As we have seen in this chapter, longer confinements did not happen. They were long before and they were long after the reform. While some defendants (12%) did return directly to the community, they were not those feared by the public. The remaining NGRI acquittees did have their movements greatly restricted and were housed in highly secure settings. Further, movements of these acquittees were much more dependent on local decisions than decisions by judges in distant counties where the state hospitals were located. From these latter perspectives, the IDRA and its dispositional reforms were quite successful. Overall, however, not as much change occurred as might have been wanted, even though the number and rate of insanity pleas did return to 1978 levels. This dispositional reform did have some impact, but its impact was not as large as we had anticipated.

7

The Impact of Adopting a Guilty but Mentally Ill Verdict in Georgia

This chapter examines the effect of enacting a guilty but mentally ill (GBMI) verdict in Georgia in 1982. Georgia passed legislation that allowed a GBMI plea and verdict shortly after John Hinckley's acquittal. Defendants found GBMI are sentenced *as if* they had been found guilty, and mental health treatment is provided within available resources of the Department of Corrections. Based on Michigan's experience from 1976 to 1982 (Smith & Hall, 1982; Blunt & Stock, 1985), we hypothesized that the addition of a GBMI verdict would not affect the volume or rate of insanity pleas, but that it would increase the seriousness of offenses committed by those raising this plea and those found GBMI.

A BRIEF HISTORICAL REVIEW

One of the most popular reforms of the insanity defense in the United States during the past 15 years has been the guilty but mentally ill (GBMI) verdict. States adopting GBMI legislation maintain their insanity defense, but the insanity defense is supplemented with another verdict that can be used for defendants who are mentally ill. That is, defendants who raise the insanity defense may be found not guilty, not guilty by reason of insanity, guilty but mentally ill, or guilty. Defendants found GBMI are sentenced as if they had been found guilty on their charges. States have varying requirements in regards to providing mental health services for GBMI defendants while they are incarcerated. A GBMI statute was first adopted in Michigan in 1975, in the aftermath of the Michigan Supreme Court ruling in *People v. McQuillan* (1974). That ruling struck down the state's automatic commitment law and ultimately resulted in the release of approximately 150 insanity acquittees who did not meet civil commitment standards (Smith & Hall, 1982). Since then, 11 other states have added a GBMI verdict to their statutes (Callahan, Mayer, & Steadman, 1987; McGraw, Farthing-Capowich, & Keilitz, 1985; Keilitz, 1987).

Advocates of GBMI reform believe that such statutes protect the public by decreasing the number of insanity acquittals and increasing incarcerations in secure settings (i.e., prisons) for those found GBMI. Keilitz (1987:307) states that "legislators hoped that the GBMI verdict would offer juries an attractive alternative to the verdict of not guilty by reason of insanity and thereby curb the use of the insanity plea and verdict and prevent the early release of dangerous individuals." But many scholars and professionals believe the GBMI verdict is conceptually flawed and procedurally problematic (Slobogin, 1985; McGraw, Farthing-Capowich, & Keilitz, 1987). They have argued that the verdict is misleading in that the phrase "but mentally ill" connotes a diminished capacity that is not part of the verdict, and that a more correct phrase would be "guilty *and* mentally ill" (Petrella, Benedek, Bank, & Packer, 1985; Smith & Hall, 1982). Others have argued that the legal definitions of mental illness and insanity overlap, making it difficult and discretionary to distinguish between them (Slobogin, 1985). Another concern is that juries will use the GBMI option as a compromise verdict and find defendants who actually fit the "legal" definition of insane GBMI to ensure their incarceration.

In fact, the empirical data on the impact of GBMI reforms generally indicate that the reforms have either had marginal or no impact on insanity proceedings (Keilitz, 1987; McGraw, Farthing-Capowich, & Keilitz, 1985; Smith & Hall, 1982). The majority of GBMI research has come from Michigan. Some results of the experiences in Illinois, Pennsylvania, and Georgia have also been reported. The issue most frequently addressed by prior research is whether GBMI legislation decreased the number of insanity acquittals. In both Michigan and Illinois, the research demonstrated that the GBMI option did not reduce the number of NGRI findings (Blunt & Stock, 1985; Criss & Racine, 1980; Klofas & Weisheit, 1986). The overall conclusion was that while the intent of the Michigan legislation was to reduce insanity acquittals, the number and rate of NGRI findings actually increased following the enactment of a GBMI statute (Smith & Hall, 1982). The Illinois data were less extensive than the data for Michigan, yet they support the same conclusion: NGRI acquittals were not reduced by the adoption of a GBMI statute.

In an effort to determine whether those found GBMI were more likely to be drawn from those previously found NGRI or guilty, Keilitz (1987) analyzed data on GBMI, NGRI, and guilty defendants in Michigan, Illinois, and Georgia. He concluded that the typical GBMI resembled the NGRI on some variables and guilty defendants on others. Utilizing data from two studies of insanity acquittees (Cooke & Sikorski, 1974; Criss & Racine, 1980), he determined that there were some changes in the population acquitted NGRI, namely, that some of the less seriously disturbed and more violent offenders may have been screened out of the NGRI population. He also compared the sentences received by a small cohort of persons found GBMI with guilty defendants and tentatively concluded that the average GBMI defendant received a longer sentence than the average guilty defendant. He stressed that more useful results would come from a study of changes in the population pleading insanity and those acquitted NGRI both before and after enactment of GBMI legislation.

This is precisely what will be done in the present chapter. While prior studies have consistently found that the GBMI verdict has had little impact on use of the insanity defense, as Keilitz noted, these studies have considered only the basic differences in the number and composition of insanity *acquittals* and GBMIs. For a more complete picture of what actually happens under the GBMI option, it is important also to examine the characteristics of the total pool of persons *pleading* insanity before and after the GBMI reform and how those found NGRI compare with those found GBMI. Without data on all defendants pleading insanity, and without controls for key factors such as offense and sociodemographic variables, conclusions drawn about the impact of GBMI legislation from NGRI acquittals alone may be misleading.

The purpose of the research reported here is to evaluate the impact of Georgia's 1982 GBMI reform on the use of the insanity defense by presenting a range of data not available in prior research. Georgia enacted the GBMI verdict in 1982 (see text from Georgia Criminal Procedure Law 27-1503 in Appendix C). As in Michigan, the GBMI verdict was adopted in Georgia by the legislature as a response to a court ruling in which the procedural safeguards for defendants acquitted on the grounds of insanity were broadened. The GBMI verdict was passed shortly after a U.S. District Court ruling in *Benham v. Edwards* (1980) that overturned the state's practice of automatically committing all persons who successfully raised the insanity defense. The court ruled that Georgia's procedures were unconstitutional. The *Benham* court also held as unconstitutional the state's release procedures for insanity acquittees, which were based on the presumption of continued insanity and were more strict than those for persons committed involuntarily. The court issued a mandatory injunction ordering that all Georgia NGRIs be given a hearing within 90 days to determine their present mental status (Hauser, 1981). After the hearings, 55 of the 127 insanity acquittees confined were released because they did not meet involuntary commitment standards. In Georgia these standards require someone to be mentally ill and presenting substantial risk to self or others or in danger of creating an imminently life-endangering crisis through their inability to care for themselves.

In response to the *Benham* case, the Georgia legislature revised the commitment procedures for insanity acquittees, effective July 1982, to require a state-initiated hearing after a 30-day evaluation period. The release procedures did not change, however. Instead the legislature waited for the results of the appeal of the *Benham* decision which was ultimately vacated in 1983 (*Benham v. Ledbetter*) after the *Jones v. United States* (1983) decision. At the same time the GBMI verdict was adopted.

Georgia's introduction of GBMI is a clear example of state efforts to safeguard the public interest in the wake of a series of judicial rulings that broadened the procedural safeguards of insanity defendants (e.g., *Baxstrom v. Herold*, 1966; *Jackson v. Indiana*, 1972; *People v. McQuillan*, 1974). The cumulative effect of these rulings mandated that the commitment and release procedures of insanity acquittees closely resemble those required for civil commitments (Harris, 1982).

In the early 1980s the flavor of federal court rulings was beginning to change toward a more conservative position. This is evidenced by *Jones* in which the Supreme Court ruled that the presumption of continued insanity could be the basis for the automatic commitment of insanity acquittees (Singer, 1985). Shortly following the *Jones* ruling, the *Benham v. Edwards* decision was vacated and remanded to the U.S. Court of Appeals for further consideration (1983). The court ultimately ruled in *Benham v. Ledbetter* (1986) that Georgia's release procedures for insanity acquittees were constitutionally sound even though they were substantially more strict than those for civil commitments.

This chapter reports data on all persons entering an insanity plea from January 1979 through December 1985 in 12 Georgia counties: Bibb, Chatham, Cherokee, Clarke, Cobb, DeKalb, Dougherty, Floyd, Fulton, Newton, Richmond, and Thomas. We gathered information on 1,956 insanity pleas and 303 insanity acquittals from 114,975 felony indictments.

VOLUME OF INSANITY PLEAS INCREASED, BUT NOT IMMEDIATELY

Prior to the 1982 reform, between 125 and 150 insanity cases were raised in each 6-month period. This volume of cases remained steady for nearly 1 year after the enactment of the GBMI statute, at which point it temporarily increased to 175 pleas per 6-month period. As the data presented in Figure 7.1 indicate, this increase—which lasted only 1 year—was the only major change in the volume of insanity pleas after the introduction of a

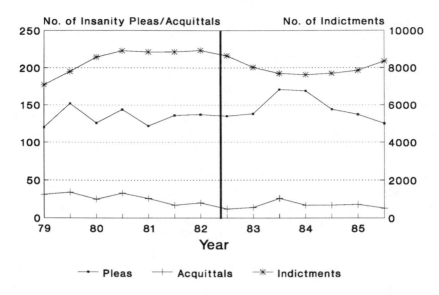

FIGURE 7.1. Number of insanity pleas, insanity acquittals, and felony indictments (right axis) in study counties of Georgia before and after the 1982 GBMI reform.

GBMI verdict. With this exception, the volume of insanity pleas remained fairly constant across the study period, averaging roughly 125 pleas per 6-month period.

The number of insanity acquittals, shown in the trend line at the bottom of Figure 7.1, was declining slightly prior to the reform, dropping from 30 to approximately 20 acquittals per 6-month period. In the first year after the reform, the number of acquittals continued to decline into the low teens before increasing again to just under 20, a level at which it remained for the rest of the study period. Not surprisingly, there was a slight increase in acquittals associated with the temporary increase in pleas noted above.

DELAYED INCREASE IN USE OF THE INSANITY DEFENSE

Figure 7.2 shows the plea rate, the number of insanity pleas per 1,000 indictments, for each observation period in Georgia. The first seven periods preceded the introduction of the GBMI verdict and the last seven periods followed its adoption. The lowest plea rate was 14 pleas per 1,000 indictments in the first half of 1981, while the highest rate was 22 per 1,000 indictments in the second half of 1983. Using a linear regression model, we did not find a significant change in the pattern of the rate of insanity pleas following the introduction of the GBMI verdict ($p = .24$).

The brief increase in the plea rate in 1983 and 1984 occurred nearly a year after the addition of the GBMI verdict. This increase could be attributable to the introduction of the GBMI verdict since it was a dispositional reform. Given that the average time from indictment to disposition for insanity cases in 1982 was between 5 and 6 months, it would take some time for defense attorneys to learn how the GBMI verdict worked and what results could be expected from the new statute. If defense attorneys believed that a GBMI finding might act as a mitigating factor in sentencing, a consequent increase in the number of insanity pleas certainly makes logical sense. Defendants could plead insanity and then bargain "down" to a GBMI plea. It is certainly possible that just such a scenario occurred in Georgia. We found that 75% of the GBMIs who had pleaded insanity were disposed of by a plea bargain. Only 19% were adjudicated by a judge and just 6% resulted from a jury verdict.

These data again highlight the misconception that juries are responsible for much of the decision making in cases involving the mentally ill. Their role is not nearly as large as most people imagine. The vast majority of cases involving an insanity plea in Georgia were resolved with a plea bargain where all parties—the defense, the prosecution, and the judge—

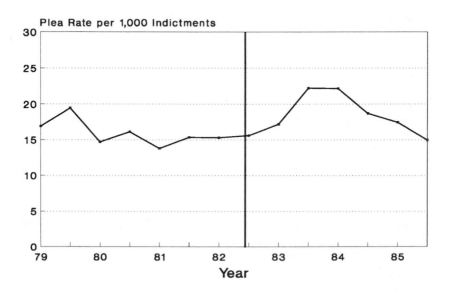

FIGURE 7.2. Insanity defense plea rate (number of insanity pleas per 1,000 felony indictments) in study counties of Georgia before and after the 1982 GBMI reform.

agreed to the verdict (68%) or by a bench (judge) trial (19%), not by a jury trial (13%).

LIKELIHOOD OF A SUCCESSFUL INSANITY DEFENSE: IT DEPENDS ON THE CRIME

The success rate, or the percentage of all insanity pleas that were found NGRI, for every 6-month period is shown in Figure 7.3. The success rate was highest (22%) in the first half of 1980 and lowest (4%) in the second half of 1985. Despite a general decline in successful pleas over the study period, we found no statistically significant effect associated with the introduction of the GBMI verdict (p = .60). There was a fairly steady decline in the success rate across the study years. The introduction of the GBMI verdict did not impact on this decline.

We also looked at the success rate by violent (murder, physical assault, rape, and kidnapping) and nonviolent crimes (robbery and other lesser felonies). The success rates for the two major categories of crime are shown in Figure 7.4. The results are striking. Prior to 1982, the success rate was nearly twice as high for those with violent offenses (between 20% and 30%)

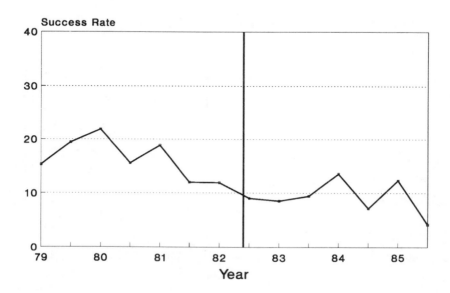

FIGURE 7.3. Percentage of insanity pleas acquitted NGRI in study counties of Georgia before and after the 1982 GBMI reform.

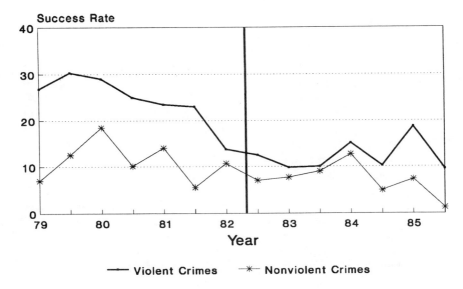

FIGURE 7.4. Percentage of insanity pleas acquitted NGRI by violent and nonviolent crimes in study counties of Georgia before and after the 1982 GBMI reform.

than it was for those committing nonviolent offenses (between 10% and 15%). Beginning in 1982, the rates for the two types of offenses became nearly identical (10%). Although we found a significant change in the success rates for violent crimes associated with the reform in the insanity defense laws in July 1982 ($p = .04$), the data presented in Figure 7.4 suggest the drop occurred prior to the 1982 reform.

Clearly, something had an impact on the success rate of the insanity plea for those committing violent offenses. It is somewhat difficult to determine exactly what caused the observed decline in the success rate of the insanity plea for defendants charged with violent offenses. The fact that the impact is seen prior to the enactment of GBMI suggests that perhaps the *Benham* court ruling that declared Georgia's policy of automatic commitment unconstitutional may have been the impetus for the change in the success rates.

Prior to the *Benham* case, trial judges had nearly total control over who was going to be committed and when they would be released. The *Benham* ruling mandated that the state initiate a commitment hearing after a 30-day evaluation period, at which the state had to prove by clear and convincing evidence that the acquittee currently met mental health commitment standards in order for confinement to continue. In effect, the trial judge lost some control over who was going to be committed. This change in the automatic commitment practice may have contributed to the decrease in the success rate for violent offenses. That is, after *Benham*, perhaps judges were less willing to acquit by reason of insanity for a violent crime when they could not be guaranteed the defendant would be institutionalized.

To more fully explore the impact of the GBMI verdict on violent crimes, we looked at all verdicts—guilty, GBMI, NGRI, and other—for defendants pleading insanity. The "other" category included not guilty, withdrawn, deferred, and dismissed. This information is presented in Figure 7.5. It is clear that in the latter half of 1981 and the first half of 1982, there was a major shift from NGRI verdicts to guilty verdicts for defendants pleading insanity for violent crimes. Prior to this time, approximately 63% of those charged with violent crimes were found guilty, 27% were acquitted NGRI, and the rest (10%) were either found not guilty, dismissed, or deferred. After this time, the proportion found NGRI was halved to 14%.

When the GBMI legislation took effect in mid-1982, the proportion found GBMI began to grow: it increased to 15% by 1983 and to 25% during 1984 and 1985. By 1984 just over half of those pleading insanity for

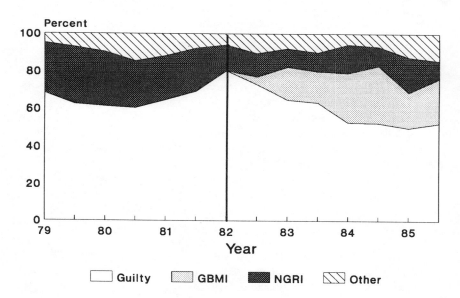

FIGURE 7.5. Distribution of verdicts for all insanity pleas charged with violent crimes in study counties of Georgia before and after the 1982 GBMI reform.

violent crimes were being found guilty, with 25% GBMI, 14% NGRI, and 10% other verdicts. These data clearly illustrate that the combination of halting the automatic commitment procedure (*Benham v. Edwards*, 1980) and creating a GBMI verdict diminished the percentage of persons successfully acquitted NGRI. Prior to the reform, someone pleading insanity for a violent crime had better than a 1 in 4 chance of being acquitted; after the reform his or her chances dropped to 1 in 7.

Although not as dramatic, a similar effect impacted nonviolent crimes. For nonviolent offenses, the percentage found NGRI was roughly 12% prior to mid-1981. After mid-1981 the percentage dropped to 7% and remained at that level throughout the study period. Guilty verdicts temporarily increased from mid-1981 through 1982 from 70% to 80%, at which point GBMI verdicts began to be used.

The same pattern is found in the trends for all crimes as well. During 1981 there was a temporary increase in guilty verdicts and a corresponding decrease in NGRI verdicts. After 1981, the proportion of cases that were acquitted NGRI remained fairly steady. These data support the view that the *Benham* decision, which occurred prior to the implementation of the GBMI verdict, affected the success rate of insanity acquittees, especially those cases involving violent offenses.

WHO USED THE INSANITY DEFENSE?

There were no statistically significant changes in the characteristics of those entering the insanity plea associated with the 1982 enactment of the GBMI verdict. Throughout the study period, defendants entering the insanity plea were typically in their late 20s and most were male (90%). The majority of defendants were nonwhite (65%) and diagnosed with a major mental illness (54%). These characteristics remained relatively stable over the study period.

THE VICTIMS IN CASES USING NGRI PLEAS

Throughout the study period approximately 40% of cases in which the insanity defense was raised were for violent offenses and 60% were for nonviolent offenses. No significant change was associated with the GBMI reform. This finding is somewhat surprising given the significant decline in the success rate for violent crimes. Apparently the defense bar either was unaware of the changes in the success rate of NGRI pleas for violent crimes or disregarded them in devising courtroom strategy. Despite the drop in successful acquittals for violent offenses, the proportion of insanity cases involving violent crimes remained essentially the same.

Regarding crimes involving a victim, we were interested in whether the sex of the victim or the victim's relationship to the defendant changed with the introduction of the GBMI verdict. Both before and after the GBMI verdict, in approximately 60% of cases with victims the victims were female. As Figure 7.6 indicates, the pattern for victim/defendant relationship was not nearly as stable. There was a peak in the percentage of related victims in the first half of 1981; perhaps this peak was associated with the initial tightening of the use of the insanity defense associated with the *Benham* decision. It is plausible that cases in which the victim was related to the defendant were more likely to be seen as acceptable for an insanity plea even in a political environment of decreasing acceptance of the appropriateness of the insanity plea.

WHO DECIDES THE CASE?

As Figure 7.7 illustrates, the majority of insanity cases both before and after the introduction of the GBMI verdict were resolved with a plea bargain. In sharp contrast to popular belief, juries rarely decide these cases. The proportion resolved by plea bargain was increasing in the early years of

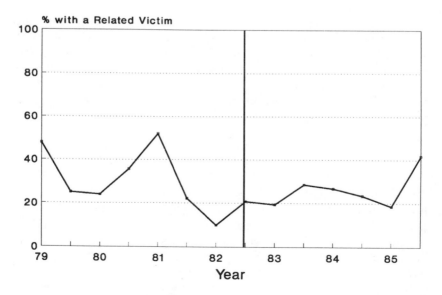

FIGURE 7.6. Percentage of victim crimes in which the victim was related to the defendant in study counties of Georgia before and after the 1982 GBMI reform.

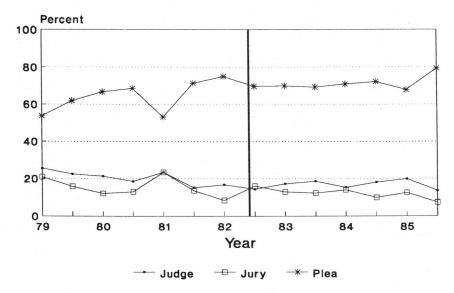

FIGURE 7.7. Percentage of insanity pleas adjudicated by a judge, jury, or plea bargain in study counties of Georgia before and after the 1982 GBMI reform.

the study and then dipped in the first half of 1981, after which it remained relatively stable at roughly 70%. The drop in plea bargained cases observed in 1981 may again be the result of the *Benham* decision. Perhaps there was a temporary drop in cases resolved by plea bargain immediately following that decision. Over the entire period, the percentage of cases decided by juries ranged from a high of 22% to a low of 8%.

THE GBMI VERDICT WAS USED FOR VIOLENT CRIMES, ESPECIALLY MURDER

Who was found GBMI when that verdict became available? To answer this question we examined the composition of the defendants who received each type of verdict before and after the introduction of the GBMI verdict. Table 7.1 contains information on those defendants found either guilty or NGRI before and after the reform and those defendants found GBMI after the reform.

The characteristics associated with being acquitted NGRI included: being older, nonwhite, female, diagnosis of major mental illness, violent crime, male victim, related victim, and adjudication by a judge. The only

TABLE 7.1. Comparative Description of Insanity Pleas by Verdict Before and After the 1982 GBMI Reform

Characteristics	Prereform			Postreform			
	Guilty	NGRI	All pleas[a]	Guilty	NGRI	GBMI	All pleas[a]
Demographic:							
Average Age	27.4	31.6	28.3	29.2	30.0	30.0	29.6
% Male	92.5	87.0	91.6	88.9	80.7	93.1	88.9
% Nonwhite	61.7	72.6	64.1	65.5	77.5	58.3	64.7
% MMI	44.3	86.2	54.9	36.0	85.3	72.5	49.6
Crime:							
% Violent	36.5	58.4	38.6	35.9	53.4	57.3	39.9
% Female Victim	60.8	47.8	57.6	56.3	32.5	67.5	56.6
% Related Victim	18.5	59.0	28.6	21.8	40.9	18.9	23.4
Adjudication:							
% Judge	3.7	69.9	15.7	3.0	88.2	18.5	14.7
% Jury	14.1	24.3	18.0	11.7	7.1	6.9	11.8

[a]Includes those found not guilty, withdrawn, dismissed, and deferred cases as well as guilty, NGRI, and GBMI.

significant change in this profile after the introduction of the GBMI verdict was in who made the ultimate decision: judges were even more likely to decide the cases after the GBMI verdict was enacted (88%) than before (70%).

The major characteristics associated with being found guilty were a diagnosis *other* than major mental illness, a nonrelated victim, and a plea bargained disposition. This profile did not change after the reform, although those found guilty were even less likely to have a major mental illness than before the reform (36% vs. 44%).

Defendants found GBMI were more likely to be male, white, and to have committed a violent offense than those found either guilty or NGRI. Most GBMIs were diagnosed with a major mental illness (73%), and had their case resolved with a plea bargain (74%). In terms of victims, GBMIs were the most likely to have victimized a female (68%) and someone to whom they were not related (81%).

As suggested by Keilitz (1987), the GBMI verdict in Georgia appeared to draw some of the more violent offenses, especially those involving unrelated victims, from both the NGRI group and those found guilty. We found that prior to the reform, 1 out of every 5 insanity cases in which the crime was murder was acquitted NGRI. After the reform, only 1 out of every 15 murder cases was acquitted NGRI. We also found that, in the postreform years, 1 out of every 4 murder cases was found GBMI. It is clear that defendants suffering from major mental illness who were charged with murder were more likely to be found GBMI than NGRI after the reform. The

GBMI verdict also drew some defendants diagnosed with a major mental illness from the guilty group. Similar to the pattern observed for the NGRIs, we found that 3 out of 4 defendants charged with murder before the reform were found guilty; after the reform it decreased to just 1 out of 2 defendants.

These data may best be understood in the context of plea bargaining. The GBMI verdict may well have been a compromise verdict for prosecutors and defense attorneys negotiating a plea bargain (C. Slobogin, personal communication, July 1992). Defense attorneys eager to avoid a death penalty may have been willing to accept a GBMI verdict rather than go to trial and risk their client's life. Similarly, prosecutors may have been willing to accept a GBMI plea with its determinate sentence and correctional confinement rather than invest the time and money in a trial.

VERDICT IS A MAJOR FACTOR IN CONFINEMENT

Part of the rationale for the enactment of the Georgia GBMI statute was a concern about insanity acquittees being released back into the community too quickly. The 1982 law specified that defendants found GBMI would be sentenced in the same manner as defendants found guilty (see Appendix C, Ga. Code 27-1503). Although the law acknowledged a defendant's mental illness, defendants were to be treated as if they had been found guilty. Psychiatric treatment was available within the resources of the Georgia Department of Corrections, but it was not mandated, nor necessarily available for those found GBMI.

We examined the confinement patterns of all defendants pleading insanity during the 7 years of our study (see Table 7.2). Both before and after the reform, the majority of defendants found guilty were sentenced to prison or jail (73% and 70%, respectively). Nearly everyone else found guilty was put on probation (26% and 29%, respectively), while fewer than 1% were hospitalized or released. Prior to the reform all NGRIs were hos-

TABLE 7.2. Comparative Description of the Disposition of Insanity Pleas Before and After the 1982 GBMI Reform

Disposition	Prereform		Postreform		
	Guilty	NGRI	Guilty	NGRI	GBMI
Prison/Jail	73.2	0.0	70.3	0.0	76.9
Probation	25.5	0.0	29.4	0.0	20.8
Hospital	0.3	100.0	0.0	97.6	2.3
Release	1.0	0.0	0.3	2.4	0.0

pitalized. Despite the court's ruling that automatic commitment was unconstitutional, virtually all (98%) of the NGRIs continued to be hospitalized after the reform. Thus the reform had little impact on the rate of institutionalization for insanity defendants found guilty or NGRI.

As we expected, the institutionalization of persons found GBMI was similar to that of defendants found guilty. A slightly larger percentage of those found GBMI went to either prison or jail (78%) and fewer were placed on probation (21%) than those found guilty. Only three people found GBMI (2%) were hospitalized.

We also looked at the sentences received by GBMI and guilty defendants. Since NGRIs did not receive a sentence, they were not included in these analyses. Table 7.3 displays the sentence data by three crime categories: murder, other violent offenses, and nonviolent offenses. The percentage of defendants receiving either a death sentence or life imprisonment is shown, as is the average sentence. The average sentence was computed only for those receiving a sentence in years. It did not include those sentenced to life imprisonment or to execution.

The average sentence for those found guilty of murder and other violent crimes after a plea of insanity did not change significantly after the reform. There was, however, a significant decrease in the average sentence for those found guilty of nonviolent offenses (5.6 years vs. 4.8 years) after the reform.

Once the GBMI verdict was available, persons found GBMI received longer sentences for both murder and other violent offenses than those who pleaded insanity but were found guilty. For cases involving murder, 52% of those found guilty received either a death sentence or life impris-

TABLE 7.3. Comparison of Sentences for Guilty and GBMI Before and After the 1982 GBMI Reform

	Prereform	Postreform	
Crime category	Guilty	Guilty	GBMI
Murder:			
% Death Sentence	5.6	7.4	0.0
% Life Sentence	45.8	44.4	70.8
Average Sentence (in years)	11.3	11.4	17.4
Other violent:			
% Life Sentence	6.9	1.9	2.0
Average Sentence (in years)	7.1	7.3	9.0
Nonviolent:			
% Life Sentence	0.5	0.0	0.0
Average Sentence (in years)	5.6	4.8	5.6

onment, while 71% of the GBMI received life imprisonment. The average sentence for the remaining guilty defendants was 11 years as compared to 17 years for the remaining GBMIs. Clearly, defendants found GBMI received harsher sentences than defendants who pleaded NGRI but were found guilty. It is important to note that none of the GBMIs received the death penalty. For nonviolent offenses, 2% of both groups received life imprisonment, and the average sentence for GBMIs was roughly 2 years longer than that given to those found guilty (9 years vs. 7 years). The difference seen in the average sentence for nonviolent offenses was not significant.

A GBMI VERDICT RESULTS IN LONG CONFINEMENT

Did harsher sentences result in longer confinements for GBMI defendants? That was the next question we examined. First, we analyzed the length of confinement patterns for those found NGRI and guilty before and after the reform. We found no significant change in their confinement patterns either as a whole or within the three crime categories we examined (murder, other violent offenses, and nonviolent offenses). That is, defendants found NGRI and guilty were confined for similar periods of time both before and after the GBMI reform. Next, we looked at the length of confinement by type of crime for the three verdicts after GBMI was enacted. The differences between the three groups were significant for murder and other violent offenses (see Figures 7.8 and 7.9). That is, the GBMIs were confined for a significantly longer period than either of the other two groups for murder and other violent offenses. All NGRIs and GBMIs charged with murder were confined for at least some period of time, while three people found guilty were placed on probation. Only 2 of the 21 GBMIs were released over the course of the follow-up (2,700 days). In comparison, roughly half of those found guilty were released within 6 years (2,200 days), and two of the six people acquitted NGRI were released within 3 years (1,000 days).

For other violent offenses, NGRIs were released the most quickly of the three groups, while GBMIs again remained in confinement the longest. Roughly half of the NGRIs were released within 1 year (300 days). Half of those found guilty were released within 2 years (636 days). For those found GBMI, however, 4½ years (1,600 days) passed before half of them were released.

There was little difference in the pattern of confinement among the three groups on nonviolent offenses, although 95% of the NGRIs were confined compared to only 60% of those found guilty or GBMI. About half of those in each group were released in less than 1 year and the bulk (80%) were released within 2 years.

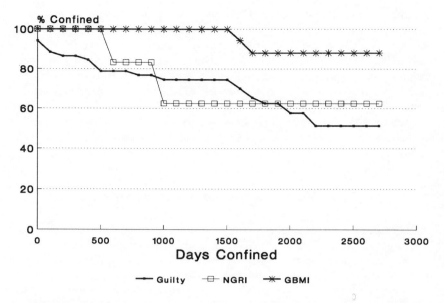

FIGURE 7.8. Confinement patterns of insanity defendants found guilty, NGRI, and GBMI on murder charges in study counties of Georgia after the 1982 GBMI reform.

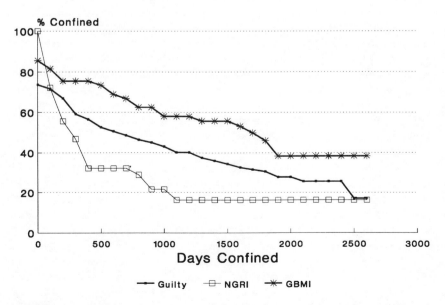

FIGURE 7.9. Confinement patterns of insanity defendants found guilty, NGRI, and GBMI for other violent crimes in study counties of Georgia after the 1982 GBMI reform.

If a major goal of the GBMI legislation was to ensure that mentally ill offenders were confined for long periods of time, our data indicate that the legislation was quite successful. Defendants found GBMI were more likely than defendants pleading insanity but found guilty to go to prison or jail and to receive a life sentence. Further, those not receiving a life sentence were given longer sentences than their guilty counterparts. They were also confined for much longer periods of time than those found NGRI.

GBMI DIMINISHES USE OF INSANITY DEFENSE

The GBMI verdict was one of the most popular reforms in the rush to reform after John Hinckley's acquittal by reason of insanity for the attempted assassination of President Ronald Reagan. Its appeal to imprisonment rather than mental hospitalization and to determinate sentences rather than indefinite commitment is undeniable. Nonetheless, its actual impact is quite uncertain. The data we have obtained on its use in Georgia, while suggesting that it may diminish use of the insanity defense, especially for those committing violent offenses, also indicate that the role of GBMI in the negotiations between defense lawyers and prosecutors is most unclear. Much more needs to be known about the actual use of the verdict before a truly informed decision can be made about the results of introducing the GBMI verdict.

Our data support Keilitz's (1987) observation that the GBMI verdict may have been used with some of the most violent offenders who, prior to the GBMI verdict, would have been found NGRI. Consistent with the idea that GBMI was drawing some of the most violent offenders among those pleading insanity, the length of confinement among defendants charged with murder and other violent offenses who were found GBMI was significantly longer than for either NGRIs or guilty. Yet it was somewhat puzzling that we found no change in the confinement patterns of defendants found NGRI or guilty after the introduction of the GBMI verdict. They were confined as long after the reform as they had been prior to the reform. This would not be expected if GBMI was really drawing the most heinous or violent offenses from these groups.

Our data do not allow us to explicate fully which factors influence a GBMI verdict and the extremely long sentences associated with that verdict. To gain insight into the factors associated with the extraordinarily long sentences seen with the GBMI verdict would require more specific information on the crimes, defendants, and court processing. Such information is crucial if we are to gain a clearer understanding of the role GBMI is playing in the criminal justice system. Is it a way to increase public safety by ensuring the lengthy confinement of the most violent, mentally ill offenders? Or is it simply a way of severely sanctioning certain mentally ill offenders whose behavior is offensive to community morals?

What is clear from our analyses is that a GBMI verdict does not miti-gate the sentence. The temporary increase in the insanity plea rate in Georgia shortly following the introduction of the GBMI verdict suggested to us that defense attorneys may have initially believed the GBMI was a compromise verdict, one that they could use to get treatment for the client or to diminish the client's sentence. This is precisely what Smith and Hall (1982) claimed was happening in Michigan after the introduction of GBMI in 1975. They found that defendants were raising the insanity plea and then using it to plea bargain for a GBMI verdict. The same thing may have oc-curred in Georgia at first. Only over time did the defense realize the nega-tive consequences for their clients of such a strategy: the likelihood of receiving a much longer sentence and period of confinement. It would appear that eventually defense lawyers realized that GBMIs received longer sentences and were confined for longer periods of time than their guilty or NGRI counterparts. As the defense became aware of the consequences, use of the plea began to decline again.

We have little reason to believe that the GBMI verdict does anything other than simply acknowledge the presence of a mental disorder. Data from a wide range of states with GBMI verdicts indicate that the treat-ment available to GBMIs is no different than that available to other pris-oners with mental health needs (Keilitz, 1987; Smith & Hall, 1982). The Georgia statute specifically states that treatment will be given to GBMIs only within available resources. It is well known that prisons have very lim-ited resources for mental health services (Fentiman, 1985). Accordingly, our data indicate that the GBMI verdict is creating a new category of pris-oner who has relatively serious mental health needs, but whose problems may be going virtually untreated. To date, courts in Michigan and Indiana that have ruled on right-to-treatment issues regarding GBMIs have deter-mined that it is not an issue of constitutional rights. These courts have recommended that legal petitions or class action suits be used to make the department of correctional services provide the mandated services (Fenti-man, 1985; McGraw, Farthing-Capowich, & Keilitz, 1985). This has yet to occur.

The addition of a GBMI verdict undoubtedly makes the insanity plea a less-appealing option for mentally ill defendants when they and their at-torneys know what the actual outcomes are. Often, neither seem to really know. In all states in which GBMI has been enacted, the defendant is required either to plead insanity or to indicate his or her intent to raise mental illness as a factor in the defense. Given the harsh reality of what can happen when a mentally ill defendant is not successful in his or her bid for an insanity acquittal, but is instead found GBMI, we would predict that, over time, defense attorneys for mentally ill defendants will be less willing to enter an insanity plea for their clients. GBMI, without question, changed the odds on a favorable outcome for an insanity plea in Georgia.

8

The Impact of Abolishing the
Insanity Defense in Montana

This chapter examines the effects of abolishing the special defense of insanity in Montana in July 1979 with the passage of the Act to Abolish the Defense of Mental Disease or Defect in Criminal Actions and to Provide an Alternative Sentencing Procedure. This law provided that "sanity" could only be considered at sentencing. The only evidence regarding a defendant's mental condition admissible for the determination of guilt was whether the defendant had the requisite intent (*mens rea*) for the crime charged, which in Montana is defined as knowingly, purposely, or negligently. This meant that, technically, the insanity defense was abolished, but a mental states concept *(mens rea)* remained as a core feature in criminal court proceedings.

A BRIEF HISTORICAL REVIEW

Abolition has been a recurring theme surrounding the insanity defense. Since the early 1960s, a number of well-known scholars have called for abolition of the insanity defense for a variety of reasons (Goldstein & Katz, 1963; Szasz, 1963; Halleck, 1967; Morris, 1968). Their arguments have ranged from ones of strict liability, that is, that all defendants should be held responsible for their actions regardless of their mental condition, to ones concerning the unfairness of recognizing lack of mental responsibility when the legal system does not recognize social injustice, to ones denouncing the insanity defense as a method of indeterminately restraining people who lack the legal requirements for conviction. On the other hand, those who oppose abolition of the insanity defense insist that it is necessary for the moral integrity of the criminal law (Morse, 1985; Bonnie, 1983; Roth, 1986–87). They feel that in order to maintain the criminal responsibility of most defendants, it is necessary to exclude from responsibility those few cases where it is impossible to impose moral blame. They contend that before there can be a crime, there must be a responsible person who can comprehend the nature and consequences of his/her actions.

Early English law was one of strict liability where the mental state of the defendant was not important. During the 13th century, the idea of moral blameworthiness became an element in the definition of crime. Most criminal offenses were defined by an *actus rea* (guilty act) and a *mens rea* (guilty mind), both of which the prosecution had to prove beyond a reasonable doubt in order to convict a defendant. Punishment became appropriate only for those who intended to do wrong (Roth, 1986–87). At that time, a successful insanity plea was like a general acquittal: the person was excused from criminal responsibility and was released. As a result, the law governing *mens rea* demanded that the defendant's madness be obvious and overwhelming. If, after acquittal, it was felt that the person was too dangerous to be released, a special hearing for civil commitment was necessary (Moran, 1985c).

With time, concerns about protecting society grew. Then, with the acquittal of James Hadfield for the attempted assassination of King George III, came the passage of the Criminal Lunatics Act of 1800. This act, which created the special defense of insanity, defined the terms by which insanity acquittees would be held upon acquittal. These included automatic and indefinite commitment procedures (Moran, 1985c).

Later, specific tests of legal insanity (such as McNaughtan, Durham, ALI) were defined for the judge and jury to use in determining criminal responsibility. Once these special insanity defense tests were incorporated into the criminal law, they superseded the *mens rea* standard in determining whether a defendant was criminally responsible for his or her behavior when his or her functioning was substantially impaired by mental disease or defect. It is also important to note that the meaning of *mens rea* has changed over time. Until recently, use of the term encompassed the concept of blameworthiness (Singer, 1983; Moran, 1985c, Brooks, 1985). It was redefined with passage of the Model Penal Code in 1962, and now it is interpreted to mean simply the intent to cause the defined act.

Most recent proposals to abolish the insanity defense call for eliminating the broader, special defense of insanity while retaining the *mens rea* requirement of the law (Brooks, 1985; American Medical Association,

1983; Morris, 1982). In essence, these proposals eliminate the special defense of insanity, but continue to allow acquittal for defendants who, due to mental disease or defect, lack the requisite state of mind to be judged guilty for the offense charged. Although the *mens rea* requirement is considerably more restrictive than the definitions of legal insanity associated with the special insanity defense (McNaughtan, ALI, Durham), defendants may still raise the issue of mental illness in their defense. Abolishing the affirmative insanity defense and leaving only the current concept of *mens rea* to assess a person's criminal responsibility is much more limiting than the earlier concept of a guilty mind.

Attempts to "completely" abolish mental disease or defect as a defense would require elimination of the *mens rea* aspect of criminal offenses (Hermann, 1983). In the early part of this century, the statutes of three states (Louisiana, Mississippi, and Washington) that abolished the defense of mental nonresponsibility were deemed unconstitutional because they had not allowed for a *mens rea* defense (Brooks, 1985).

Since then, three other states have passed legislation abolishing the affirmative insanity defense while maintaining the *mens rea* doctrine: Montana in 1979, Idaho in 1982, and Utah in 1983. Little information has been available on the effect of abolishing the affirmative insanity defense in any of these states, all of which had very few insanity acquittals either before or after their abolition. A study of acquittals due to mental status in Utah indicated that there were as many of these acquittals ($N = 7$) in the 2 years following the abolition of the defense as there were insanity acquittals during the 9 years prior to the reform (Heinbecker, 1986). The author concluded that the more restrictive law had not limited insanity acquittals. In fact, in only one of the seven postreform cases did the defendant's mental functioning actually meet the *mens rea* definition. Yet the lawyers in the other six cases were able to successfully negotiate an acquittal due to mental disease or defect in spite of the fact that the person's mental functioning did not meet the legal criteria for a *mens rea* defense.

Utah's experience with abolition appears to have confirmed some of the critics' observations that attempts to replace the insanity defense with a *mens rea* standard would not be good law reform (Monahan, 1973; Bayer, 1983). Bonnie (1983) predicted that such reform attempts would force judges and juries into stretching the new standard to include defendants with severe mental disorders because they would be morally unable to hold them responsible for their actions.

MONTANA'S EXPERIENCE WITH ABOLITION

In contrast to most insanity defense reforms, the abolition of the insanity defense in Montana was not precipitated by a notorious case. Rather, a freshman legislator, Michael Keedy, simply attacked the old law. In an interview with our project staff in 1985, Keedy said that his reasons for sponsoring a change in the insanity defense were both legal and social. He said that, legally, a separate insanity defense was not necessary because establishing the requisite state of mind is an essential element of the state's case and, socially, he was motivated to change the law because of the public's view of the insanity defense as a way of "beating a rap."

Prior to 1979, Montana used a modified ALI test that required the defendant to prove by a preponderance of evidence that mental problems made him or her unable to understand or control his or her actions. With the 1979 Reform Act, the ALI test for insanity was shifted to the sentencing phase of the criminal process and any reference to mental disease or defect as an affirmative defense was stricken (Bender, 1984). These changes were meant to shift the focus of the defendant's mental condition from the trial phase to the sentencing phase. Sentencing procedures were also changed. For those acquitted due to mental disease or defect (using the *mens rea* defense), dangerousness to others was the primary factor in disposition. If found to be dangerous, the defendant was committed to the Montana State Hospital for custody and treatment. At the initial release hearing, which was required within 180 days, the defendant could gain release by establishing, by a preponderance of the evidence, that he or she was no longer dangerous. Conditional release was also available as a disposition for those cases acquitted due to mental nonresponsibility.

Those found guilty and, at the sentencing hearing, found to be suffering from mental disease or defect (guilty and mentally ill), were automatically committed to the state hospital. The term of hospitalization was equal to the maximum sentence imposed under sentencing statutes, with no provisions made for "good time." As a result, guilty defendants who had raised mental disease or defect in their defense or at sentencing were subject to longer periods of confinement than their counterparts where mental disease or defect was not raised since inmates in the prison system earned "good time" credits to apply against their maximum sentences.

OBTAINING THE DATA

In Montana anyone who filed notice that he or she intended to raise the issue of mental disease or defect in his or her defense (which meant the lack of requisite mental state in the postreform years) was required to undergo a psychiatric examination; moreover, such an exam was also required whenever the court had reason to doubt a defendant's fitness to proceed. We collected data on all defendants for whom a psychiatric examination was ordered from January 1, 1976, through December 31, 1985, in seven study counties: Missoula, Cascade, Flathead, Gallatin, Lewis and

Clark, Silver Bow, and Yellowstone. To obtain our sample of 816 insanity pleas and 58 acquittals, we examined over 14,000 indictments in the court records of the seven study counties.

ABOLITION OF THE INSANITY DEFENSE DID NOT STOP ITS USE

The title for this section may sound odd because *abolition* means "to do away with or destroy completely." The fact that "abolition" did not stop use of the insanity defense would suggest that it did not meet the definition of *abolition*. It is apparent from the information presented in Figure 8.1 that, despite the abolition of the affirmative insanity defense in July 1979, the number of defendants pleading "insanity" did not show any noticeable decline until mid-1984. At that point the number began to decline sharply. Clearly, the number of insanity acquittals did drop dramatically after the reform, but during each 6-month period, between 40 and 50 of those indicted on felony charges continued to raise the issue of mental disease or defect in their defense. Prior to the reform, the number of insanity acquittals ranged from 3 to 14 in a 6-month period, with an aver-

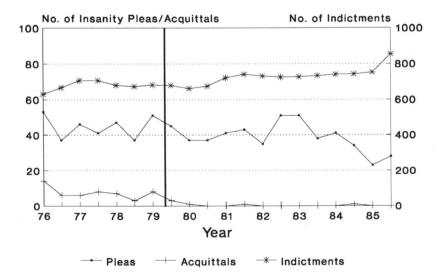

FIGURE 8.1. Number of insanity pleas, insanity acquittals, and felony indictments (right axis) in the study counties of Montana before and after the 1979 reform.

age of 7 per period. But in the 6½ years after the reform, there were only 5 insanity acquittals in the seven study counties.

The plea rate, which represents the number of mental disease or defect pleas per 1,000 felony indictments, is shown in Figure 8.2. The plea rates for the first 7 periods preceded the 1979 reform, while the plea rates for the remaining 13 periods followed the reform. It is clear that abolishing the affirmative insanity defense did not effect the rate at which defendants raised the issue of their mental responsibility. In fact, there was no statistically significant change in the plea rate following the 1979 reform.

The data presented in Figure 8.2 indicate that use of the insanity defense began to decline in the last 2 years of the study. Possibly the observed decline was a delayed response to the reform, although 3 years is a long time for such a delay effect. Another potential explanation for the 1983 decline in the plea rate was John Hinckley's acquittal in July 1982 for the attempted assassination of President Ronald Reagan. This highly publicized trial stimulated a nationwide outcry for reform or abolition of the insanity defense during which 34 states made changes in their insanity defense statutes (Callahan, Mayer, & Steadman, 1987).

Three legal experts with whom we talked while collecting data in Montana felt that the Hinckley trial had had a major effect on the insanity defense in Montana, despite the fact that the affirmative defense had been

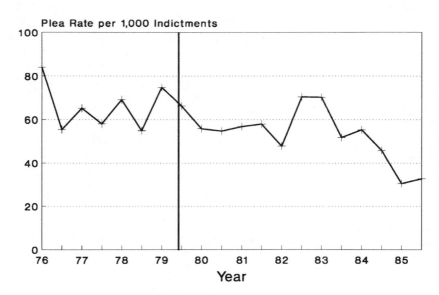

FIGURE 8.2. Insanity defense plea rate (number of pleas of mental disease or defect per 1,000 felony indictments) in study counties of Montana before and after the 1979 reform.

abolished 3 years before. Marc Raicot, a state prosecutor, John Maynard an assistant attorney general, and Ted Lympus, Flathead County attorney, all felt that the publicity surrounding the Hinckley trial led to an awareness that Montana had abolished its insanity defense and that "it couldn't happen here." Maynard went so far as to state that he believed that most prosecutors, judges, and defense attorneys had been largely unaware of or had ignored the changes in the 1979 law. There had been no formal effort to educate the legal practitioners about the changes contained in the law. To some extent, it seemed that with Hinckley's acquittal and the national focus on the insanity defense, people in Montana became aware of the changes contained in the reform for the first time.

WHO USED THE INSANITY DEFENSE?

Abolition of the insanity defense in 1979 did not substantially diminish the frequency with which the issue of mental disease or defect was raised in criminal proceedings, but did it effect the type of defendant who used the defense? We compared the demographic characteristics and criminal charges of defendants raising the insanity plea before the reform to those of defendants raising the mental disability plea after the reform. They were very similar in terms of age, diagnosis, and the type of criminal charge. The average age increased slightly from 29 years prior to the reform to 31 years after the reform. About a quarter of the plea group was diagnosed with schizophrenia or a major affective disorder both before (21%) and after (23%) the reform. Only a small percentage (7%) of the plea group was charged with murder, a third (33%) with other violent offenses, and more than half (60%) with minor felonies both before and after the reform.

The percentage of female and minority (primarily Native American) defendants raising the insanity defense did increase significantly after the reform. The percentage of females raising the defense actually doubled, increasing from 5% to 10%. An examination of this data revealed that the trend began shortly before the reform in the latter half of 1978 and continued throughout the study years. We found a similar increase in the proportion of women using the defense in all our study states despite the widely varying nature of reforms between states. This pattern suggests that it was a national phenomenon, rather than an immediate fallout of the reforms. However, the increase in minority defendants raising the plea from 9% before the reform to 17% after the reform appeared to coincide with the date of the actual reform; therefore it probably was the result of the change. We have no idea why this may have occurred, nor were any of our informants in Montana willing to speculate on the increase.

We also looked at the characteristics of the victim of the crime and the method of adjudication, but again found no changes. Of those crimes with victims, just over one-half had a female victim both before (52%) and after (55%) the reform, and roughly one-quarter of the defendants were related to the victim (23% prereform; 21% postreform). The vast majority of cases involving an insanity plea both before (85%) and after (82%) the reform were disposed of by a judge in a bench trial.

VIRTUALLY NO ONE WAS ACQUITTED AFTER THE REFORM

While we found no relationship between the 1979 reform and the number of people raising mental disease or defect as their defense, and little change in the characteristics of those raising the defense, we did find a very strong relationship between the enactment of the reform and a decrease in the number of acquittals due to mental disease or defect. Figure 8.3 illustrates the success rate of mental disease or defect pleas, which is the number of acquittals due to mental disease or defect divided by the number of persons raising the issue in their defense, for each 6-month period during the study. While the success rate was declining prior to the 1979 reform, there was a marked *drop* following the reform ($p < .001$). In the 6 years after the reform, only five people in the seven study counties were successfully

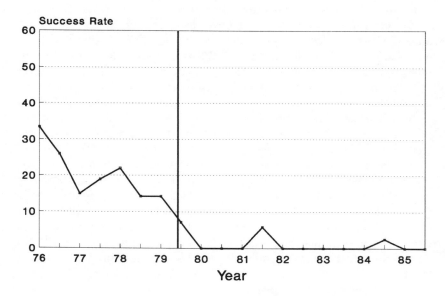

FIGURE 8.3. Percentage of insanity pleas acquitted NGRI in study counties of Montana before and after the 1979 reform.

acquitted due to their mental state at the time of the crime. This represented 5 defendants out of the 466 (1%) who raised the issue in their defense. Three of the acquittals occurred within the first year following the reform and may have been tried under the old law.

These data clearly indicate that after the reform in Montana it became virtually impossible for anyone to be acquitted due to lack of *mens rea* or requisite mental state. This suggests that the reform had an immediate and large impact, even though it did not affect the number or rate at which the insanity defense was raised. Further, it implies that the judges who were presiding over these cases were well aware of the changes in the law regardless of whether defense attorneys were clear about its contents or implications. On the other hand, our findings may simply mean that the plea rate did not change because the ultimate disposition of these cases really did not change that much. Even though the chances of obtaining an acquittal on the grounds of insanity were virtually eliminated with the reform, perhaps it was still somehow advantageous for a defendant to raise the plea.

ALTERNATIVE METHODS CREATED TO DEAL WITH INSANITY PLEAS CASES

When an earlier paper (Steadman, Callahan, Robbins, & Morrissey, 1989) reporting the initial results of Montana's abolition of the insanity defense was published, a senior staff member at Montana State Hospital (formerly Warm Springs State Hospital) indicated that it was her belief that those who were found NGRI before the reform were now being found incompetent to stand trial (IST). People who, prior to the reform, would have gone to the hospital for an IST and/or NGRI evaluation and who then would have been returned to the court to stand trial were now being civilly committed to the hospital after being found IST with charges dismissed.

Since we had information about IST evaluations for our sample, we looked at trends in the frequency of its use before and after the reform. We found that the proportion of felony indictments evaluated for IST remained virtually the same before (14%) and after (16%) the reform. We then looked at the verdicts of those found IST. Prior to the reform, the large majority of those found IST were acquitted NGRI (72%), while smaller percentages had their charges dismissed or deferred (22%), or were found guilty (6%). In contrast, after the reform, the vast majority of those found IST had their charges dismissed or deferred (79%), while only small percentages were found NGRI (8%), guilty and mentally ill (3%), or guilty (10%). These data are striking. They clearly indicate that even though the proportion of ISTs remained the same, the eventual verdicts in these cases changed dramatically. Prior to the reform, less than a quarter of the group had their charges dismissed or deferred, while after the reform, the large majority had their charges dismissed or deferred.

This dispositional change is clearly illustrated in Figure 8.4. As suggested above, the trends of the NGRI group and the IST group were inversely related to one another. The percentage found NGRI decreased dramatically at the time of the reform, while the percentage of persons found IST and had their charges dismissed or deferred began to increase. The percentage found guilty remained relatively stable until 1982 when it increased temporarily for a couple of years. These results would support the local staffperson's suggestion that many of the people who prior to the reform were found NGRI were now being found IST with charges dismissed or deferred. Subsequently, we also determined that many of the IST cases were civilly committed to the same unit of the hospital as those who were acquitted NGRI. A different legal statute was being used to produce nearly identical results for defendants raising a mental disease or defect defense. It appears that IST became the surrogate for the insanity defense in the years following the reform.

We were also interested to see whether people found guilty were raising the issue of their mental illness at sentencing as permitted under the new law. We were able to identify seven cases, two before the reform and five after the reform, where it was clear that the defendant's mental illness was considered at sentencing. In all seven of these cases the defendant

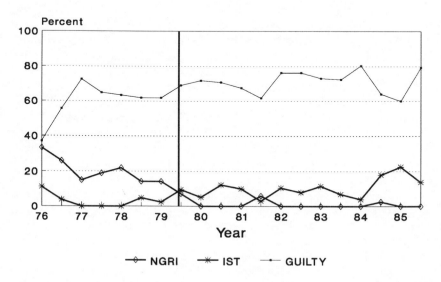

FIGURE 8.4. Percentage of insanity pleas acquitted due to insanity (NGRI), found incompetent to stand trial (IST), and found guilty in study counties of Montana before and after the 1979 reform.

was found guilty, but each was sentenced to serve a term at Montana State Hospital as specified in the law. We refer to these cases as guilty *and* mentally ill (GAMI).

There were a number of other cases where it was not clear what had transpired. Seven defendants were found guilty, but had their sentences suspended under the condition that they receive inpatient hospitalization, and a larger group were found guilty and given probation with conditions specifying that they receive mental health treatment. Not surprisingly, we found a few more cases with a guilty verdict and a disposition of mental health treatment after the reform (9%) than before (4.5%). In fact, the prevalence of such cases more than doubled after the reform.

WHO RECEIVED MENTAL HEALTH DISPOSITIONS BEFORE AND AFTER THE REFORM

In an effort to determine whether those defendants who were found IST and had the charges dismissed or deferred after the reform were similar to the group found NGRI before the reform, we defined a group that consisted of all defendants with a mental health–related outcome (MHRO) before and after the reform. This group was composed of:

1. Those found NGRI before the reform ($N = 50$) and those found not guilty due to mental disease or disorder after the reform ($N = 6$).
2. Those found IST with charges dismissed or deferred either before ($N = 7$) or after the reform ($N = 53$).
3. Those found guilty *and* mentally ill (GAMI) but sentenced to serve their term in the mental hospital before ($N = 2$) and after the reform ($N = 6$).

The verdicts of the MHRO group (NGRI, IST, or GAMI) both before and after the reform are shown in Figure 8.5. Prior to the reform, the vast majority of the group were found NGRI (85%), and after the reform the majority were found IST (82%).

Figure 8.6 displays the characteristics of those with a mental health–related outcome (MHRO) before and after the reform. There were no major differences associated with the reform in their age, gender, or ethnicity. The average age was 31 years before and 33 years after the reform. The percentage of females and minority defendants remained virtually the same before and after the reform. Women comprised 9% of the MHRO group before and after the reform, while minority defendants increased from 6% to 9%.

There were significant pre- to postreform changes in diagnosis and crime for this group. Whereas 53% of the MHRO group were diagnosed

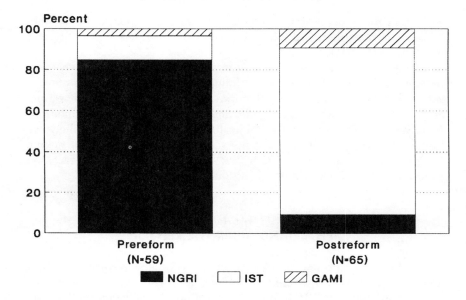

FIGURE 8.5. Composition of the mental health related outcome (MHRO) group in study counties of Montana before and after the 1979 reform.

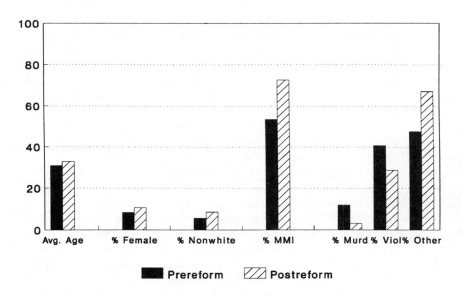

FIGURE 8.6. Characteristics of the mental health related outcome (MHRO) group and their arrest charges in study counties of Montana before and after the 1979 reform.

with schizophrenia or a major affective disorder before the reform, 72% of the postreform MHRO group were so diagnosed. In terms of criminal charges, a significantly larger percentage of the MHRO group were charged with nonviolent offenses after the reform period than before. While 12% of this group were charged with murder before the reform, after the reform only 3% faced murder charges. Similarly, the percentage of persons charged with other violent offenses dropped from 41% before the reform to 30% afterward. Overall, defendants with mental health dispositions after the reform were more likely to have a major psychiatric diagnosis and were more likely to have committed a nonviolent offense than those with a MHRO before the reform. These data suggest that the reform may have decreased the likelihood of a mental health outcome for certain defendants: those with less serious mental disorders and those who committed violent offenses.

The method by which cases were adjudicated did not change substantially across the study period, although there was a small increase (from 2% to 5%) in the percentage of cases adjudicated by a jury after the reform. In terms of victims, the percentage with a female victim was fairly consistent before (52%) and after the reform (59%). There was, however, a more substantial change in the relationship of the victim to the defendant associated with the reform. Prior to the reform, in 19% of the cases where there was a victim, the victim was related to the defendant; after the reform, this figure dropped to 11%.

Despite these diagnosis and criminal offense differences, the characteristics of the MHRO group were fairly similar before and after the reform. These findings add further support to the hypothesis that the types of cases that were found NGRI before the abolition of the special insanity defense were being found IST in the years after the reform. The same type of defendants were coming through the courts but were simply being disposed of differently.

HOW DID ABOLITION EFFECT PATTERNS OF RELEASE?

To assess how these legal reforms impacted on the confinement histories of the MHRO group, we looked at both their dispositions and their lengths of confinement. Figure 8.7 shows the disposition of those found guilty and those acquitted or found IST or GAMI before and after the reform. The results suggest that after the 1979 reform fewer people were confined, either in hospitals or in prisons. Of those found guilty, a smaller percentage were sentenced to prison or jail after the reform (62%) than before (69%), and a larger percentage were placed on probation or conditionally released after the reform (29%) than before (22%).

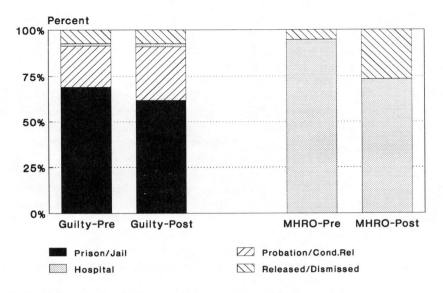

FIGURE 8.7. Number of insanity pleas, insanity acquitals, and felony indictments (right axis) in the study counties of Montana before and after the 1979 reform.

In fact, 27% of the MHRO group (those found NGRI, IST, or GAMI) were released or dismissed after the reform compared to only 5% before the reform ($p <. 01$). This is largely due to the fact that many defendants found IST with charges dismissed or deferred were released (36%), whereas nearly everyone acquitted NGRI was hospitalized. Since most of the MHRO group was found NGRI prior to the reform, most were hospitalized. After the reform, fewer were hospitalized, as one-third of those found IST with charges dismissed or deferred were released when they were found incompetent.

Figures 8.8 and 8.9 present the length of stay for the MHRO group before and after the reform in terms of violent and nonviolent crimes. The mean length of stay for those charged with violent offenses was roughly the same prior to the reform (750 days) as after the reform (668 days), while the median length of stay dropped considerably, from 305 days to 123 days, after the reform. The fact that the median length of stay was so much shorter after the reform reflects our finding that a large percentage of the MHRO group was released after the IST finding and not hospitalized. Those who were hospitalized for violent crimes after the reform tended to stay almost as long as those hospitalized before the reform. The pattern of hospitalization displayed in Figure 8.8 reflects these data as well.

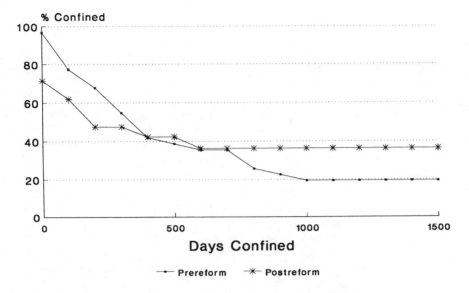

FIGURE 8.8. Confinement patterns of mental health related outcome (MHRO) group charged with violent crimes in study counties of Montana before and after the 1979 reform.

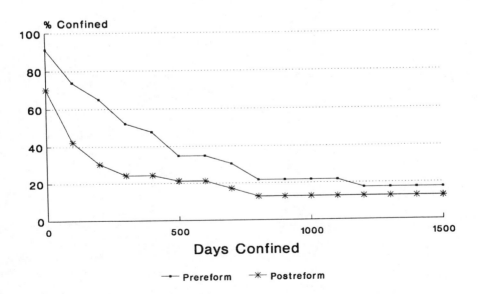

FIGURE 8.9. Confinement patterns of mental health related outcome (MHRO) group charged with nonviolent crimes in study counties of Montana before and after the 1979 reform.

In contrast, the length of stay for nonviolent offenses was significantly shorter after the reform than before ($p < .02$). The mean length of stay was 640 days prior to the reform compared to 205 days after the reform, while the median decreased from 328 days to 77 days.

DID MONTANA REALLY ABOLISH THE INSANITY DEFENSE?

One of the most interesting results from Montana's abolition experience is the fact that the plea rate remained nearly the same after the reform as before. People continued to raise mental illness in their defense at the same rate despite the fact that virtually no one was acquitted due to lack of *mens rea* after that standard went into effect. Initially, this was a very puzzling result to us. We asked ourselves why, if the insanity defense had been abolished, did people continue to raise the plea? Did defendants and defense attorneys not understand that the insanity defense had been abolished? Or was there some kind of incentive in the process that still made it worthwhile to enter a plea of mental disease or defect? Our analyses of the data strongly suggest that the latter question must be answered with a resounding "yes."

After the reform, most mental disease or defect cases were being eliminated from criminal justice processing prior to adjudication. They were being found IST, their charges were dismissed or deferred, and they ended up being hospitalized in the same settings where NGRI cases had been sent. Faced with the loss of one avenue, the legal and mental health systems simply found another way to accomplish the same end. If a person's mental status was seen as sufficient to warrant reduced criminal responsibility, they were found IST and committed to the same hospital and the same wards where they would have been confined if they had been found NGRI.

Montana's experience with abolition, like Utah's, supports the argument of the critics of abolition who contend that there will always be a certain group of offenders who are so severely impaired as to make their punishment repugnant and who need special consideration. Further, our data suggest that abolishing the special insanity defense does not necessarily result in the majority of cases being found guilty, with mental illness considered only at sentencing, as many reformers have advocated. In fact, we found such a scenario occurred for only a small proportion of cases. Rather, the majority of cases were either transferred from the criminal justice system to the civil system, or they were simply released into the community with little or no treatment.

These data again highlight the necessity of adopting a systemic approach when assessing insanity defense reforms. If we had not collected information on IST evaluations, we might have concluded that only a handful of people were actually acquitted under the *mens rea* alternative and a few more were convicted and sentenced to mental health treatment. We would have overlooked the most frequent way by which insanity cases were being disposed. Our conclusions would have been considerably different.

Also of interest in Montana was the increasing incidence of mandatory mental health treatment for those convicted after the 1979 reform. This group of defendants was similar, psychiatrically, to those in our cohort who were found guilty and sentenced to terms of incarceration or probation. Yet during our study period there was a twofold increase in court-ordered mental health treatment. Our data indicated that these were *not* cases that would have been found NGRI before the abolition; instead, they closely resembled those found guilty. The increase in mental health dispositions for those convicted was not anticipated.

Montana did abolish the insanity defense, but mentally ill offenders did not disappear. They were still being processed through the courts and criminal justice system. Having one avenue of confinement blocked (NGRI), the courts have made more liberal use of another option (IST) to manage mentally ill offenders. Moreover, we found little evidence that consideration of mental illness was shifted to sentencing.

9

The Next Wave of Reform

There will be another wave of insanity defense reform. We cannot say where, we cannot say when, but it is inevitable. In 1992, in Milwaukee, Wisconsin, Jeffrey Dahmer seemed to offer a strong prospect for such a surge, but he was convicted of 15 counts of murder rather than being acquitted by reason of insanity. His conviction stifled further cries for reforming the insanity defense for now. Regardless of the outcome of the Dahmer trial, however, every time a heinous, high-visibility criminal defendant pleads insanity, more than the defendant is put on trial.

Look at the headlines about Dahmer and John Hinckley a decade earlier:

- "Why Insanity Defense Is Breaking Down"—*National Law Journal*, May 3, 1982
- "The Insanity Plea on Trial"—*Newsweek*, June 24, 1992
- "Is the System Guilty?: A Stunning Verdict Puts the Insanity Defense on Trial"—*Time*, July 5, 1982
- "The Insanity Plea on Trial"—*New York Times Magazine*, August 8, 1982

The media recognize that the insanity defense itself is tested in the public's eye in every one of these cases. In Chapter 1 we noted Tighe's (1983:224) observation that periodic, high-visibility insanity defense trials "have been a regular feature of American life since the early nineteenth century and have just as regularly resulted in legal reform campaigns." But no previous reform campaign equaled the magnitude of reform following John Hinckley's acquittal.

WHY STUDY INSANITY DEFENSE REFORM?

The main goal of our research has been to document exactly what the Hinckley-era reforms really produced. Within 2½ years of John Hinckley's 1982 acquittal, 34 states had changed their insanity defense statutes. We sought to document what happened as a result of these legislative changes so that when the next cry for reform occurs a more reasoned and factual response might be possible. We are not so naive as to expect empirical data alone to set the directions or pace of change in such a volatile and politically charged arena as insanity and public safety. We do believe, however, that the public's interests are best served by reasoned discourse about alternative courses of action.

Often there is little relationship between the stated goals and the actual accomplishments of legal reforms. As documented in our research, the victories of insanity defense reform can be illusory and totally symbolic. Black letter law is altered, but actual practices are barely modified. This is clear from our assessment of California's 1982 insanity test changes (see Chapter 3). Alternatively, the consequences of reform can be far different than the intended outcomes. This is illustrated by our analysis of Montana's 1978 "abolition" of the insanity defense (Chapter 8) and our examination of Georgia's 1982 introduction of a guilty but mentally ill statute (Chapter 7). Very rarely have the results of legal reforms in the insanity defense been so well documented. It is costly and time-consuming work, and it is not highly valued. As a result, there was little factual knowledge available when the rush to reform surged in 1982.

SENATE JUDICIARY SUBCOMMITTEE
ON CRIMINAL LAW HEARINGS

Three days after John Hinckley's acquittal by reason of insanity on June 21, 1982, the Subcommittee on Criminal Law of the Committee on the Judiciary of the United States Senate began hearings on "Limiting the Insanity Defense." Over the course of 3 days of hearings, a total of 25 witnesses offered their opinions, anecdotes, and observations, but provided precious little data on how the insanity defense was operating in the United States. These hearings were a preview of what was to transpire repeatedly in legislative hearing rooms in many states over the next 2½ years. What the Senate Committee's deliberations so well illustrate is the dearth of real data that the reformers could draw upon to inform their proposals.

The Committee's acting chair, Arlen Specter, the senior senator from Pennsylvania, opened the hearing with this statement:

> This hearing has been convened promptly because of the public concern engendered by the acquittal of Mr. Hinckley. The American public has raised the question appropriately as to whether the criminal justice system can deal with violent crime and whether or not the legal technicalities weigh too heavily in favor of defendants. That has been a recurrent issue in the criminal justice system and has been posed in the Hinckley trial with respect to the insanity defense.
>
> This hearing has been convened as promptly as possible so that the public will be aware that the law can respond to correct errors where such errors are found in the criminal justice system.

The Committee's goal apparently was to correct the errors inherent in John Hinckley's insanity acquittal by obtaining relevant information from expert witnesses. A bill "To Amend Title 18 to Limit the Defense of Insanity" (S. 2669) had been submitted in the U.S. Senate on June 23, 1982, the day before the Senate hearings began. Thus proposed legislation to solve the errors had already been introduced before any testimony from these witnesses was heard. Nonetheless, it is instructive to review the quality of the information that the witnesses offered.

Many facts and figures were cited. However, not one number, not one study was based on more than a single jurisdiction. No study cited by any witness addressed questions about what could be expected from the changes proposed in any of the seven bills pending before the Senate. One of us (Steadman) was the next-to-last witness. In prepared testimony, he cited ten studies with data on insanity acquittals and one on insanity pleas. Additional statistics, published and unpublished, were presented by other witnesses such as Dr. James L. Cavanaugh, Jr., Dr. Jonas R. Rappeport, and Dr. Stuart Silver. Relevant reports were cited on the characteristics of insanity acquittees, their crimes and lengths of confinement, especially as compared to defendants who were convicted of similar charges and incarcerated. Conspicuous by their absence, however, were any studies on the characteristics of defendants who *plead* insanity, the success rates of these *pleas*, and how the insanity *plea* and acquittal systems changed as a result of specific legal reforms.

From its inception in 1985, the goal of our research was to fill these data gaps, to the extent that any one study could. This book is based on 5,302 insanity pleas culled from over 600,000 felony indictments. We tracked the impact of five major types of legal reforms for at least 6 years in each of the four study states. We hoped that when the next wave of insanity defense reforms occurred these data would be used to inform the debates. Our findings will not resolve the inherent tensions between punishment and exculpation in the insanity defense, but we do hope that the dialogue about these competing interests might proceed more rationally as a result of their availability.

In approaching the issue of insanity defense reform, we found it useful to categorize specific reforms by the judicial processing point at which they were targeted. *Adjudication* ("front-end") reforms occur at the earliest stages of this processing. They focus on the determination of insanity at the verdict phase. In our study, we examined two types of adjudication reforms: the *test* of insanity and the *burden* of proof. The first type of reform is represented by California's change from an ALI test to a restrictive form of the McNaughtan test in 1982, and the second is represented by the shift of the burden of proof from the state to the defendant in Georgia in 1978 and in New York in 1984. Both of these latter reforms also included a change in the standard of proof from beyond a reasonable doubt to beyond a preponderance of the evidence.

Dispositional ("back-end") reforms include the wide array of changes that focus on the detention or release of a defendant after being found not guilty by reason of insanity. In our research, we examined the dispositional reforms made in New York in 1980. To a great extent, perceived abuses in this postverdict phase most infuriate the public and generate the rush to reform. As Ellis (1986:963) has observed,

> [I]t cannot be doubted that the public's principal concern is the likelihood that an acquitted defendant will be released from custody more quickly than the public deems desirable. Indeed, the popular dissatisfaction with other issues, such as allocation of the burden of proof on the insanity issue and insanity standard, is fueled ultimately by concern over the possibility that too many defendants are "getting off," which to many in the general public means "going free."

Combination reforms involve "front-end" as well as "back-end" changes. The two examples of this type of reform that we studied are Montana's 1978 abolition of the traditional insanity defense and Georgia's 1982 introduction of a guilty by mentally ill (GBMI) verdict. These reforms impacted both the verdict and the dispositional stage by altering the test for exculpation and by changing the procedures and standards by which a defendant would be released.

WHAT WERE THE BOTTOM LINES?

We obtained some relatively clear results about the impacts of these three types of reform.

Adjudication Reforms

California's 1978 Insanity Defense Test Reform

In 1982 California shifted from a relatively liberal ALI standard for insanity that required a substantial incapacity to appreciate the nature of the act or to recognize that it was wrong. It moved to a McNaughtan test that was much more restrictive by requiring that the defendant both did not know right from wrong *and* could not appreciate the nature of his or her conduct. The intent was to make it much more difficult for defendants to be acquitted by reason of insanity. We found that:

- No significant changes occurred in the rate of insanity pleas, the rate of insanity acquittals, or the success rate of insanity pleas.
- There was a steady decline in the rate of insanity pleas throughout the study period (1979–84). It began prior to the 1980 reform and continued at a similar pace after the change from ALI to McNaughtan.
- There were no significant changes in the characteristics of or the criminal charges for defendants pleading insanity or being acquitted not guilty by reason of insanity.
- There were no significant changes in the confinement patterns of insanity acquittees.
- The declining rate of insanity pleas throughout the study period seemed to result from a 1979 change in confinement terms of insanity acquittees (a dispositional reform). This reform set a maximum term of commitment for insanity acquittees equal to the sentence they would have received if they had been convicted with no allowance for "good time."

Burden and Standard of Proof: Georgia (1978) and New York (1984)

Both Georgia, in 1978, and New York, in 1984, made changes in their adjudication phases of insanity defense pleas consistent with the major pieces of legislation before the U.S. Senate Judiciary Subcommittee on Criminal Law in 1982 discussed earlier in this chapter. They placed the burden on the defendant to prove he or she was insane, rather than requiring the state to prove that the defendant was sane. Both also shifted the standard of proof from beyond a reasonable doubt to a preponderance of evidence. We found that:

- In both states there was a significant *decrease* in the insanity plea rate (i.e., there were fewer insanity pleas per 1,000 felony indictments).
- Although many scholars predicted a decline in the success rate, we

found no change in Georgia and an increase in the success rate in New York.

- We explained the unexpected findings in the success rate by the observed changes in the population pleading insanity and those acquitted. The most dramatic change was in the significant increase in defendants both pleading insanity and acquitted NGRI who had a diagnosis of major mental illness. In New York there was also an increase in success rate for women and those committing violent offenses.
- These adjudication changes drastically altered the type of person raising the defense: those with questionable cases were less likely to plead insanity; hence the decline in the plea rate and no changes in the success rate.

Dispositional Reform

Changes in Commitment and Release Procedures: New York (1980)

We studied New York's Insanity Defense Reform Act of 1980 which defined specific procedures for the commitment and release of insanity acquittees. Primary among the changes were: (1) a 30-day evaluation period to assess current mental status rather than automatic commitment based on presumed insanity; (2) a postverdict evaluation classification system for acquittees to distinguish between those considered dangerous and those not dangerous and then between those mentally ill and those not; and (3) increased court review of those considered dangerous such that the criminal courts had the final say on release, furlough, and transfer decisions while the acquittee was under the auspice of the state Office of Mental Health.

Our major findings were:

- There were no significant changes in the plea rate, although there was a gradual decline after the reform.
- There was a temporary, but significant, increase in the success rate of insanity pleas, especially for defendants charged with violent crimes. We concluded this was due to changes in the law that gave the trial judges and district attorneys nearly total control over any release decisions. They did not need to be concerned about any premature release of persons considered dangerous.
- No change was observed in the characteristics or crimes of insanity defendants who were acquitted, or in the types of crimes with which they were charged.
- There were changes in their processing. Roughly 85% were plea bargained after the reform compared to just 8% before the reform.

This was a part of the change in the law. Acquittals could be the result of a plea bargain, whereas before there was no formal process to plea bargain for an insanity acquittal.

- We did find one change in disposition. A small percentage (12%) of acquittees were released after the 30-day evaluation period following acquittal rather than being committed. Despite the immediate release of a small group of acquittees, there was no significant change in their lengths of hospitalization.
- Across all crime categories, insanity acquittees stay confined longer than those convicted. The fact that they stay so long may well influence the very low use of the plea in New York as compared to other states.

Combination Reforms

Guilty but Mentally Ill Statute: Georgia (1982)

Immediately following John Hinckley's acquittal in 1982, Georgia enacted a guilty but mentally ill verdict (GBMI). The intent of this verdict was to give the jury an alternate mental health verdict. This verdict acknowledges that the defendant was mentally ill at the time of the offense, but that he or she still meets the criminal law standards for being responsible for his or her conduct. As such, they are given a regular criminal sentence with a requirement that they receive mental health treatment. Regardless of the course of that treatment, the full sentence, with any earned "good time," must be served. We found:

- There was a temporary and delayed increase in the rate of insanity pleas.
- There was no change in the success rate overall, although there was a significant decline in the success rate for violent crimes associated with the reform.
- The actual change appeared to be due to the *Benham* decision which occurred about one year before the GBMI was enacted. That decision declared Georgia's policy of automatic and indefinite commitment unconstitutional. The judiciary appears to have become more conservative after that finding; certainly, there was a major shift from NGRI to guilty verdicts for those raising insanity. Shortly thereafter the GBMI was enacted. Once it was available, it began drawing cases from the guilty group, who prior to *Benham* probably would have been found NGRI.
- Those who were found GBMI were more likely to have committed a violent offense than either those found guilty or NGRI. They were also seriously mentally ill, used a plea bargain, and were likely to have committed crimes involving unrelated, female victims.

- Despite the fact that the law specified that anyone found GBMI would be sentenced in the same manner as someone found guilty, we found that the former received longer sentences and longer periods of confinement than those who pleaded insanity but were found guilty.
- The enactment of a GBMI verdict made the insanity plea a less-appealing option for those with serious mental illness. It definitely reduced the odds of a favorable outcome with such a plea.

Abolition of an Insanity Defense: Montana (1979)

We examined Montana's abolition of the insanity defense in 1979. Although there was no longer a special defense, defendants could still raise the issue of mental disease or defect in their defense as part of *mens rea*. We determined that:

- Much to our surprise, there was no change in either the volume or rate of insanity pleas.
- There was also little change in the population raising the plea before and after the reform.
- The success rate of insanity pleas dropped dramatically.
- After further investigation we found that a large majority of people who probably would have been found NGRI prior to the reform were simply being found IST after the reform and their charges were being dismissed or deferred.
- The postreform IST group was somewhat more likely to have a serious mental illness and less likely to be violent; otherwise they closely resembled the prereform NGRI population.
- There were some changes in dispositions postreform. More defendants were being released rather than hospitalized. Those committing violent offenses were confined for roughly the same period of time, while those with nonviolent offenses were not confined as long.
- Rather than eliminating mental illness dispositions with abolition, the types of cases previously being found NGRI were being found IST and being detained in the same units of the same facility.

THE MESSAGE FOR FUTURE REFORMERS

As we noted in Chapter 3, well over 100 reforms were made in laws pertaining to the insanity defense from 1978 to 1990. The large majority (85%) of these reforms closely followed the acquittal of John Hinckley. These reforms represented efforts by 34 states to strike a balance between individual rights and the public's concerns of safety. We examined the effects of five major types of reforms in this book and found that the reforms did have significant impact on the operation of the insanity defense, some more so than others. Our work would suggest, as have others' (Morse, 1985; Hermann, 1983; Ellis, 1986), that if states desire to restrict use of the insanity defense, it is better to reform those specific aspects of the defense deemed in need of change, rather than to either abolish the insanity defense or offer a compromise verdict such as the GBMI. The fact that some of the reforms resulted in the anticipated or desired results suggests that, with careful consideration, the insanity defense can be molded and structured in such a way as to safeguard the rights of defendants and to provide for the protection of the public. It is not a static doctrine, but rather is very flexible. Who is eligible, who is acquitted, and how they are treated depends upon how the defense is structured.

Generally, the two most frequently cited goals of insanity defense reform are to limit its use and to prevent the premature release of danger- ous people. We found that shifting the burden of proof to the defense, a reform that the majority of states have made, resulted in a major reduc- tion in use of the defense. Not only was there a significant decline in the plea rate, but the composition of those using the defense also changed. This reform seemed to ensure that those who were using the defense, both those pleading and those acquitted, were seriously mentally ill. Since the majority of states have already made this reform, it is likely that use of the insanity defense has already been restricted in these states and is currently being used by a more limited group of mentally ill offenders.

Changing the burden of proof appeared to be much more effective in limiting use of the defense than California's change in the insanity test. However, the fact that California had shifted the burden of proof to the defense prior to changing the test may have limited the possible effects of the latter reform. This may be an instance of a reform having differential effects depending upon when it is enacted. Common perception and a number of studies indicate that changing the test from McNaughtan to the ALI standard did indeed broaden the class of defendants eligible for the insanity defense. Yet when we examined the opposite reform, making the test more restrictive, we found no evidence of an effect. Perhaps the change occurred not at the beginning, but in the middle of a politically conserva- tive climate in which other factors were operating to limit use of the defense.

What did seem to have an impact on a declining use of the insanity defense in California was a change in commitment laws. The major decline we found in use of the insanity plea in California seemed to correlate with the introduction of a "maximum period of confinement" given to the NGRI acquittee at the time of confinement that equaled the maximum term of incarceration applicable to someone convicted of the same charge. The maximum period of confinement represented a longer period of confine- ment for the insanity acquittee than what he or she could expect if, for example, he or she plea bargained to a lesser offense. Moreover, the maximum term of confinement did not take into account any "good time," otherwise a common procedure in the correctional setting. As a result, little incentive was left for someone to plead insanity. The fact that the term of confinement was given to the defendant at the time of acquittal or confinement would facilitate feedback within the system. The defense attorney would know the expected term of confinement almost immediately, which would then be considered in the next case involving the insanity defense.

New York's reform in commitment and release procedures also resulted in changes, although they were not as dramatic as those associated with California's dispositional change. New York replaced its automatic commitment procedure with a process that included an evaluation period (30 days) followed by classification based on dangerousness and mental illness which influenced the type and length of confinement. We found that the reform resulted in a significant change in whether someone was hospitalized, although it did not significantly affect the length of confinement. We also found that the length of stay for insanity acquittees was long—indeed, longer than for other defendants who raised the defense, but who were found guilty. We hypothesized that this was probably due to restrictive release procedures which require notification of the prosecuting attorney and judicial approval for acquittees initially considered dangerous, as well as the aggressive use of conditional release.

Although we did not conduct a community follow-up of those released, another study in New York found that less than 5% of acquittees released were subsequently arrested for violent offenses including murder, attempted murder, or aggravated assault (McGreevy & Dollard, 1989). These data would suggest that laws pertaining to the confinement and release of insanity acquittees can be formulated in such a way as to positively impact on the public's concerns regarding the premature release of dangerous people. Our work suggests that changes in the burden and standard of proof and on commitment and release procedures had direct effects on the use of, and outcomes associated with, the insanity defense.

In contrast, efforts to limit use of the insanity defense by abolishing the defense or enacting a GBMI plea and verdict seemed less effective. Montana's abolition was little more than slight of hand. The large majority of those who probably would have been found NGRI prior to the 1979 abolition were simply found IST, with charges either dismissed (lesser offenses) or deferred (more serious offenses), after the reform. They were treated in the same hospital, the same wards, just under a different legal label. Our study would support the contentions of critics (Bonnie, 1983; Cobun, 1984) that there are some mentally ill offenders who are so seriously ill that the legal profession could not, morally, hold them criminally responsible. So, regardless of the law, a mechanism is found to accommodate this need.

Similarly, efforts to restrict use of the insanity defense by enacting a GBMI plea and verdict were not "clearly" successful. It did not seem to limit the rate at which the defense was raised, although there was a decline in successful use of the defense for certain types of violent offenses. The fact that the large majority of those found GBMI were diagnosed with major mental illnesses seemed to support concerns that the GBMI verdict would allow for the conviction of those who would otherwise be found NGRI. Another troubling aspect of the GBMI verdict was that it appeared to create a new class of prisoners, a group with serious mental illness who were sentenced to extremely long periods of incarceration and were actually incarcerated for longer periods than defendants found guilty of similar charges. Without further "process-oriented" research in which more-detailed information on the defendants' criminal background and the commission of the crime are obtained, it is impossible to determine why they were given such long sentences. On the surface, it appears to be discriminatory.

SOME MAJOR RESEARCH ISSUES REMAINING

As with most research studies, there were as many questions raised during the process of our project as answered by the data collected and analyzed. One terribly significant issue that emerged from our data, but which could not be adequately addressed with our research, is the wide variation both within and across states in use of the insanity defense. There were substantial differences across states with similar procedures, and even more interestingly across the study counties within the same states. Not only did we see major differences in the rates of use of the insanity plea, but also in its rates of success, in the types of crime for which the defense is usually successful, and in the lengths of subsequent confinements. The source of such variations may lie within the workings of the court system, perhaps in the discretion vested in the prosecutors and the judges presiding in each jurisdiction. A more in-depth understanding of the operation of the insanity defense requires comprehensive study of the factors influencing decisions to enter an insanity defense and all of the negotiations leading to an insanity acquittal.

It was apparent that in New York and California insanity acquittees were charged with more serious offenses than insanity acquittees in Georgia and Montana. This may have been due to the fact that the length of confinement for nonviolent offenses was considerably longer for insanity acquittals in New York and California than it was for those convicted, thereby making an insanity acquittal less desirable in these states. Perhaps the fact that the prosecutor was given notification of all release hearings in New York and California contributed to their longer lengths of confinement than in Georgia and Montana.

Although our data serve to illuminate the workings of some key insanity defense elements and to counteract many of the myths about the defense, they do not address more systemic concerns. For instance, we have seen that the insanity defense has gone through periods of expansion and contraction in the last two decades, but we have little understanding as to any impact these changes may have on either the larger mental health system or the criminal justice system. Although the overall number of persons utilizing the defense is small, it is a population which receives great public attention and one with many needs. Do these needs have major implications in the other systems?

Throughout the last decade the insanity defense has become less expansive. It is less receptive to a wide range of defendants in terms of diagnosis and crimes. Have there been any effects on the civil mental health system as a result? Has the civil commitment system become more restrictive? Or was it able to maintain a clear delineation between its civil and criminal populations? Conversely, what are the affects of more restrictive use of the insanity defense on the criminal justice system? How adequately are the needs of mentally ill offenders being addressed in the jails and prisons of this country, especially those defendants being found GBMI?

These questions are further highlighted by the observed effects of Montana's efforts to abolish the insanity defense and Georgia's enactment of a GBMI verdict. In Montana many potential insanity acquittees were diverted to the civil system, while their criminal charges were either dismissed or deferred. Our data did not allow us to examine how this diversion may have affected the quality of care or the structure of the civil system. Nor were we able to examine how the GBMI verdicts for defendants with serious mental illnesses affected the prison system in Georgia. Were mental health services available for them? Did the correctional system have the resources to expand its mental health services for this class of inmates?

Now that we have a baseline of information on both the operation of the insanity defense and the effects of certain reforms, there is need for research on these and other systemic questions to inform the design and financing of the systems of care and detention for persons being found not criminally responsible as a result of mental disorder.

THE INSANITY DEFENSE: A NEW BALANCE

Our review of statutory changes since 1978 showed that the majority of states made major changes in how the defense operates. The most common reform was assigning the burden of proof to the defense. This change has undoubtedly restricted the use of the insanity defense in these states. Also, the majority of states are again utilizing the more restrictive McNaughtan standard rather than the ALI standard. Most states have also made changes in their commitment and release procedures for insanity acquittees. Currently, there is wide variation in how states treat insanity acquittees: some states automatically commit acquittees; others automatically commit for evaluation followed by a hearing to determine the disposition; still others follow civil commitment procedures. Release procedures also vary widely across the United States. We know considerably less about how specific changes in these procedures impact on use of the defense, although we continue to believe that they do have major effects. What is much clearer is the trend recently documented by LaFond and Durham (1992:150) that a "wealth of evidence confirms the onset of an era in which the rights of the community are protected at the expense of individual freedom." They suggest that state legislatures have taken the initiative in recent years to formulate new mental health laws and policies designed to protect the community. At the same time, the courts, a bastion for individual civil liberties in the past, have taken a back seat to state legislatures, thereby producing a new balance which tips toward overprotection of the community. One notable exception to this trend is the May 1992 U.S. Supreme Court decision *Foucha v. Louisiana*, which reversed the Louisiana Court of Appeals ruling that allowed the detention of insanity acquittees if they were deemed dangerous even in the absence of mental illness. The ultimate impact of this important decision awaits the passage of time and, hopefully, follow-up research.

LaFond and Durham (1992:157) contend that many of the recent reforms to the insanity defense will "symbolically reassure the community that the law is in step with their basic values." Perhaps this new balance will satisfy the public's concerns about safety and there will be less need for more drastic reforms like abolition or the GBMI verdict whose actual impacts in any given state may be most uncertain.

Is all of the furor over the insanity defense warranted? Probably not. In the decade since John Hinckley's acquittal, there probably were fewer insanity acquittals than during the 10 years before his NGRI verdict. Moreover, there never have been many insanity pleas or acquittals. In our four study states there was less than one (0.9) insanity plea for every 100 felony indictments during our study years. For those states, this meant that 586,063 felony indictments produced only 5,302 insanity pleas, of which only 22.7% (1,204) were successful. What happens, of course, is that every once in a while one of those insanity pleas involves a defendant whose crimes are particularly heinous. The possibility of such a person being able to return to the community "soon" or being detained in a facility from which escape is thought to be easy spreads fear throughout the population and incites calls for drastic actions. These emotions are associated with ideas of widespread abuses of the justice system and a push for statutory reform to ensure long-term, secure detention of *all* insanity acquittees.

As we have shown here, murder defendants are a minority of all defendants who raise the insanity plea. To approach the structuring of state and federal laws or master plans for detention/treatment facilities as though this were not the case can make for poor law and poorly managed, overly expensive, state forensic systems. Changing a state's insanity standard is likely to be only an illusory, symbolic change. Abolition will stop insanity acquittals in a narrow sense, but criminal defenses relying on mental status, that is, *mens rea*, can be expected to continue at rates similar to traditional insanity pleas. Altering the conditions of confinement may detain acquittees longer, but will accomplish little else concerning the volume of pleas or the characteristics of defendants. Introducing a GBMI verdict may change the composition of who ends up in the mental health system as NGRI, but it also produces a particularly disadvantaged group of prisoners who have disproportionately longer sentences and who are unlikely to receive any increase in specialized mental health treatment commensurate with their disadvantaged status. Shifting the burden of proof to the defendant and also increasing the standard of proof would appear to be the most effective mechanism for reducing both the number of insanity pleas and the number of insanity acquittals. This is especially true if a determinate sentence is attached to an NGRI verdict, as was the case in California during the period we studied.

There are surely suggestions for future reformers imbedded in the results of our research on what some of the major legislative wranglings with the insanity defense over the past 10 to 15 years have produced. The result from our work that is probably most clear is that legislative reforms are likely to have subtle and often unintended consequences. We believe that if the framework that guided this research is incorporated into the planning of proposed legislation, then the probable outcomes can be more obvious and less unexpected. That framework requires a consideration not only of the number of acquittals that may need to be treated and detained, but also of the number of pleas and their disposition in the courts; not only of the number of pleas and acquittals, but also of their characteristics, for example, their gender and their criminal charges.

Just as this book's framework has been systemic, so should assessments of proposed statutory changes concerning the insanity defense. Nowhere in our data was this made clearer than in our study of how California's 1982 reform of its insanity defense standard was completely muted by a determinate sentencing statute as it applied to insanity acquittees. When the periodic surges for insanity defense reform peak, it is essential that proposed reformers reflect on the data we have presented here and consider its application to the judicial, mental health, and correctional *systems* in their states. The ultimate results of their reforms are dependent on the legal, fiscal, political, and administrative infrastructure that define and surround the statutes and regulations that comprise the insanity defense. In this arena, good policy, good law, and good research demand the same things: a systemic perspective and solid empirical data, not the usual anecdote, hysteria, and hyperbole.

EPILOGUE: DATA CAN HELP TO INFORM THE DEBATE ON THE INSANITY DEFENSE

We were pleased to have our data widely solicited by the press during its coverage of the Jeffrey Dahmer trial in 1992. We saw at firsthand how empirical data can help shape the perspectives of future reformers and the public. In one of the stories about Dahmer, *Newsweek* (February 3, 1992:49) acknowledged that, "Public perceptions to the contrary, the insanity plea is relatively rare; lawyers consider it a defense of last resort. . . . Few felons actually 'get off' thanks to the insanity defense."

Likewise, an editorial in *USA Today* (February 6, 1992) observed,

> Insanity is so difficult to prove that it's rarely used in even the most grisly, infamous cases: Mass murderers Ted Bundy, Richard Speck and Son of Sam all decided against the insanity defense. In an eight-state study funded by the National Institute of Mental Health, the plea was used in only 1% of all felony cases. Of those, 64% were found guilty anyway. Only 15% involved murder. Even if the defense succeeds, chances are remote that Dahmer will ever go free. Release must be approved not just by doctors but by a judge or jury.

The authors of the news report and the editorial had contacted us while doing their background work. Because we had some data to contribute, we were able to counteract common misperceptions and affect what they ultimately put into print. To what extent, if any, these stories influenced public opinion or legislators' intents, we will never know. We do know that our data were able to influence how the insanity defense was depicted for millions of Americans. We do know that without these data some very different opinions might have been put forward to the same readers. While the fuller elaboration of our findings presented in this book will be seen by a small fraction of the people who read *Newsweek* and *USA Today*, we hope the added depth offered here will be a valuable source when the next inevitable wave of insanity reform smashes into the legal shore.

References

Appelbaum, P. (1982). The insanity defense: New calls for reform. *Hospital and Community Psychiatry, 33*, 13–14.

American Bar Association, Standing Committee on Association Standards for Criminal Justice. (1984). *Criminal justice and mental health standards*. Chicago: American Bar Association.

American Law Institute. (1962). *Model Penal Code § 4.01.74, Proposed Official Draft*. Philadelphia.

American Medical Association, Board of Trustees. (1984). The insanity defense in criminal trials and limitations of psychiatric testimony. *Journal of American Medical Association, 251*, 2967–2981.

American Psychiatric Association Insanity Defense Work Group. (1983). American Psychiatric Association Statement on the Insanity Defense. *American Journal of Psychiatry, 140*, 681–688.

Arenella, P. (1982). Reflections on current proposals to abolish or reform the insanity defense. *American Journal of Law and Medicine, 8*(3), 272–282.

Arens, R. (1967). The Durham rule in action: Judicial psychiatry and psychiatric justice. *Law and Society Review, 2*, 41–84.

Azumi, K., & Haque, J. (1972). *Organizational systems*. Lexington, MA: D. C. Heath.

Bagby, R. M. (1987). The effects of legislative reform on admission rates to psychiatric units of general hospitals. *International Journal of Law and Psychiatry, 10*, 383–394.

Bardach, E. (1977). *The implementation game: What happens after a bill becomes a law*. Cambridge, MA: MIT Press.

153

Bayer, R. (1983). The insanity defense in retreat. *Hastings Center Report, 13*(6), 13–16.

Bender, J. M. (1984). After abolition: The present state of the insanity defense in Montana. *Montana Law Review, 45,* 133–150.

Blossfeld, H., Hamerle, A., & Mayer, K. V. (1989). Event history analysis: Statistical theory and application in the social sciences. Hillsdale, NJ: Erlbaum.

Blunt, L. W., & Stock, H. V. (1985). Guilty but mentally ill: An alternative verdict. *Behavioral Sciences and the Law, 3,* 49–67.

Boehnert, C. (1989). Characteristics of successful and unsuccessful pleas. *Law and Human Behavior, 13,* 31–39.

Bonnie, R. J. (1983). The moral basis of the insanity defense. *American Bar Association Journal, 69,* 194–197.

Bowers, W. J., Givelber, D. J., & Blitch, C. L. (1986). How did Tarasoff affect clinical practice? *Annals of the American Academy of Political and Social Science,* 70–85.

Boyce, J. N., & Jackson, D. S. (1982). Is the system guilty? *Time* July 5: 26.

Braff, J., Arvanites, T. M., & Steadman, H. J. (1982, October 7). *Insanity acquittals 1980–1982.* New York State Office of Mental Health Special Projects Research Unit. Albany, NY.

Brooks, A. (1974). *Law, psychiatry, and the mental health system.* Boston: Little, Brown.

Brooks, A. D. (1985). The merits of abolishing the insanity defense. *Annals of the American Academy of Political and Social Sciences, 477,* 125–136.

Buckley, W. (1967). *Sociology and modern systems theory.* Englewood Cliffs, NJ: Prentice-Hall.

Callahan, L., Mayer, C., & Steadman, H. J. (1987). Insanity defense reform in the United States—Post Hinckley. *Mental and Physical Disability Law Reporter, 11*(1), 54–59.

Callahan, L. A., & Steadman, H. J. (1990). Insanity defense reform in Ohio: Does the court of jurisdiction matter? *Capitol University Law Review, 19*(3), 809–824.

Campbell, D. T., & Stanley, J. C. (1963). Experimental and Quasi-experimental Designs for Research. Chicago: Rand McNally.

Caplan, L. (1984, July 2). The insanity defense. *New Yorker,* pp. 45–78.

Carter, R. A. (1982). History of the insanity defense in New York State. New York State Library Legislative and Governmental Services Cultural Education Center. Albany, N.Y.

Caulfield, J. M. (1974). Ohio commitments of the mentally ill offender. *Capitol University Law Review, 4*(1), 1–36.

Chan, M.K.M. (1982). Outpatient status: Beyond the term of commitment. *Pacific Law Journal, 13,* 1180–1205.

Cicourel, A. (1968). *The social organization of juvenile justice.* New York: Wiley.

Cobun, L. (1984). The Insanity Defense: Effects of Abolition Unsupported by a Moral Consensus. *American Journal of Law & Medicine, 9*(4) Winter: 471–500.

Cohen, L., & Kluegel, J. (1978). Determinants of juvenile court dispositions. *American Sociological Review, 43,* 162–176.

Comment. (1977). Mental Health Litigation: Implementing Institutional Reform. *Harvard Law Review,* September-December 221–233.

Cook, T. D., & Campbell, D. T. (1979). Quasi-experimentation: Design and Analysis Issues for Field Settings. Chicago: Rand McNally.

Cooke, G., & Sikorski, C. (1974). Factors affecting length of hospitalization in persons adjudicated not guilty by reason of insanity. *Bulletin of the American Academy of Psychiatry and Law, 2,* 251–261.

Criss, M. L., & Racine, R. D. (1980). Impact of change in legal standard for those adjudicated not guilty by reason of insanity 1975–1979. *Bulletin of the American Academy of Psychiatry and Law, 8*(3), 261–271.

Ellis, J. W. (1986). The consequences of the insanity defense: Proposals to reform post-acquital commitment laws. *Catholic University Law Review, 35,* 961–1020.

Ennis, B. J. (1982, July 24–31). Straight talk about the insanity defense. *Nation,* pp. 70–72.

Faulkner, L. R., Bloom, J. D., McFarland, B. H., & Stern, T. O. (1985). The effect of mental health system changes on civil commitment. *Bulletin of the American Academy of Psychiatry and the Law, 13,* 345–357.

Fentiman, L. C. (1985). "Guilty but mentally ill": The real verdict is guilty. *Boston College Law Review, 26*(3), 610–653.

Finkel, N. J. (1989). The insanity defense reform act of 1984: Much ado about nothing. *Behavioral Sciences and the Law, 7*(3), 403–419.

Finkel, N. J., & Handel, S. F. (1989). How jurors construe "insanity." *Law and Human Behavior, 13*(1), 41–59.

Fox, J. (1984). Detecting changes of level and slope in repeated measures data. *Sociological Methods and Research, 12,* 263–277.

German, J. R., & Singer, A. C. (1976). Punishing the not guilty: Hospitalization of persons acquitted by reason of insanity. *Rutgers Law Review, 29,* 1011–1083.

Goldstein, A. (1967). *The insanity defense.* New Haven: Yale University Press.

Goldstein, A., & Katz, J. (1963). Abolish the "insanity defense"—Why not? *Yale Law Journal, 72,* 853.

Government Accounting Office. (1987). Sentencing Guidelines: Potential Impact on Federal Criminal Justice System. Washington D.C.

Halleck, S. L. (1967). *Psychiatry and the dilemmas of crime: A study of causes, punishment and treatment.* New York: Harper and Row.

Halpern, A. L. (1989). The American Psychiatric Association Insanity Rule—A metaphysical subtlety. In R. Rosner & R. B. Harmon (Eds.), *Criminal court consultation.* New York: Plenum.

Hans, V. P. (1986). An analysis of public attitudes toward the insanity defense. *Criminology, 24*(2), 393–413.

Harris, J. D. (1986). Guilty but mentally ill: A critical analysis. *Rutgers Law Journal, 14,* 453–477.

Hauser, S. (1981). Commitment and release of persons found not guilty by reason of insanity: A Georgia perspective. *Georgia Law Review, 15,* 1065–1101.

Hawkins, M. R., & Pasewark, R. A. (1983). Characteristics of persons utilizing the insanity plea. *Psychological Reports, 53,* 191–195.

Heinbecker, P. (1986). Two year's experience under Utah's mens rea insanity law. *Bulletin of the American Academy of Psychiatry and Law, 14*(2), 185–191.

Hermann, D. (1983). Assault on the insanity defense: Limitations on the effectiveness and effect of the defense of insanity. *Rutgers Law Journal, 14,* 241–371.

Hess, C. A. (1980). Release from confinement of persons acquitted by reason of insanity in Ohio. *Akron Law Review, 13*(3), 582–592.

Hiday, V. A. (1983). Representing respondents under new civil commitment statutes: An analysis of counsel's role in and out of the court room. *Law and Policy Quarterly, 5,* 438–454.

Howell, L. (1985, October 2). Insanity defense still plagues state juries. *Missoulian,* Oct. 2: pg 2 (Newspaper).

Institute on Mental Disability and the Law. (1985). *The guilty but mentally ill verdict: An empirical study. Final report.* National Center for State Courts. Williamsburg, Va. (Rev.)

Janofsky, J. S., Vandewalle, M. B., & Rappeport, J. R. (1989). Defendants pleading insanity: An analysis of outcome. *Bulletin of the American Academy of Psychiatry and Law, 17,* 203–211.

Jeffrey, R. W., Pasewark, R. A., & Beiber, S. (1988). Insanity plea: Predicting not guilty by reason of insanity adjudications. *Bulletin of the American Academy of Psychiatry and Law, 16,* 35–39.

Jones, L. R., & Parlous, R. R. (1981). *Wyatt v. Stickney: Restrospective and perspective.* New York: Grune and Stratton.

Jordan, M. (1982). The Insanity Defense. *Western Law Journal, 3,* 2–6.

Katz, D., & Kahn, R. (1978). *The social psychology of organizations.* (2d ed.). New York: Wiley.

Kaufman, I. R. (1982, August 8). The insanity plea on trial. *New York Times Magazine,* pp. 16–20.

Keilitz, I. (1987). Researching and reforming the insanity defense. *Rutgers Law Review, 39,* 289–322.

Klofas, J., & Weisheit, R. (1986). Pleading guilty but mentally ill: Adversarial justice and mental health. *International Journal of Law and Psychiatary, 9,* 1–18.

Koshland, D. E. (1992). Elephants, monstrosities, and the law. *Science, 255*(5046), 777.

Krash, A. (1961). The Durham rule and judicial administration of the insanity defense in the District of Columbia. *Yale Law Journal, 70,* 905–951.

Krausz, F. R. (1983). The relevance of innocence: Proposition 8 and the diminished capacity defense. *California Law Review, 71,* 1197–1215.

LaFond, J. Q., & Durham, M. L. (1992). *Back to the asylum: The future of mental health law and policy in the United States.* New York: Oxford University Press.

Lauter, D. (1982). Why insanity defense is breaking down. *National Law Journal, 4*(34), 11–13.

Leo, J. (1982, July 5). Is the system guilty? *Time,* pp. 26–27.

Lottman, M. S. (1976). Enforcement of judicial decrees: Now comes the hard part. *Mental Disability Law Reporter, 1*(1), 69–76.

Mathews, T., Springen, K., Rogers, P., & Cerio, G. (1992, 3 February). Secrets of a serial killer. *Newsweek,* pp. 45–51.

Matthews, A. R., Jr. (1970). *Mental disability and the criminal law.* Chicago: American Bar Association.

Mayer, C. (1987, 10 June). *Insanity defense reforms: Pre- and post-Hinckley.* Paper presented at the Law and Society Association annual meeting, Washington, D.C.

McClellan, D. S. (1986). *The New York State Insanity Defense Reform Act of 1980: Impact and prospects*. Rockefeller Institute Special Reports. Albany, NY. No. 14 Fall 1986.

McClellan, D. S. (1989). The New York State Insanity Defense Reform Act of 1980: A legislative experiment. *Bulletin of the American Academy of Psychiatry and Law, 17*(2), 129–151.

McGarry, A. L., Schwitzgebel, R. K., Lipsitt, P. D., & Lelos, D. (Eds.). (1981). *Civil commitment and social policy: An evaluation of the Massachusetts Mental Health Reform Act of 1970*. Rockville, MD: U.S. Department of Health and Human Services, National Institute of Mental Health, Center for Studies of Crime and Delinquency.

McGinley, H., & Pasewark, R. A. (1989). National survey of the frequency and success of the insanity plea and alternate pleas. *Journal of Psychiatry and Law, 169*, 205–221.

McGrath, J. J. (1985).The insanity defense: A difficult necessity. *Hospital and Community Psychiatry, 36*(1), 54–55.

McGraw, B. D., Farthing-Capowich, D., & Keilitz, I. (1985). The "guilty but mentally ill" plea and verdict: Current state of the knowledge. *Villanova Law Review, 30*, 117–191.

McGreevy, M. A., & Dollard, N. (1989). Striking a balance: An assessment of the conditional release program in New York State. Bureau of Survey and Evaluation Research, New York State Office of Mental Health Final Report. Albany, N.Y.

Melton, G. B., Petrila, J., Poythress, N. G., & Slobogin, C. (1987). *Psychological evaluations for the courts*. New York: Guilford Press.

Mental Disability Law Reporter. (1983). The insanity defense: ABA, APA proposals for change. *Mental Disability Law Reporter*, March/April, pp. 136–147.

Mesritz, G. D. (1976). Guilty but mentally ill: An historical and constitutional analysis. *Journal of Urban Law, 53*, 471–496.

Miller, J. G. (1978). *Living systems*. New York: McGraw-Hill.

Mishler, E., & Waxler, N. (1963). Decision processes in psychiatric hospitalization. *American Sociological Review, 29*, 576–587.

Monahan, J. (1973). Abolish the insanity defense?—Not yet. *Rutgers Law Review, 26*, 719.

Moran, R. (1985a). Preface: The insanity defense. *Annals of the American Academy of Political and Social Sciences, 477*, 9–11.

Moran, R. (1985b). The modern foundation for the insanity defense: The cases of James Hadfield (1800) and Daniel McNaughtan (1843). *Annals of the American Academy of Political and Social Sciences*, 31–42.

Moran, R. (1985c). The origin of insanity as a special verdict: The trial for treason of James Hadfield (1800). *Law and Society Review, 19*(3), 602–631.

Morgan, D. W., McCullough, T. M., Jenkins, P. L., & White, W. M. (1988). Guilty but mentally ill: The South Carolina experience. *Bulletin of the American Academy of Psychiatry and Law, 16*(1), 41–48.

Morris, N. (1968). Psychiatry and the dangerous criminal. *Southern California Law Review, 41*, 514–547.

Morris, N. (1982). *Madness and the criminal law*. Chicago: University of Chicago Press.

Morris, N., Bonnie, R., & Finer, J. J. (1986–87). Should the insanity defense be abolished? An introduction to the debate. *Journal of Law and Health, 1,* 113–139.

Morrissey, J. P., & Goldman, H. H. (1985). The alchemy of mental health policy: Homelessness and the fourth cycle of reform. *American Journal of Public Health, 75,* 727–731.

Morrissey, J. P., & Tessler, R. (1982). Selection processes in state mental hospitalization: Policy issues and research directions. In M. Lewis, (Ed.), *Social problems and public policy: A research annual.* (Vol. 2). Greenwich, CT: JAI Press.

Morse, S. J. (1985). Retaining a modified insanity defense. *Annals of the American Academy, 477,* 137–147.

Nagatani, F., & Nakles, N. J. (1981). Procedural changes in civil commitment for those found to be not guilty by reason of insanity in Ohio. *University of Dayton Law Review, 6*(2), 295–336.

National Mental Health Association. (1983). *Myths and realities: A report of the National Commission on the Insanity Defense.* Arlington, VA: National Mental Health Association.

New York Times. (1984, May 17). Editorial: Shift the insanity burden. *New York Times,* p. A26.

Northrup, J. A. (1983). Guilty but mentally ill: Broadening the scope of criminal responsibility. *Ohio State Law Journal, 44,* 797–820.

Packer, I. K. (1987). Homicide and the insanity defense: A comparison of sane and insane murderers. *Behavioral Sciences and the Law, 5,* 25–36.

Padavan, F. (1979, July 25). An alternative to the insanity plea. *New York Daily News,* 32.

Page, S. (1980). New civil commitment legislation: The relevance of commitment "criteria." *Canadian Journal of Psychiatry, 26,* 419–420.

Pasewark, R. A., Jeffrey, R. W., & Beiber, S. (1987). Differentiating successful and unsuccessful insanity plea defendants in Colorado. *Journal of Psychiatry and Law, 15,* 55–71.

Pasewark, R. A., & Pantle, M. (1979). Insanity plea: Legislators' view. *American Journal of Psychiatry, 136,* 222.

Pasewark, R. A., Randolph, R. L., & Bieber, S. (1984). Insanity plea: Statutory language and trial procedures. *Journal of Psychiatry and Law,* Fall, 399–422.

Pasewark, R. A., & Seidenzahl, D. (1979). Opinions concerning the insanity plea and criminality among mental patients. *Bulletin of the American Academy of Psychiatry and Law, 7,* 199–202.

Perr, I. N. (1984). The insanity defense: Effects of abolition unsupported by a moral consensus. *American Journal of Law and Medicine, 9*(4), 472–500.

Peters, R., Miller, K. S., Schmidt, W., & Meeters, D. (1987). The effects of statutory change on the civil commitment of the mentally ill. *Law and Human Behavior, 11,* 73–99.

Petrella, R. C., Benedek, E. P., Bank, S. C., & Packer, I. K. (1985). Examining the application of the guilty but mentally ill verdict in Michigan. *Hospital and Community Psychiatry, 36*(3), 254–259.

Phillips, M. R., Wolf, A. S., & Coors, D. J. (1988). Psychiatry and the criminal justice system: Testing the myths. *American Journal of Psychiatry, 145,* 605–610.

Press, A., et al. (1982, May 24). The insanity plea on trial. *Newsweek,* pp. 56–61.

Rackmill, S. J. (1991). The impact of determinate sentencing ideology upon prison overcrowding. *Criminal Law Bulletin,* 230–246.

Rappeport, J. R. (1983). The insanity plea and scapegoating the mentally ill—Much ado about nothing? *South Texas Law Journal,* 686–707.

Reynolds, S. (1984). Battle of the experts revised: 1983 Oregon legislation on the insanity defense. *Williamette Law Review, 20,* 303–317.

Riley, W. D., & George, B. J. (1984). Reform not abolition. *Journal of the American Medical Association, 251*(22), 2947–2948.

Roesch, J. L., & Golding, S. (1980). *Competency to stand trial.* Urbana: University of Illinois Press.

Rogers, R. (1987). APA's position on the insanity defense. *American Psychologist, 42*(9), 840–848.

Roth, L. H. (1984). Tighten but do not discard. *Journal of the American Medical Association, 251*(22), 2949–2950.

Roth, L. H. (1986–87). Preserve but limit the insanity defense. *Psychiatric Quarterly, 58*(2), 91–105.

Sales B., & Hafemeister T. (1984). Empircism and legal policy on the insanity defense. In L. Teplin, (Ed.), *Mental health and criminal justice.* Newbury Park, CA: Sage.

Scott, W. R. (1981). *Organizations: Rational, natural, and open systems.* Englewood Cliffs, NJ: Prentice-Hall.

Simon, R. J. (1967). *The jury and the defense of insanity.* Boston: Little, Brown.

Simon, R. J., & Aaronson, D. E. (1988). *The insanity defense: A critical assessment of law and policy in the post-Hinckley era.* New York: Praeger.

Singer, R. G. (1983). Abolition of the insanity defense: Madness and the criminal law. *Cardozo Law Review, 4,* 683–707.

Singer, R. G. (1985). The aftermath of an insanity acquital: The Supreme Court's recent decision in *Jones v. United States. Annals of the American Academy of Political and Social Science, 1,* 114–124.

Slobogin, C. (1985). The guilty but mentally ill verdict: An idea whose time should not have come. *George Washington Law Review, 53*(4), 494–526.

Slovenko, R. (1988). The continuing saga of the insanity defense. In *Festschrift in Honor of Dean Paul K. Ryu.* Seoul, Korea: 8th Annual Congress of the Australian and New Zealand Association of Psychiatry, Psychology and Law Melbourne, Australia, November 1987.

Smith G. A., & Hall, J. A. (1982). Evaluating Michigan's guilty but mentally ill verdict: An empirical study. *Journal of Law Reform, 16*(1), 75–112.

Smith, W. F. (1982). Limiting the insanity defense: A rational approach to irrational crimes. *Missouri Law Review, 47,* 605–620.

Steadman, H. J. (1979). *Beating a rap: Defendants found incompetent to stand trial.* Chicago: University of Chicago Press.

Steadman, H. J. (1980). Insanity acquittals in New York State, 1965–1978. *American Journal of Psychiatry, 137,* 321–326.

Steadman, H. J. (1985). Empirical research on the insanity defense. *Annals of the American Academy of Political and Social Sciences, 477,* 58–71.

Steadman, H. J., Callahan, L. A., Robbins, P. C., & Morrissey, J. P. (1989). Maintenance of an insanity defense under Montana's "abolition" of the insanity defense. *American Journal of Psychiatry, 146*(3), 357–360.

Steadman, H. J., & Cocozza, J. J. (1974). *Careers of the criminally insane.* Lexington, MA: Lexington Books.

Steadman, H. J., & Cocozza, J. J. (1978). Public perceptions of the criminally insane. *Hospital and Community Psychiatry, 29,* 457–459.

Steadman, H. J., Keitner, L., Braff, J., & Arvanites, T. (1983). Factors associated with a successful insanity plea. *American Journal of Psychiatry, 140,* 401–405.

Steadman, H. J., Rosenstein, M. J., MacAskiel, R. L., & Manderschied, R. W. (1988). A Profile of Mentally Disordered Offenders Admitted to Inpatient Psychiatric Services in the United States. *Law & Human Behavior, 12,* 91–99.

Stokman, C.L.J., & Heiber, P. G. (1984). The Insanity Defense Reform Act in New York State, 1980–1983. *International Journal of Law and Psychiatry, 7,* 367–384.

Stone, A. A. (1982). The insanity defense on trial. *Hospital and Community Psychiatry, 33*(8), 636–640.

Szasz, T. S. (1963). *Law, liberty, and psychiatry.* New York: MacMillan.

Tighe, J. A. (1983). Francis Wharton and the nineteenth-century insanity defense: The origins of a reform tradition. *American Journal of Legal History, 27,* 224–253.

Thornberry, T. P., & Jacoby, J. E. (1980). *The criminally insane.* Chicago: University of Chicago Press.

Toufexis, A. (1992, 3 February). Do mad acts a madman make? *Time,* p. 17.

Troetti, T. J. (1980). Criminal procedures affecting the mentally ill offender. *University of Dayton Law Review, 5*(2), 527–538.

Turner, W. B., & Ornstein, B. (1983). Distinguishing the wicked from the mentally ill. *California Lawyer, 3,* 41–45.

U.S. Department of Justice, Bureau of Justice Statistics. (1991). Sourcebook of criminal justice statistics—1990. Albany, NY: Hindelang Criminal Justice Research Center.

U.S. Department of Justice, Bureau of Justice Statistics. (1988). Sourcebook of criminal justice statistics—1986. Albany, NY: Hindelang Criminal Justice Research Center.

U.S. Senate Subcommittee on Criminal Law of the Committee on the Judiciary. (1982, June 24, 30, and July 14). Limiting the insanity defense. Hearings before the United States Senate.

Urmer, A. H. (1972). *A study of California's new mental health.* Chatsworth, CA: ENKI Research Institute.

Van Hirsh, A. (1976). Doing Justice: The Choice of Punishments. New York: Hill and Wang.

Weiner, B. A. (1985). The insanity defense: Historical development and present status. *Behavioral Sciences and the Law, 3*(1), 3–35.

Wettstein, R. M., Mulvey, E. P., & Rogers, R. (1991). A prospective comparison of four insanity defense standards. *American Journal of Psychiatry, 148*(1), 21–27.

Weyant, J. L. (1981). Reforming insanity defense procedures in New York: Balancing societal protection against individual liberty. *Albany Law Review, 45,* 679–716.

Wexler, D. B. (1985). Redefining the insanity problem. *George Washington Law Review, 53*(3–4), 528–561.

Case References

Ake v. Oklahoma, 105 S.Ct. 1087 (1985).

Baxstrom v. Herold, 383 U.S. 107 (1966).

Benham v. Edwards, 501 F. Supp. 1050 (N.D. Ga.) 678 F.2d 511 (1980).

Benham v. Ledbetter, 103 S.Ct. 3043 (1983), 785 F.2d 1480 (11th Cir. 1986)

Bolton v. Harris, 395 F.2d 642 (D.C. Cir. 1968).

California v. Horn, 205 Cal. Rept. 119 (Cal. Ct. App.) (1984).

Davis v. United States, 160 U.S. 469 (1895).

Dixon v. Attorney General of the Commonwealth of Pennsylvania 323, F. Suppl. 966 (1971).

Durham v. United States, 214 F.2d 862 (D.C. Cir. 1954).

Foucha v. Louisiana, 563 So. 2d 1138 (1992).

Harris v. State, 499 N.E.2d 723 (Ind. 1986).

In re Moye, 22 Cal.3d, 457, 584 P.2d at 1099, 149 Cal Rptr 491 (1978).

In re Torsney, 47 N.Y.2d 667, 394 N.E.2d 262, 420 N.Y.2d 192 (1979).

In re Winship 397 U.S. 358 (1970).

Jackson v. Indiana, 406 U.S. 715 (1972).

Jones v. United States, 463 U.S. 354 (1983).

Leland v. Oregon, 343 U.S. 790 (1952).

M'Naghten, 101 Cl. & Fin. 200 8 Eng. Rep. 718 (H.L. 1843).

Patterson v. New York, 432 U.S. 197 (1977).

People v. McQuillan, 392 Mich. 511, 221, K.W. 2d 569, 575 (1974).

Rivera v. Delaware, 429 U.S. 877 dismissing appeal from 351 A.2d 561 (1976).

State v. Field, 77 N.J. 282, 390 A.2d 574 (1978).

State v. Krol, 68 N.J. 236, 344 A.2d 289 (1975).

Tarasoff v. The Regents of California 17 Cal.3d 425, 551 P.2d 334, 131 Cal. Rept. 14 (1976).

Wilson v. State, 359 Ind. 375, 287 N.E.2d 875 (1972).

Wyatt v. Stickney, 325 F. Suppl. 781 (M.D. Alc.) (1971).

APPENDICES

APPENDIX A

Research Methodology

The grant application for this research was first submitted to the National Institute of Mental Health (NIMH) on June 1, 1983, by Henry J. Steadman and Joseph P. Morrissey. After two reviews, resubmissions, and a site visit, the research was funded on September 1, 1985. The funding concluded on February 29, 1992. What happened over the intervening period of almost 9 years?

What happened from June 1983 to September 1985 is grist for another book about the grant-seeking and grant-review processes. Only about 20% of research applications are funded, so we were fortunate to receive a grant. That part is as fascinating as anything we have written in this book, and it is just as critical to the research process as any other stage of a project. Without funding there is no study.

But, in this case, there was a study. This appendix describes in great detail what we did over its nearly 7 years of operation. We have organized the presentation around two sets of ideas: first, the logic of the research that guided the innumerable day-to-day decisions about project design and project logistics, and second, a road map for how to do this kind of research. As in any research study, what is required is balancing the desire to meet every tenet of quality scientific research with the constraints imposed by cost, time, and available data. All research is a series of compromises. By laying out all of our project's key decisions, their rationales and results, we hope to make the way smoother for future investigators and to provide further support for the data and conclusions reported in this book.

PROJECT RATIONALE

The independent variable in this study was legal reform. We wanted to discover whether different types of legal reforms would produce distinct outcomes with regard

165

to the volume and characteristics of insanity cases. As we noted in Chapter 2, we recognized that reforms of the insanity defense fall into three types: adjudication, disposition, and a mixed or combined type. Thus, our first task was to find a sample of states that had enacted the types of reforms we wanted to study.

To be eligible for selection a state not only had to have adopted one of the types of reform we wanted to study, but it also had to have a sufficient number of insanity pleas and acquittals to make such data significant enough to be useful. That is, the pleas and acquittals were our dependent variables, and we had to make sure that any observed variations would not be produced by so few cases as to render inferences about the impact of reform totally suspect. Intimately associated with the issue of a sufficient number of cases was the problem of getting access to the pertinent records. While certain documents such as indictments and court verdicts are public records, other data we needed, for example, information about diagnosis and length of confinement, were confidential. Just how we addressed these issues and how they forced us to modify our original design is explained later in this appendix.

A large number of other issues flowed from our choice of dependent or outcomes variables. On the basis of prior research, we decided that there were four major types of outcomes to be investigated: (1) volume and rate of insanity pleas; (2) volume and rate of insanity acquittals; (3) the characteristics of the defendants pleading insanity and acquitted by reason of insanity; and (4) the confinement patterns of successful and unsuccessful insanity pleas. Obtaining such information meant gaining access to a wide variety of agencies. Plea data required going to county courthouses. Acquittal data were obtained from state mental health authorities, both at their central offices and at their individual state mental hospitals. The confinement patterns of defendants acquitted by reason of insanity were available at the same mental health institutions, but those defendants who were unsuccessful were often sent to state prisons, so confinement data for them had to be gathered from state correctional agencies.

Our decisions about the number and scope of our independent and dependent variables led to 5 years of data collection of one type or another in ten states. Four stages of data collection were involved: (1) setup; (2) staffing and training; (3) data abstracting and coding; and (4) data management. After first describing our sample of states with regard to the legal reforms adopted, we will discuss each stage of the research process. The amount of detail presented here is unusual for research monographs. All too often we found precious little guidance for the "nuts and bolts" decisions we needed to make when we were planning our own major research initiatives. Such information becomes, at best, part of the oral folklore of researchers working in a field. We have taken the time in this book to document our procedures so that future researchers can learn from our experiences and mistakes. One of the things we learned from this experience is that needles *can* be found in haystacks, but the search takes forethought, planning, and teamwork!

SAMPLE OF STATES

The research design in the grant application called for ten study states. We proposed to look at seven states that had made reforms in the insanity defense (reform states) and three states that had made no substantial changes (comparison states). The comparison states were included in the design at the suggestion of the NIMH review group to allow us to determine whether any significant changes observed in the study states were indeed a result of the target reform and not simply due to a larger national trend.

We had done some preliminary work and had proposed ten states for study when the grant application was resubmitted and approved, but nearly a year had elapsed between resubmission and funding. So it was necessary to revisit our decisions once the study had been funded. Accordingly, we first conducted a national survey to update information on insanity defense reforms enacted by all 50 states and the federal system. We completed this survey in the summer of 1986. This survey consisted of a review of the statutes and case law for all 51 jurisdictions; if the statutes were unclear, we made telephone calls to the state forensic director or other knowledgeable officials to clarify the nature of the reforms. This information on the number and types of reforms enacted by each state provided the sampling frame for our decisions on which states to examine more closely. The study states were chosen not only for the type of reform (or lack of reform), but also for their volume of insanity cases. We were forced to exclude some of the states that had made substantial changes in their insanity defense statutes just because the number of cases occurring in these states was too small to permit any meaningful analyses. In fact, relatively few states met our volume criterion. Beyond these two major considerations, we also made an effort to ensure that the chosen states were geographically distributed across the country in order to increase generalizability.

Ultimately, ten states were chosen: California, Georgia, Missouri, Montana, New Jersey, New York, Ohio, Pennsylvania, Washington, and Wisconsin. During the initial set-up stage, it was necessary to drop two of the reform states before data collection had begun. We decided not to include Pennsylvania for two reasons. First, our method for selecting study counties would have required us to focus on Philadelphia and adjacent counties, but members of our project advisory board alerted us to the fact that Philadelphia was very different in regard to its judicial and mental health systems practices than the rest of the state. Second, Pennsylvania had enacted many types of reform over a relatively short period of time. After considering several options, we decided it would be impossible to disentangle the separate effects of the different reforms.

In our preliminary conversations with the court administrator in St. Louis, we were told that courts in Missouri did not keep data on cases in which the disposition was not guilty or not guilty by reason of insanity. Since we felt our request for data might have been misunderstood, we visited the "Show Me" state, where we discovered that the indictment records we required were in fact expunged on all not guilty cases, including cases in which the verdict was not guilty by reason of insanity. Thus retrospective data collection was not possible.

While choosing substitutes for these two states was a possibility, we soon realized that our funding would only allow for data collection in the eight remaining states. Rather than jeopardize the viability of the overall study, we decided to proceed with eight states: five reform states and three comparison states.

Table A.1 displays the eight states included in the study, along with the target reform and the length of the data collection period. In every state we collected data for a minimum of 3 years *before* and 3 years *after* the target reform so that we could detect any postreform changes in the outcome variables. In two states with multiple reforms (New York and Georgia), we extended our data collection window to examine both reforms. In these two states we decided to capitalize on the fact that we were already collecting data there and that it could be cost-effective to study the additional reforms. In Georgia, chosen originally so that we could examine the 1982 GBMI reform, we also studied the 1978 burden and standard of proof change. Similarly, in New York we decided to look not only at the 1984 burden and standard reform but also to study the 1980 "back-end" changes in release procedures. Thus we were able to obtain much additional information at much lower costs since the data collection framework arrangements had already been negotiated and our coders were already in place. These decisions helped to compensate for the loss of Pennsylvania and Missouri as reform states.

In most states data on insanity defense pleas are maintained at the county level. Thus, in order to even identify insanity defense cases, it is necessary to go to each individual county to review court records. We realized that a complete enumeration of all insanity pleas in a state would be very labor-intensive, too labor-intensive for a study designed to produce multistate comparisons. Since it was not feasible to gather data in all counties in each study state, we selected a sample of counties for inclusion. This research strategy was cost-effective and still quite thorough. We first identified the number of acquittals in each county for the years surrounding the reforms. Using this list, we identified the counties that contributed two-thirds of the states' insanity acquittals. This strategy assumed that there was a strong positive correlation between the number of acquittals and the number of pleas in a given county, an assumption that seemed entirely plausible.

This approach introduced one major bias, however, the overinclusion of "high-volume," urban counties. Those more densely populated counties produced the most NGRI acquittals. A sampling strategy was necessary since the costs of collecting data from every county were prohibitive. We came very close or exceeded our goal of including 66% (ranging from 60% in Georgia to over 90% in Montana) of the counties in each study state. We collected data on all pleas during the designated years in all counties sampled except Los Angeles County, California, where due to size considerations we only collected data from half of the districts (including Central District). Table A.2 provides a list of the 49 counties in the eight study states where data were collected.

Not all the data that were collected in these eight states are reported in this

TABLE A.1. Timing of Insanity Defense Reforms in Study States

State	'76	'77	'78	'79	'80	'81	'82	'83	'84	'85	'86	'87
California	Δ		O			O	▲			Δ	O	
Georgia	Δ		▲				▲			Δ		
Missouri	Δ						▲			Δ		
Montana	Δ			▲						Δ		
New York	Δ				▲			O	▲			Δ
Ohio			Δ	O		▲			Δ			
Pennsylvania	ΔO	O						▲O		Δ		
New Jersey	Δ			No reforms						Δ		
Washington	Δ			No reforms						Δ		
Wisconsin	Δ			No reforms						Δ		

California:
1978—ALI adopted
1981—Delete auto commitment
1982—McNaughtan adopted
1984—McNaughtan clarified
1986—Release procedures changed

Georgia:
1978—Burden and standard
1982—GBMI added; new release criteria

Missouri:
1982—Discharge/release proc. reformed

Montana:
1979—Special plea of insanity abolished

New York:
1980—Release procedures changed
1983—Appellate procedures added for commitment and release
1984—Burden and standard

Ohio:
1978—Probate court jurisdiction, end of automatic commitment
1980—Criminal court jurisdiction

Pennsylvania:
1976—Bifurcated trial
1977—Presumption of dangerousness
1983—GBMI added (focal change)
1983—Burden and standard

Note: Δ—Start/end of study window. ▲—Target reform. O—Other reforms.

book. Our findings for Ohio are reported in the *Capitol University Law Review* (Callahan & Steadman, 1990). We have not included data from Ohio in this book because we ultimately determined that multiple changes that had occurred in the insanity defense in Ohio during the study interval confounded interpretation of the effects of a particular reform. In addition, we were unable to use the data from two counties in New York as there was no way to identify persons who had raised the insanity defense but were unsuccessful with the plea. Most notably, for reasons dis-

TABLE A.2. Sample Counties in Four Study States

State	Study counties	State	Study counties
California	Alameda	New York	Albany
	Los Angeles		Bronx
	Orange		Erie
	Sacramento		Kings
	San Diego		Nassau
	San Francisco		New York
	Santa Clara		Queens
Georgia	Bibb	Ohio	Cuyahoga
	Chatham		Franklin
	Cherokee		Hamilton
	Clarke		Montgomery
	Cobb		Summit
	DeKalb		
	Dougherty		
	Floyd	Washington	King
	Fulton		Pierce
	Newton		Spokane
	Richmond		
	Thomas		
Montana	Cascade	Wisconsin	Brown
	Flathead		Milwaukee
	Gallatin		Racine
	Lewis and Clark		Waukesha
	Missoula		
	Silver Bow		
	Yellowstone		
New Jersey	Camden		
	Essex		
	Mercer		
	Monmouth		
	Passaic		
	Union		

cussed in the Data Collection section below, we have not presented any data from our three comparison states.

DATA COLLECTION

Staffing and Training

Most of the data were collected by field researchers recruited in each state who were supervised by a state research coordinator we hired to oversee the work in each state. These researchers and coordinators were hired and trained by the project director and the assistant project director. Continual contact was maintained throughout the data collection process between the field staff and the project staff in Albany, New York. In one state, New Jersey, the project director and the assistant project director acted as the research coordinators. They also did the data collection at each county courthouse and in three of the five state hospitals (they were joined by the principal investigators on several occasions) in order to acquire some "hands-on" data collection experience.

The first step in hiring the staff in each state was to identify the county that was the preferred location for the research coordinator, a decision based on which counties had the most cases and the site that was geographically central to them. We then contacted colleagues in local universities to find persons with research experience for the job of research coordinator. All resumes were reviewed and potential candidates were interviewed by the project director during one of her scouting visits. State coordinators were recruited from a number of academic departments including sociology, criminal justice, public administration, and political science. Each state had one research coordinator with the exception of California, where we hired northern (based in Oakland) and southern (based in Los Angeles) coordinators due to the size of the state and the large volume of cases. In one case, the same person was the supervisor in two different states (Ohio and Washington).

The same networking approach used to find and hire the research coordinators was used to recruit field interviewers. A typical field researcher was a graduate assistant in one of the departments listed above or a law student with modest research experience. Prior work in courts or with court records was given considerable weight. The fact that we scheduled much of the data collection to begin in the early summer gave us a greater pool of students. Field researchers were hired to work in a particular county(ies), and a subset of these researchers participated in the state-level data collection. When interviewing and hiring the field staff, we stressed the tedious nature of the work and the attention to detail required. One field researcher began work for the project one summer in Missoula, Montana, and then worked the next summer on data collection in Cleveland, Ohio. He also did some quality control in the other counties in Ohio as well. Moreover, the third summer he worked in Spokane, Washington, and then relocated to northern California to collect data in two counties. This researcher gave us a bonus of data reliability. Overall, the number of field researchers hired in a given state ranged from 6 to 20, depending on the size of the data collection task. Estimating the number of staff required was usually not a problem since we had an idea of the procedures that would be involved from our scouting expeditions.

The field staff reported directly to the research coordinators on all facets of the project. The research coordinators were responsible not only for arranging time and space for the data abstractors at each county site, but also for reviewing their time cards, checking completed abstract forms, and performing a myriad of other clerical tasks. In addition, the coordinators were responsible for recoding random forms completed by the abstractors to ensure that the information coded was accurate and complete.

Once staff was hired, the project director and the assistant project director conducted a two-day, on-site training seminar in each state. This training seminar involved a combination of classroom teaching on the abstracting and coding procedures used in data collection, and orientation at a courthouse to learn procedures for examining the records and docket books. The training covered the sequence of events for data collection, identification of pleas from the records, instructions for completing the abstract form, coding, data handling, confidentiality, and other employment details (e.g., time cards, mileage reimbursement). Field researchers were told how to organize the information they would find in the typical court file, and they were shown the specific sections where they would be likely to find the data for completing each section of the abstract form.

This approach to staffing and training worked exceedingly well. It might have been preferable to have had centralized training for all of the field researchers from all the study states, but this was not possible given the staggered approach to data collection that we followed. The research coordinators played a crucial role in the data collection. Our one major mistake was deciding not to hire an on-site state coordinator in New Jersey. Our attempt to perform that function from Albany, New York, led to some minor supervision problems and a very elongated data collection period.

Data Abstracting and Coding

Data collection began in the fall of 1985 and was completed in the summer of 1990. The most challenging and time-consuming task was identifying every NGRI plea that was entered during our study years in all 49 study counties. Once the records with pleas were identified (described below), we used a standardized data collection instrument to abstract the desired information. A copy of the abstract form is attached as Appendix B. The original data collection form was used in Montana. Soon after the abstract form was first used, we discovered that several of the data elements on the form did not correspond to what was actually available from court records. So we substantially revised the form. In effect, Montana, our first state, served as a pilot test for the data collection form. The revised form was used in the remaining states. It includes sections on sociodemographics, target crimes, criminal justice processing, diagnoses, target confinement, known prior criminal justice and mental health histories, and release information.

The information required to complete the abstract form came from multiple sources. The primary location for the data was the criminal case records at the county courts. As much data as possible were collected at the county level. We followed up defendants who were found NGRI with state mental health departments. For persons found guilty and sent to prison, we followed up with state departments of corrections. Information was obtained on length of confinement at the facility or facilities where the defendant was confined and/or at the centralized information source. We did not attempt to follow any defendants who were released directly into the community following trial. Details regarding data collection efforts for county and state information are summarized below.

County-Level Data

As is readily apparent from the information presented in Tables A.3 and A.4, the process of gathering information about insanity pleas is extremely complicated. We examined nearly 1 million indictments to find a total of 8,953 insanity pleas. The most common method of identifying cases was to hand-search the individual criminal dockets that are maintained in county clerks' offices. This entailed reviewing every docket page of every indictment for the inclusive years, searching for any reference to an insanity defense. Often this procedure led to oversampling, for we had originally instructed the field researchers to include any cases with a reference to the mental health of the defendant (e.g., "NGRI," "expert witness," "mental illness," "psychiatrist," "state hospital"). This criterion for identifying cases required the field researchers to review dockets for 597,957 indictments.

In those counties where the dockets were not available, we relied upon other techniques for identifying insanity cases. In five counties the researchers pulled every case file for the study years from storage shelves or file drawers and reviewed each to determine whether an insanity plea was ever raised. Although this was a much more time-consuming task than reviewing the docket pages, we followed this procedure in pulling and reviewing a total of 89,554 individual case files across the eight study states. Another time-consuming procedure was required in four New York counties where the dockets contained none of the necessary information for identifying insanity pleas. There our field researchers had to review all cases where an incompetent to stand trial (IST) exam was ordered. In this way, we anticipated that we would capture most cases in which an insanity plea was used, as an IST exam is often the first step to an NGRI plea in New York. We were able to rely on a computerized search for only three counties in New York which accounted for 11% of the total indictments. In one county we were given the indictment number of all defendants who were evaluated for insanity, information that greatly simplified the search procedures.

All cases identified by one or another of these procedures were then reviewed. The initial scan was made to determine if an insanity plea was, in fact, ever entered. This was much like searching for a needle in a haystack. Documentation of an insanity plea ranged from a formal notice or motion to rely on the defense to a casual reference to the plea in the case minutes. Once documentation was found, the case became a study case and a data abstraction form was completed.

Completing the abstract form for study cases was fraught with frustrations. Aside from misplaced criminal records, some of "these types" of cases were kept in the judges' chambers for special reasons, including mandated periodic court hearings, the notoriety of the defendant, and the unpopularity of the outcome. Within case files it was not uncommon for key documents to be missing. Because the clerks' records are the only permanent case record, there was no other place to search for missing court data. At some sites the clerks allowed the researchers to go into the stacks to pull their own records. In other counties the researchers were required to fill out a request form for every file they wanted to review, and often were allowed to examine only a few files at one time. In one county in Georgia each individual

TABLE A.3. Information Sources for Insanity Pleas and Acquittal by Study State

State	No. study counties	Study years	% of counties where plea information obtained from:				Statewide acquittal information obtained from:		
			Court dockets	Computer	Case records	Other	Computer	No. state hospitals visited	Central records
California	7	7/78–6/87	57%	14%	28%		1		
Georgia	12	1/76–12/85	92%		8%			1	
Montana	7	1/76–12/85	100%					1	
New Jersey	6	1/76–12/85	83%		17%			5	
New York	5	10/77–9/87				100%			1
Ohio	5	1/77–12/83	100%				1	12	
Washington	3	7/79–12/87		67%	33%			2	
Wisconsin	4	7/79–6/85	100%					2	
TOTAL	49		74%	6%	10%	10%	2	23	1

TABLE A.4. Volume of Insanity Cases by Study State

States	No. felony indictments	No. insanity pleas	No. NGRI[a] acquittals	Plea[b] rate	Acquittal[c] rate	Success[d] rate
California	225,152	1,300	665	0.58	0.30	45.52
Georgia	151,669	2,630	426	1.73	0.28	13.11
Montana	14,227	816	58	5.74	0.41	7.31
New Jersey	125,951	670	295	0.53	0.23	43.34
New York	195,015	556	226	0.30	0.12	39.78
Ohio	147,477	2,005	342	1.36	0.23	15.30
Washington	74,105	442	387	0.60	0.52	87.36
Wisconsin	33,613	534	156	1.59	0.46	28.24
TOTAL	967,209	8,953	2,555	.93	.26	26.27

[a]NGRI acquittals includes all acquittals identified through county records as well as acquittals (in study counties) who were identified via state-level records (State Hospitals).
[b,c]Plea and Acquittal Rates are per 100 felony indictments.
[d]Success Rate is the percentage of NGRI pleas that result in acquittal. It is based *only* on data obtained through county-level records which are not reported in this table (see Note 1). We did not use acquittals identified through state records in the success rate because we could not identify comparable insanity pleas from such records.

indictment, rolled up and tied with a red ribbon, was filed separately from the other court documents. That meant that the field researchers had to search the drawers for the indictments and then unroll each one to abstract several data elements. In several other counties it was necessary to go to archive buildings or storage facilities or, when we were lucky, to microfiche to access the older court records.

Despite these obstacles encountered in the county data collection process, we were able to complete this portion of the study within the expected time frame. Many court clerks expressed their disbelief about our goals and said we were "crazy" for trying to dig through the boxes, stacks, shelves, and drawers of files. Many were convinced that we would either fail to find any insanity pleas or never find the files. They expressed surprise at the number of pleas we did find (they tended to remember only successful pleas), and they were genuinely amazed that we did uncover most of the information we were seeking.

State-Level Data

We obtained two kinds of information from record systems maintained by state mental health authorities. The first was hospitalization data for persons found NGRI in our county sample, and the second was the same data for all the *other* persons found NGRI in the state during the study years. In some instances we found a number of additional cases from our study county. This last information was important because from our county sample we could identify NGRI acquittals from sample counties, but not those from the rest of the state. The state data also provided confinement information for the acquittals in sample and nonsample counties. The level of completeness of the county-level data in identifying NGRI acquittals varied considerably from state to state. In Montana all of the acquittals in the state came from our study counties, whereas in California 23% of the acquittal data for cases from our study counties came from the state-level source. This was largely due to the identification of cases at the state level for the five unsampled districts of Los Angeles County.

Case records on NGRIs committed to state mental health systems were not necessarily maintained in one location. As Table A.3 demonstrates, it was necessary to rely on a number of procedures to obtain follow-up information. In California we were able to obtain most of our information through a number of customized computer reports that were made available to us by exceedingly cooperative staff at the state mental health department. In New York we used centralized (paper files) records. The most common procedure for collecting follow-up mental health data, however, was to go directly to the state mental hospitals where the persons found NGRI were hospitalized. Montana had only one such facility. The follow-up phase included data collection at two hospitals in Georgia, Washington, and Wisconsin; five facilities in New Jersey (often returning many times to locate the complete case files); and 16 state psychiatric centers in Ohio.

The data collection procedures for unsuccessful insanity pleas (those who were found guilty and sent to prison) were simplified by the fact that most state departments of corrections maintain centralized paper or computerized records. Generally, we were able to request information on all of our cases and receive the data directly from state agency data sources. This was the easiest phase of our field work.

Data Management

The data management requirements for this study were formidable. Each abstract form was completed by a field researcher, coded later that same day, checked for internal inconsistencies by the coder, and then submitted to the research coordinator for that state. The research coordinator rechecked the forms and submitted all clean abstract forms to the project research staff in Albany, New York. The forms were then rechecked by our central project staff. To maintain central control over project coding decisions and to ensure consistency across states, any forms with coding problems were resolved in Albany via consultation with the research coordinators. This was a huge undertaking. One of the most demanding and frustrating parts of this stage of the research process was connected to the discovery of new information; when new information became available we had to go back and recode some portion of all the previously coded forms. The entire state of Montana, for example, was recoded when we revised the abstract form. In various states it was necessary for the field researchers to go back to the court records in order to clarify coding questions about some cases. Once coded, all of the data were keypunched and verified centrally using an SPSS-PC data entry program. We achieved some relief from the enormous volume of data received and the daily coding decisions by staggering our data collection so that we had only two states active at any time.

Data Collected but Not Used

We collected data from eight states, but not all that information has been presented in this monograph. First, we did not present our analysis for Ohio's 1980 reform in which the court of jurisdiction was changed from the probate court to the criminal court. The target reform was enacted to ensure that potentially dangerous persons found NGRI would not be released without adequate judicial scrutiny (Nagatani & Nakles, 1981). There was widespread concern that decisions to release insanity acquittees would be made by judges in the probate courts who were not responsive to community concerns. Essentially, the reform reassigned jurisdiction over commitment and release decisions to the criminal court, specifically, the trial court. We chose to study this reform because we believed it represents one type of combination reform where changes are made at the front and back end of the process.

However, subsequent to data collection, we became aware of an insanity defense reform that had been enacted by the Ohio legislature in November 1978. That reform had transferred the court of jurisdiction for commitment and release from the criminal court to the probate court. This meant that the probate court was the court of jurisdiction for only a very brief period of time (November 1978 to April 1980). The Ohio data were drawn for a 6-year period from 1977 through 1982. Regrettably, this time frame did not offer sufficient time periods pre-1978 to evaluate the first reform or post-1980 to adequately assess the second reform. The lack of sufficient time periods introduced several complications for analysis, but there was an even greater problem with use of these data. Prior to the 1978 reform, the Ohio system was based on automatic and indefinite commitment. The earlier reform had eliminated that approach and created a system consistent with civil commitment standards. This change remained in effect even after the 1980 reform. After careful scrutiny we decided that we could not readily disentangle the effects of the reforms given the close proximity of the two reforms, the effect of the elimination of automatic and indefinite commitment crossing over the time periods associated with both reforms, and the paucity of time intervals. The validity of any conclusion we might draw from these data would be tenuous, at best. Although the results for Ohio are not reported in this book, they were published with a clear statement of their limitations in the *Capitol University Law Review* published by Ohio Law School (Callahan & Steadman, 1990).

We also did not report data for the three comparison states that did not enact reforms over the study period. These states were New Jersey, Washington, and Wisconsin. They were originally included to provide an assessment of national trends against which the data from the study states could be interpreted. Ultimately, we concluded that the data from these states were not useful comparisons for the states that had enacted reforms. One reason for this conclusion was the difficulty of pooling the data from these three states to estimate a national trend. Pooling the data was difficult because the study periods in those states were not consistent (New Jersey—1976 through 1985; Washington—1980 through 1987; Wisconsin—1980 through 1985). We had mistakenly assumed that having the study years for the reform states covered by at least one comparison state would be sufficient. We also found it difficult to use the data from the comparison states because the pattern of insanity use in these states did not always match the pattern in the reform states *prior* to the enactment of the reform. In effect, the comparison states and the reform states did not match up very well, and it did not make sense to us to identify impacts on outcome variables in the reform states only if they were significantly different than the trend in the comparison states. We could only determine the lack of comparability after we had analyzed the data.

In some instances during our early analyses the comparison states appeared to be useful. In these instances, we included the comparison states in our analyses, but found our conclusions regarding the impact of the reforms were the same whether or not the comparison states were included. The inclusion of data from the comparison states made a much more complicated presentation of the results with no gain in understanding. Accordingly, we excluded them from consideration in this book.

To sum up, the data reported in this monograph were collected from California, Georgia, Montana, and New York. Across these four states, we collected data in 31 counties. We found a total of 5,274 insanity pleas and 1,369 insanity acquittals over the study period.

DATA ANALYSIS

The analyses presented throughout this book focus on insanity pleas as well as insanity acquittals. The analysis of insanity pleas allows for an assessment of the frequency of use of the insanity defense, the characteristics of the people using the insanity defense, the methods of adjudication associated with the defense, and the crimes for which insanity pleas were raised. We use data from both state and county sources for these analyses. Use of both data sources provides a more complete estimate of frequency of use and a more complete description of who used the insanity defense in study counties. The analysis of acquittals, on the other hand, allows us to assess the probability of being acquitted by reason of insanity, to determine those characteristics associated with successful pleas, and to estimate the confinement patterns for persons found NGRI.

To measure use of the insanity defense, we examine the plea *rate* rather than simply the number of insanity pleas. The plea rate controls for the volume of crimes in a state as measured by felony indictments. The plea rate for a given 6-month period is equal to the number of insanity pleas entered during that 6-month period per 1,000 felony indictments recorded during that 6-month period. We measured the chances of being acquitted by reason of insanity (the "success rate") as the percentage of insanity pleas actually acquitted NGRI.

For adjudication reforms, the change in test in California and the burden and standard reforms in Georgia and New York, the success rate was calculated using the date of indictment. Regarding Montana's abolition of the insanity defense, the GBMI reform in Georgia, and the IDRA reform in New York, the success rate was calculated using the date of disposition. The latter reforms primarily affected the disposition of insanity defendants. Thus, we wanted to ensure that we were placing cases in time periods based on the date when the case was disposed. The other reforms were associated with the processing of the case, and we were interested in when the case entered the system.

Virtually all of the analyses of rates and most of the analyses of characteristics were based on an interrupted time series design (Fox, 1984). A time series design requires the periodic measurement of some phenomenon, such as a plea rate. Several observations were made prior to the enactment of the reform and several were made subsequent to the reform. We then used a linear regression model to assess the impact of the reform. The regression model included four terms: the linear trend (slope) prior to the reform, the level (intercept) prior to the reform, the linear trend subsequent to the reform, and the level subsequent to the reform. The statistical test for a reform effect was the test of the equivalence across time of both the trend and level. The advantage of the time series over a pre–post test is that it does account for trends (Campbell & Stanley, 1963; Cook & Campbell, 1979). Whenever necessitated by a small number of cases, we relied on *t*-tests and contingency tables to assess differences based on a pre–post design.

The use of a time series design in this study was not without its problems. While the design does account for trends, the number of observation points associated with our data limited the extent to which we could assess those trends. What may be a long time period when gathering the raw data becomes a small number of observations over time for the purpose of statistical analysis. The short study periods (typically 6 years, 3 prior to the reform and 3 subsequent to the reform) rendered impossible the determination of the extent to which the pattern observed was consistent with that for time periods outside of our observation period. For example, Georgia's plea rate was declining in 1984 and 1985, but we could not determine whether such a decrease was sustained beyond 1985. Likewise, the plea rate in Georgia was increasing in 1976 and 1977, and we could not determine the extent to which this increase was the result of a continued increase over a long period of time. While the short study periods did present limitations, both resources and the selection of recent reforms made lengthier observation periods impossible to obtain. Because of the limitations caused by the short study intervals, our data and analyses are best suited to the assessment of short-term impacts of the reforms.

Because the basic design was limited to 3 years pre- and 3 years postreform, there were not enough yearly data points for a time series analysis. The best we could do was to divide the data into 6-month time intervals, thereby doubling the number of observations in each state. There were a total of 12 observations for the analyses of both reforms in New York, 10 observations for Georgia's 1978 reform in the burden and standard of proof, 20 for Montana's 1978 abolition, and 11 for California's change of test. These are still a relatively small number of observations to detect trends over time and the types of effects that reforms might have had on the plea and success rates. As a result, the power of any statistical tests that we employed to assess the significance of the reform effects was limited.

While using shorter time intervals, for example, quarterly or monthly data, would have provided more observations, there were a number of data limitations that prevented us from employing these shorter intervals. For example, to compute the 6-month plea rates, we needed to determine the number of insanity pleas and the number of felony indictments for each 6-month period. When collecting data on persons raising the insanity defense, we recorded the actual day the plea was entered. Our data on felony indictments was based upon official records, and they were reported as the number of indictments per year. With a computer-based estimation program developed by Dr. Steven Banks, we used the yearly data to estimate the numbers of felony indictments for each 6-month period. Such a procedure would not have been acceptable for estimates for time intervals shorter than 6 months. Another constraint on using time intervals shorter than 6 months is the paucity of cases. Whenever the analysis centered on persons who raised the insanity defense (both the success rate and the characteristics of those raising the defense) or on persons found NGRI (characteristics of insanity acquittals), the number of cases observed in each 6-month time interval is generally low. Shorter time intervals would only have exacerbated this problem.

We used event history analysis to examine confinement patterns. This approach is particularly well suited for data such as ours where many of the defendants were still confined after data collection ceased. These data are referred to as "censored." Data on their length of confinement could be used up until the point that they became censored. The statistical procedures were the Kaplan-Meier method of estimating the proportion of persons who were confined for a given period of time and the log rank test to assess differences in confinement patterns (Blossfeld, Hamerle, & Mayer, 1989). The Kaplan-Meier estimator did not require us to make assumptions regarding the distribution of the probability of release.

An issue that may have played a role in the validity of the conclusions drawn from our analyses was the near simultaneity of different reforms, the Hinckley case, and other court cases. For example, Georgia enacted the GBMI reform in the second half of 1982. Only months earlier John Hinckley was found NGRI, and the *Benham* decision, which overturned Georgia's commitment procedures for insanity acquittees, had occurred in November 1980. Furthermore, the reform was enacted only 4½ years after a reform in the burden and standard of proof. As a result, it was difficult to disentangle the unique effects of these various factors. All of these issues would be threats to validity regardless of the design. In fact, the time series design allowed for some measure of control against certain threats, such as the *Benham* case, because it would allow for the detection of effects for which there was some (at least 6 months) difference in the time of occurrence. The purpose of collecting data in New Jersey, Washington, and Wisconsin was to provide a control for national changes, particularly those due to the Hinckley case. As mentioned earlier, these data proved to be limited. Although, it is important to note that when the comparison states were considered, our conclusions did not change.

The other primary investigation was into the length of confinement for persons acquitted by reason of insanity and for others who raised the insanity defense (persons found guilty or guilty but mentally ill). The length of confinement for a given person was equal to the number of days the person was hospitalized or confined from the date of admission until either subsequent release or the end of data collection—whichever came first. The final dates of data collection for confinement in the four study states were: February 1, 1990, in California; November 14, 1989, in Georgia; December 31, 1985, in Montana; and February 1, 1990, in New York.

THE RESULT

The product of the multiplicity of decisions that we have recounted in this appendix is this book. It is hard to recount all of the decisions made that shape any research project. However, it is a worthwhile endeavor to make one's conclusions more persuasive and to better equip future researchers in all areas of law and mental health to do their task. Careful guidance in these areas is all too rare. We encourage other researchers to commit to this activity more often in future monographs. These day-to-day decisions and the factors that impinge on them are too frequently glossed over in order to make data cleaner than they are. Such illusion does not benefit science well. We trust this appendix will prove useful in these regards.

APPENDIX B

Data Abstraction Form

INSANITY DEFENSE REFORM PROJECT
262 Delaware Avenue, Delmar, NY 12054

Abstract Form

Study I.D.# _ _ _ _ _ _ _ _ _

Source: 1 ☐ County
2 ☐ State

Choose ONE box for each question

DEMOGRAPHICS

Date of Birth ___ / ___ / ___
Month / Day / Year

(If no date of birth is available, give age at the time of the arrest) _____

Sex
1 ☐ Male
2 ☐ Female
9 ☐ No Information

Ethnicity
1 ☐ White
2 ☐ Black
3 ☐ Hispanic
4 ☐ Asian
5 ☐ Native American/Eskimo
7 ☐ Other (Specify) _____
9 ☐ No Information

Education *(Check highest grade completed at the time of the offense)*
0 ☐ Did not attend
1 ☐ 1-8 grades
2 ☐ 9-11 grades
3 ☐ High school graduate
4 ☐ Technical school
5 ☐ Some college
6 ☐ College degree
7 ☐ Graduate studies
9 ☐ No information

Marital Status *(at the time of the offense)*
1 ☐ Single
2 ☐ Married
3 ☐ Separated
4 ☐ Divorced
5 ☐ Widowed
6 ☐ Unmarried
9 ☐ No Information

HISTORY OF TARGET CHARGE(S)

Date of Arrest ___ / ___ / ___
Month / Day / Year

Date of Indictment ___ / ___ / ___
Month / Day / Year

Date of Verdict ___ / ___ / ___
Month / Day / Year

Other Information
For Target Charge(s)
was defendant evaluated for:

IST
1 ☐ Yes
2 ☐ No
9 ☐ No Information

NGRI
1 ☐ Yes
2 ☐ No
9 ☐ No Information

Other Psych Exam
1 ☐ Yes
2 ☐ No
9 ☐ No Information

For Target Charge(s)
was defendant found:

IST
1 ☐ Yes
2 ☐ No
9 ☐ No Info.

NGRI
1 ☐ Yes
2 ☐ No
9 ☐ No Info.

Original Charge(s)
(List specific charges)

Charge 1:
Victim: 1 ☐ Male 3 ☐ No Victim 9 ☐ No Info
2 ☐ Female 4 ☐ Multiple

Relation:
1 ☐ Spouse
2 ☐ Child of
3 ☐ Other Family
4 ☐ Other Child
5 ☐ Friend
6 ☐ Other Acquaintance (eg. Neighbor)
7 ☐ Stranger
8 ☐ No Victim (Business)
9 ☐ No Information

Plea:
1 ☐ Not Guilty
2 ☐ Guilty
3 ☐ NGRI
4 ☐ GBMI
5 ☐ Withdrawn
6 ☐ Pending
7 ☐ Nolo Contendere
9 ☐ No Information

Charge 2:
Victim: 1 ☐ Male 3 ☐ No Victim 9 ☐ No Info
2 ☐ Female 4 ☐ Multiple

Relation:
1 ☐ Spouse
2 ☐ Child of
3 ☐ Other Family
4 ☐ Other Child
5 ☐ Friend
6 ☐ Other Acquaintance (eg. Neighbor)
7 ☐ Stranger
8 ☐ No Victim (Business)
9 ☐ No Information

Plea:
1 ☐ Not Guilty
2 ☐ Guilty
3 ☐ NGRI
4 ☐ GBMI
5 ☐ Withdrawn
6 ☐ Pending
7 ☐ Nolo Contendere
9 ☐ No Information

Charge 3:
Victim: 1 ☐ Male 3 ☐ No Victim 9 ☐ No Info
2 ☐ Female 4 ☐ Multiple

Relation:
1 ☐ Spouse
2 ☐ Child of
3 ☐ Other Family
4 ☐ Other Child
5 ☐ Friend
6 ☐ Other Acquaintance (eg. Neighbor)
7 ☐ Stranger
8 ☐ No Victim (Business)
9 ☐ No Information

Plea:
1 ☐ Not Guilty
2 ☐ Guilty
3 ☐ NGRI
4 ☐ GBMI
5 ☐ Withdrawn
6 ☐ Pending
7 ☐ Nolo Contendere
9 ☐ No Information

Verdict:
- 01 Not Guilty
- 02 Guilty
- 03 NGRI
- 04 GBMI
- 05 Withdrawn
- 06 Pending
- 07 Dismissed
- 09 Deferred
- 10 Died During Trial
- 99 No Information

Final Charge(s)

Charge 1:

Sentence:
- 01 Prison
- 02 Jail
- 03 Parole
- 04 Probation
- 05 Hospital
- 06 Outpatient
- 07 Release
- 08 Conditional Release
- 09 Pending
- 10 Dismissed
- 11 Deferred
- 13 Died
- 77 Other (Specify)
- 98 Not Applicable
- 99 No Information

Was sentence suspended?
- 1 Yes
- 2 No
- 8 Not Applicable
- 9 No Information

Disposition:
- 01 Prison
- 02 Jail
- 03 Parole
- 04 Probation
- 05 Hospital
- 06 Outpatient
- 07 Release
- 08 Conditional Release
- 09 Pending
- 10 Dismissed
- 11 Deferred
- 13 Died
- 77 Other (Specify)
- 98 Not Applicable
- 99 No Information

Conditions:

Length of Sentence (in years)

Verdict:
- 01 Not Guilty
- 02 Guilty
- 03 NGRI
- 04 GBMI
- 05 Withdrawn
- 06 Pending
- 07 Dismissed
- 08 Merger
- 09 Deferred
- 10 Died During Trial
- 99 No Information

Final Charge(s)

Charge 2:

Sentence:
- 01 Prison
- 02 Jail
- 03 Parole
- 04 Probation
- 05 Hospital
- 06 Outpatient
- 07 Release
- 08 Conditional Release
- 09 Pending
- 10 Dismissed
- 11 Deferred
- 12 Merger
- 13 Died
- 77 Other (Specify)
- 98 Not Applicable
- 99 No Information

Was sentence suspended?
- 1 Yes
- 2 No
- 8 Not Applicable
- 9 No Information

Disposition:
- 01 Prison
- 02 Jail
- 03 Parole
- 04 Probation
- 05 Hospital
- 06 Outpatient
- 07 Release
- 08 Conditional Release
- 09 Pending
- 10 Dismissed
- 11 Deferred
- 12 Merger
- 13 Died
- 77 Other (Specify)
- 98 Not Applicable
- 99 No Information

Conditions:

Length of Sentence (in years)

Verdict:
- 01 Not Guilty
- 02 Guilty
- 03 NGRI
- 04 GBMI
- 05 Withdrawn
- 06 Pending
- 07 Dismissed
- 08 Merger
- 09 Deferred
- 10 Died During Trial
- 99 No Information

Final Charge(s)

Charge 3:

Sentence:
- 01 Prison
- 02 Jail
- 03 Parole
- 04 Probation
- 05 Hospital
- 06 Outpatient
- 07 Release
- 08 Conditional Release
- 09 Pending
- 10 Dismissed
- 11 Deferred
- 12 Merger
- 13 Died
- 77 Other (Specify)
- 98 Not Applicable
- 99 No Information

Was sentence suspended?
- 1 Yes
- 2 No
- 8 Not Applicable
- 9 No Information

Disposition:
- 01 Prison
- 02 Jail
- 03 Parole
- 04 Probation
- 05 Hospital
- 06 Outpatient
- 07 Release
- 08 Conditional Release
- 09 Pending
- 10 Dismissed
- 11 Deferred
- 12 Merger
- 13 Died
- 77 Other (Specify)
- 98 Not Applicable
- 99 No Information

Conditions:

Length of Sentence (in years)

Trial:
- 1 Judge
- 2 Jury
- 3 Both
- 4 Pending
- 5 Plea
- 6 Not Applicable
- 9 No Information

Additional Charges (more than the 3 recorded?)
- 1 Yes
- 2 No
- 9 No Information

Was there a plea bargain agreement?
- 1 Yes
- 2 No
- 3 Informal Charge
- 4 No Information

(Code as 1 or 3 if there was a change of plea)

Found NGRI on additional charges?
- 1 Yes
- 2 No
- 8 Not Applicable
- 9 No Information

HISTORY OF TARGET CHARGE(S) *(Continued)*

Diagnosis *(For diagnoses and dates, give most recent diagnoses [those associated with insanity plea if NGRI]; code 9's for unknown, and when DSM code unknown, write in specific diagnosis in pencil)*

Purpose
1 - NGRI
2 - IST
3 - Other
4 - NGRI and IST
5 - NGRI and Other
6 - NGRI, IST & Other
9 - No Information

Evaluator
1 - Psychiatrist
2 - Psychologist
3 - Social Worker
4 - Other
9 - No Information

Finding
1 - Yes
2 - No
8 - Not Applicable
9 - No Information/
     No Conclusion

	Purpose	Date of Exam	Axis 1 (or primary)	Axis 2 (or secondary)	Evaluator		Was defendant found to be:
							IST NGRI GBMI
1.	_____	___/___/___ Month Day Year	_____	_____	_____	Exam 1	☐ ☐ ☐
2.	_____	___/___/___ Month Day Year	_____	_____	_____	Exam 2	☐ ☐ ☐
3.	_____	___/___/___ Month Day Year	_____	_____	_____	Exam 3	☐ ☐ ☐

Total # exams included in case file _____

MENTAL HEALTH HISTORY

	Yes	No	No Info
Prior hospitalizations?	01 ☐☐☐☐	00 ☐☐☐☐	99 ☐☐☐☐
Prior NGRI?	01 ☐☐☐☐	00 ☐☐☐☐	99 ☐☐☐☐
Prior IST?	01 ☐☐☐☐	00 ☐☐☐☐	99 ☐☐☐☐
Prior GBMI?	01 ☐☐☐☐	00 ☐☐☐☐	99 ☐☐☐☐

CRIMINAL HISTORY

	Yes	No	No Info
Prior juvenile arrests?	01 ☐☐☐☐	00 ☐☐☐☐	99 ☐☐☐☐
Prior adult arrests?	01 ☐☐☐☐	00 ☐☐☐☐	99 ☐☐☐☐
Prior violent arrests?	01 ☐☐☐☐	00 ☐☐☐☐	99 ☐☐☐☐
Prior prison incarcerations?	01 ☐☐☐	00 ☐☐☐	99 ☐☐☐

HISTORY OF TARGET CONFINEMENT

Date of admission ___/___/___ Facility: _____
Month Day Year

Institutional Length of Stay: *(Code # of days and type of confinement)*

Number of Days: **Type of Confinement:**

1. _____ _____ ☐
2. _____ _____ ☐
3. _____ _____ ☐

Date of Change From NGRI Status? ___/___/___ ☐☐
Month Day Year

Date of Release? ___/___/___
Month Day Year

Type of Release:
1 - Discharge
2 - Conditional Release or
    Parole (list terms)

Discharged to:
01 ☐ Community/No Designation
02 ☐ Community Treatment/
      Halfway House

4. _____

5. _____

6. _____

7. _____

8. _____

9. _____

10. RELEASE FACILITY _____

3 Leave Without Consent
4 Escape
5 Died
7 Other (Specify)
8 Not Applicable
9 No Information

03 Outpatient
04 Family/Friend
05 Prison
06 Jail
07 Court
08 Other Hospital
09 Home for the Aged
77 Other (Specify)
98 Not Applicable
99 No Information

Terms:

1.

2.

3.

4.

Diagnosis (For diagnoses and dates, code 9's for no information and when DSM code unknown, write in specific diagnosis in pencil)

Axis I (or primary)	Axis 2 (or secondary)	Evaluator
Admission		
Discharge (or current)		

Medication (at discharge or from most recent treatment plan)

Psychotropic Medication?

1 ☐ Yes If yes, specify:

2 ☐ No

9 ☐ No Information

1.

2.

3.

4.

COMPLETE FOR NGRI ACQUITTEES:

Were conditions of release violated?

1 ☐ Yes (1-3)
2 ☐ Yes (4-6)
3 ☐ Yes (7 or more)
4 ☐ No
8 ☐ Not Applicable
9 ☐ No Information

If yes, list dates of readmission and facilities:

Date Admitted	Name of Facility	Date Released
1. __/__/__	1.	1. __/__/__
2. __/__/__	2.	2. __/__/__
L. __/__/__	L.	L. __/__/__

APPENDIX C

Criminal Procedure Laws: Applicable Sections from the Four Study States

GEORGIA'S CRIMINAL PROCEDURE LAW

27-1503. Insanity and incompetency.

(a) Definitions. For purposes of this Code section:

(1) "Insane at the time of the crime" means meeting the criteria of Code Section 26-702 or 26-703. However, the term shall not include a mental state manifested only by repeated unlawful or antisocial conduct.

(2) "Mentally ill" means having a disorder of thought or mood which significantly impairs judgment, behavior, capacity to recognize reality, or ability to cope with the ordinary demands of life, or having a state of significantly subaverage general intellectual functioning existing concurrently with defects of adaptive behavior which originates in the developmental period. The term "mentally ill" shall not include a mental state manifested only by repeated unlawful or antisocial conduct.

(b) Verdict; finding as to insanity. In all cases in which the defense of insanity is interposed the jury, or the court if tried by it, shall find whether the defendant is:

(1) Guilty;

(2) Not guilty;

(3) Not guilty by reason of insanity at the time of the crime; or

(4) Guilty but mentally ill at the time of the crime, but the finding of guilty but mentally ill shall be made only in felony cases.

(c) Jury instructions; finding as to insanity. In all criminal trials of any of the courts of this state wherein an accused shall contend that he was insane or otherwise mentally incompetent under the law at the time the act or acts charged against him were committed, the trial judge shall instruct the jury that they may consider, in addition to verdicts of "guilty" and "not guilty," the additional verdicts of "not guilty by reason of insanity at the time of the crime" and "guilty but mentally ill at the time of the crime."

(1) The defendant may be found "not guilty by reason of insanity at the time of the crime" if he meets the criteria of Code Section 26-702 or 26-703 at the time of the commission of the crime. If the court or jury should make such finding, it shall so specify in its verdict.

(2) The defendant may be found "guilty but mentally ill at the time of the crime" if the jury, or court acting as trier of facts, finds beyond a reasonable doubt that the defendant is guilty of the crime charged and was mentally ill at the time of the commission of the crime. If the court or jury should make such finding, it shall so specify in its verdict.

(d) Evaluation of present mental condition. Whenever a defendant is found not guilty by reason of insanity at the time of the crime, the court shall retain jurisdiction over the person so acquitted and shall order such person to be detained in a state mental health facility, to be selected by the Department of Human Resources, for a period not to exceed 30 days from the date of the acquittal order, for evaluation of the defendant's present mental condition. Upon completion of the evaluation, the proper officials of the mental health facility shall send a report of the defendant's present mental condition to the trial judge, the prosecuting attorney, and the defendant's attorney, if any.

(e) Post evaluation commitment procedures. After the expiration of the 30 days' evaluation period in the state mental health facility, if the evaluation report from the Department of Human Resources indicates that the defendant does not meet the commitment criteria of Code Chapter 88-5 or Code Chapter 88-25, the trial judge may issue an order discharging the defendant from custody without a hearing. If the defendant is not so discharged, the trial judge shall order a hearing to determine whether the defendant should be committed to the Department of Human Resources. The defendant shall be detained in custody until completion of the hearing. The hearing shall be conducted at the earliest opportunity after the expiration of the 30 days' evaluation period but in any event within 30 days after receipt by the prosecuting attorney of the evaluation report from the mental health facility. The court may take judicial notice of evidence introduced during the trial of the defendant and may call for testimony from any person with knowledge concerning whether the defendant is currently a mentally ill person in need of involuntary treatment or currently mentally retarded and in need of being ordered to receive services, as provided in subsection (v) of Code Section 88-501 and Code Section 88-2504. The prosecuting attorney may cross-examine the witnesses called by the court and the defendant's witnesses and present relevant evidence concerning the issues presented at the hearing. If the judge determines that the defendant meets the commitment criteria of Code Chapter 88-5 or 88-25, the judge shall order the defendant to be committed to the Department of Human Resources to receive involuntary treatment under Code Chapter 88-5 or to receive services under Code Chapter 88-25. The defendant is entitled to the rights specified below and shall be notified in writing of these rights at the time of his admission for evaluation under subsection (d). Such rights are:

(1) A notice that a hearing will be held and the time and place thereof;

(2) A notice that the defendant has the right to counsel and that the defendant or his representatives may apply immediately to the court to have counsel appointed if the defendant cannot afford counsel and that the court will appoint counsel for the defendant unless he indicates in writing that he does not desire to be represented by counsel;

(3) The right to confront and cross-examine witnesses and to offer evidence;

(4) The right to subpoena witnesses and to require testimony before the court in person or by deposition from any person upon whose evaluation the decision of the court may rest;

(5) Notice of the right to have established an individualized service plan or individualized program plan specifically tailored by the person's treatment needs, as such plans are defined in subsection (w) of Code Section 88-501 and subsection (i) of Code Section 88-2502;

(6) A notice that the defendant has the right to be examined by a physician or a licensed clinical psychologist of his own choice at his own expense and to have that physician or psychologist submit a suggested service plan for the patient which conforms with the requirements of subsection (w) of Code Section 88-501 or subsection (i) of Code Section 88-2502, whichever is applicable.

(f) Release of persons found not guilty by reason of insanity. A defendant who has been found not guilty by reason of insanity at the time of the crime and is ordered committed to the Department of Human Resources under subsection (e) of this Code section may only be discharged from that commitment by order of the committing court in accordance with the procedures specified in this subsection:

(1) Application for the release of a defendant who has been committed to the Department of Human Resources under subsection (e) of this Code section upon the ground that he does not meet the civil commitment criteria under Code Chapter 88-5 or Code Chapter 88-25 may be made to the committing court, either by such defendant or by the superintendent of the state hospital in which the defendant is detained.

(2) The burden of proof in such release hearing shall be upon the applicant. The defendant shall have the same rights in the release hearing as set forth in subsection (e) of this Code section.

(3) If the finding of the court is adverse to release in such hearing held pursuant to subsection (f) on the grounds that such defendant does meet the civil commitment criteria under Code Chapter 88-5 or Code Chapter

88-25, a further release application shall not be heard by the court until twelve months have elapsed from the date of the hearing upon the last preceding application.

(g) Sentencing of defendant found guilty but mentally ill. Whenever a defendant is found guilty but mentally ill at the time of a felony, or enters a plea to that effect that is accepted by the court, the court shall sentence him in the same manner as a defendant found guilty of the offense. If a defendant who is found guilty but mentally ill at the time of the felony is committed to an appropriate penal facility, he shall be further evaluated and then treated, within the limits of state funds appropriated thereof, in such manner as is psychiatrically indicated for his mental illness. Treatment may be provided by:

(1) The penal facility; or

(2) The Department of Human Resources after transfer pursuant to procedures set forth in regulations of the Department of Offender Rehabilitation and the Department of Human Resources.

(h) Probation. If a defendant who is found guilty but mentally ill at the time of a felony is placed on probation under Chapter 27-27, the "Statewide Probation Act," the court may require that the defendant undergo available outpatient medical or psychiatric treatment or seek similar available voluntary inpatient treatment as a condition of probation. Persons required to receive such services may be charged fees by the provider of the services.

NEW YORK'S CRIMINAL PROCEDURE LAW

Part Two—The Principal Proceedings

Title J—Prosecution of Indictments in Superior Courts—Plea to Sentence

Article 330—Proceedings from Verdict to Sentence

§ 330.10—Disposition of defendant after verdict of acquittal

1. Upon a verdict of complete acquittal, the court must immediately discharge the defendant if he is in the custody of the sheriff, or, if he is at liberty on bail, it must exonerate the bail.

2. Upon a verdict of not responsible by reason of mental disease or defect, the provisions of section 330.20 of this chapter shall govern all subsequent proceedings against the defendant.

§ 330.20—Procedure following verdict or plea of not responsible by reason of mental disease or defect

6. Initial hearing; commitment order. After the examination reports are submitted, the court must, within ten days of the receipt of such reports, conduct an initial hearing to determine the defendant's present mental condition. If the defendant is in the custody of the commissioner pursuant to an examination order, the court must direct the sheriff to obtain custody of the defendant from the commissioner and to confine the defendant pending further order of the court except that the court may direct the sheriff to confine the defendant in an institution located near the place where the court sits if that institution has been designated by the commissioner as suitable for the temporary and secure detention of mentally disabled persons. At such initial hearing, the district attorney must establish to the satisfaction of the court that the defendant has a dangerous mental disorder or is mentally ill. If the court finds that the defendant has a dangerous mental disorder, it must issue a commitment order. If the court finds the defendant does not have a dangerous mental disorder but is mentally ill, the provisions of subdivision seven of this section shall apply.

7. Initial hearing; civil commitment; and order of conditions. If at the conclusion of the initial hearing described in subdivision six of this section, the court

finds that the defendant is mentally ill but does not have a dangerous mental disorder, the provisions of articles nine or fifteen of the mental hygiene law shall apply at that stage of the proceedings and at all subsequent proceedings. Having found that the defendant is mentally ill, the court must issue an order of conditions and an order committing the defendant to the custody of the commissioner. The latter order shall be deemed an order made pursuant to the mental hygiene law and not pursuant to this section, and further retention, conditional release or discharge of such defendant shall be in accordance with the provisions of the mental hygiene law. If, at the conclusion of the initial hearing, the court finds that the defendant does not have a dangerous mental disorder and is not mentally ill, the court must discharge the defendant either unconditionally or subject to an order of conditions.

8. First retention order. When a defendant is in the custody of the commissioner pursuant to a commitment order, the commissioner must, at least thirty days prior to the expiration of the period prescribed in the order, apply to the court that issued the order, or to a superior court in the county where the secure facility is located, for a first retention order or a release order. The commissioner must give written notice of the application to the district attorney, the defendant, counsel for the defendant, and the mental health information service. Upon receipt of such application, the court may, on its own motion, conduct a hearing to determine whether the defendant has a dangerous mental disorder, and it must conduct such hearing if a demand, therefore, is made by the district attorney, the defendant, counsel for the defendant, or the mental health information service within ten days from the date that notice of the application was given to them. If such a hearing is held on an application for retention, the commissioner must establish to the satisfaction of the court that the defendant has a dangerous mental disorder or is mentally ill. The district attorney shall be entitled to appear and present evidence at such hearing. If such a hearing is held on an application for release, the district attorney must establish to the satisfaction of the court that the defendant has a dangerous mental disorder or is mentally ill. If the court finds that the defendant has a dangerous mental disorder it must issue a first retention order. If the court finds that the defendant is mentally ill but does not have a dangerous mental disorder, it must issue a first retention order and, pursuant to subdivision eleven of this section, a transfer order. If the court finds the defendant does not have a dangerous mental disorder and is not mentally ill, it must issue a release order and an order of conditions pursuant to subdivision twelve of this section.

9. Second and subsequent retention orders. When a defendant is in the custody of the commissioner pursuant to a first retention order, the commissioner must, at least thirty days prior to the expiration of the period prescribed in the order, apply to the court that issued the order, or to a superior court in the county where the facility is located, for a second retention order or a release

order. When a defendant is in the custody of the commissioner prior to the expiration of the period prescribed in a second retention order, the procedures set forth in this subdivision for the issuance of a second retention order shall govern the application for and the issuance of any subsequent retention order.

10. Furlough order. The commissioner may apply for a furlough order, pursuant to this subdivision, when a defendant is in his custody pursuant to a commitment order, or retention order, and the commissioner is of the view that, consistent with the public safety and welfare of the community and the defendant, the clinical condition of the defendant warrants a granting of the privileges authorized by a furlough order. The application for a furlough order may be made to the court that issued the commitment order, or to a superior court in the county where the secure facility is located. The commissioner must give ten days written notice to the district attorney, the defendant, counsel for the defendant, and the mental health information service. Upon receipt of such application, the court may, on its own motion, conduct a hearing to determine whether the application should be granted, and must conduct such hearing if a demand therefore is made by the district attorney. If the court finds that the issuance of a furlough order is consistent with the public safety and welfare of the community and the defendant, and that the clinical condition of the defendant warrants a granting of the privileges authorized by a furlough order, the court must grant the application and issue a furlough order containing any terms and conditions that the court deems necessary or appropriate. If the defendant fails to return to the secure facility at the time specified in the furlough order, then, for purposes of subdivision nineteen of this section, he shall be deemed to have escaped.

11. Transfer order and order of conditions. The commissioner may apply for a transfer order, pursuant to this subdivision, when a defendant is in his custody pursuant to a retention order or a recommitment order, and the commissioner is of the view that the defendant does not have a dangerous mental disorder or that, consistent with the public safety and welfare of the community and the defendant, the clinical condition of the defendant warrants his transfer from a secure facility to a non-secure facility designated by the commissioner. The application for a transfer order may be made to the court that issued the order under which the defendant is then in custody, or to a superior court in the county where the secure facility is located. The commissioner must give ten days written notice to the district attorney, the defendant, counsel for the defendant, and the mental health information service. Upon receipt of such application, the court may, on its own motion, conduct a hearing to determine whether the application should be granted, and must conduct such hearing if the demand therefore is made. The court must reject the transfer order if it finds the defendant has a dangerous mental disorder or that the issuance of a transfer order is inconsistent with the public safety and welfare

of the community. The court must grant the application and issue a transfer order if the court finds that the defendant does not have a dangerous mental disorder, or if the court finds that the issuance of a transfer order is consistent with the public safety and welfare of the community and the defendant and that the clinical condition of the defendant, warrants his transfer from a secure facility to a non-secure facility. A court must also issue a transfer order when, in connection with an application for a first retention order pursuant to subdivision eight of this section or a second or subsequent retention order pursuant to subdivision nine of this section, it finds that a defendant is mentally ill but does not have a dangerous mental disorder. Whenever a court issues a transfer order it must also issue an order of conditions.

12. Release order and order of conditions. The commissioner may apply for a release order, pursuant to this subdivision, when a defendant is in his custody pursuant to a retention order or recommitment order, and the commissioner is of the view that the defendant no longer has a dangerous mental disorder and is no longer mentally ill. The application for a release order may be made to the court that issued the order under which the defendant is then in custody, or to a superior court in the county where the facility is located. The application must contain a description of the defendant's current mental condition, the past course of treatment, a history of the defendant's conduct subsequent to his commitment, a written service plan for continued treatment which shall include the information specified in subdivision (g) of section 29.15 of the mental hygiene law, and a detailed statement of the extent to which supervision of the defendant after release is proposed. The commissioner must give ten days written notice to the district attorney, the defendant, counsel for the defendant, and the mental health information service. Upon receipt of such application, the court must promptly conduct a hearing to determine the defendant's present mental condition. At such hearing, the district attorney must establish to the satisfaction of the court that the defendant has a dangerous mental disorder or is mentally ill. If the court finds that the defendant has a dangerous mental disorder, it must deny the application for a release order. If the court finds that the defendant does not have a dangerous mental disorder but is mentally ill, it must issue a transfer order pursuant to subdivision eleven of this section to a non-secure facility. If the court finds that the defendant does not have a dangerous mental disorder and is not mentally ill, it must grant the application and issue a release order. A court must also issue a release order when, in connection with an application for a first retention order pursuant to subdivision eight of this section or a second or subsequent retention order pursuant to subdivision nine of this section, it finds that the defendant does not have a dangerous mental disorder and is not mentally ill. Whenever a court issues a release order it must also issue an order of conditions. If the court has previously issued a transfer order and an order of conditions, it must issue a new order of conditions upon issuing a release order.

The order of conditions issued in conjunction with a release order shall incorporate a written service plan prepared by a psychiatrist familiar with the defendant's case history and approved by the court, and shall contain any conditions that the court determines to be reasonably necessary or appropriate. It shall be the responsibility of the commissioner to determine that such defendant is receiving the services specified in the written service plan and is complying with any conditions specified in such plan and the order of conditions.

13. Discharge order. The commissioner may apply for a discharge order, pursuant to this subdivision, when a defendant has been continuously on an outpatient status for three years or more pursuant to a release order, and the commissioner is of the view that the defendant no longer has a dangerous mental disorder and is no longer mentally ill and that the issuance of a discharge order is consistent with the public safety and welfare of the community and the defendant. The application for a discharge order may be made to the court that issued the release order, or to a superior court in the county where the defendant is then residing. The commissioner must give ten days written notice to the district attorney, the defendant, counsel for the defendant, and the mental health information service. Upon receipt of such application, the court may, on its own motion, conduct a hearing to determine whether the application should be granted, and must conduct such hearing if a demand therefore is made by the district attorney. The court must grant the application and issue a discharge order if the court finds that the defendant has been continuously on an outpatient status for three years or more, that he does not have a dangerous mental disorder and is not mentally ill, and that the issuance of the discharge order is consistent with the public safety and welfare of the community.

   (n) "Discharge order" means an order terminating an order of conditions or unconditionally discharging a defendant from supervision under the provisions of this section.

14. Recommitment order. At any time during the period covered by an order of conditions an application may be made by the commissioner or the district attorney to the court that issued such order, or to a superior court in the county where the defendant is residing, for a recommitment order when the applicant is of the view that the defendant has a dangerous mental disorder. The applicant must give written notice of the application to the defendant, counsel for the defendant, and the mental health information service, and if the applicant is the commissioner he must give such notice to the district attorney or if the applicant is the district attorney he must give such notice to the commissioner. Upon receipt of such application the court must order the defendant to appear before it for a hearing to determine if the defendant has a dangerous mental disorder. Such order may be in the form of a written notice,

specifying the time and place of appearance, served personally upon the defendant, or mailed to his last known address, as the court may direct. If the defendant fails to appear in court as directed, the court may issue a warrant to an appropriate peace officer directing him to take the defendant into custody and bring him before the court. In such circumstance, the court may direct that the defendant be confined in an appropriate institution located near the place where the court sits. The court must conduct a hearing to determine whether the defendant has a dangerous mental disorder. At such hearing, the applicant, whether he be the commissioner or the district attorney, must establish to the satisfaction of the court that the defendant has a dangerous mental disorder. If the applicant is the commissioner, the district attorney shall be entitled to appear and present evidence at such hearing; if the applicant is the district attorney, the commissioner shall be entitled to appear and present evidence at such hearings. If the court finds that the defendant has a dangerous mental disorder, it must issue a recommitment order. When a defendant is in the custody of the commissioner pursuant to a recommitment order, the procedures set forth in subdivisions eight and nine of this section for the issuance of retention orders shall govern the application for and issuance of a first retention order, a second retention order, and subsequent retention orders.

17. Rights of defendants. Subject to the limitations and provisions of this section, a defendant committed to the custody of the commissioner pursuant to this section shall have the rights granted to patients under the mental hygiene law.

18. Notwithstanding any other provision of law, no person confined by reason of a commitment order, recommitment order or retention order to a secure facility may be discharged or released unless the commissioner shall deliver written notices, at least four days excluding Saturdays, Sundays, and holidays, in advance of such discharge or release to all of the following:

(a) the district attorney.

(b) the police department having jurisdiction of the area of which the defendant is to be discharged or released.

(c) any other person the court may designate.

21. Appeals. (a) A party to proceedings conducted in accordance with the provisions of this section may take an appeal to an intermediate appellate court by permission of the intermediate appellate court as follows:

(i) the commissioner may appeal from any release order, retention order, transfer order, discharge order, order of conditions, or recommitment order, for which he has not applied;

(ii) a defendant, or the mental health information service on his behalf, may appeal from any commitment order, retention order, recommitment order, or, if the defendant has obtained a rehearing and review of any such order pursuant to subdivision sixteen of this section. A defendant who takes an appeal from a commitment order, retention order, or recommitment order may not subsequently obtain a rehearing and review of such order pursuant to subdivision sixteen of this section;

(iii) the district attorney may appeal from any release order, transfer order, discharge order, order of conditions, furlough order, or order denying an application for a recommitment order which he opposed.

(b) An aggrieved party may appeal from a final order of the intermediate appellate court to the court of appeals by permission of the intermediate appellate court granted before application to the court of appeals, or by permission of the court of appeals upon refusal by the intermediate appellate court or upon direct application.

(c) An appeal taken under this subdivision shall be deemed civil in nature, and shall be governed by the laws and rules applicable to civil appeals; provided, however, that a stay of the order appealed from must be obtained in accordance with the provisions of paragraph (d) hereof.

CALIFORNIA'S PENAL CODE

§ 1026. Pleas of insanity; separate trials; presumption of sanity; trial of sanity issue; verdict; sentence; confinement in state hospital or mental facility; outpatient status; restoration to sanity; transfers between facilities; reports by hospitals or facilities.

(a) When a defendant pleads not guilty by reason of insanity, and also joins with it another plea or pleas, the defendant shall first be tried as if only such other plea or pleas had been entered, and in that trial the defendant shall be conclusively presumed to have been sane at the time the offense is alleged to have been committed. If the jury shall find the defendant guilty, or if the defendant pleads only not guilty by reason of insanity, then the question whether the defendant was sane or insane at the time the offense was committed shall be promptly tried, either before the same jury or before a new jury in the discretion of the court. In that trial, the jury shall return a verdict either that the defendant was sane at the time the offense was committed or was insane at the time the offense was committed. If the verdict or finding is that the defendant was sane at the time the offense was committed, the court shall sentence the defendant as provided by law. If the verdict or finding is that the defendant was insane at the time the offense was committed, the court, unless it shall appear to the court that the sanity of the defendant has been recovered fully, shall direct that the defendant be confined in a state hospital for the care and treatment of the mentally disordered or any other appropriate public or private treatment facility approved by the county mental health director, or the court may order the defendant placed on outpatient status pursuant to Title 15 (concerning with Section 1600) of Part 2. The court shall transmit a copy of its order to the county mental health director or a designee, and if the defendant is ordered confined in a state hospital or other treatment facility, copies of the arrest reports and the report of the county mental health director required under subdivision (b) shall accompany the person to the state hospital or other treatment facility where the defendant is to be confined.

(b) Prior to making such order directing the defendant be confined in a state hospital or other treatment facility or placed on outpatient status, the court shall order the county mental health director or a designee to evaluate the defendant and to submit to the court within 15 judicial days of the order a written recommendation as to whether the defendant should be placed on outpatient status or confined in a state hospital or other treatment facility. No person shall be admitted to a state hospital or other treatment facility or placed on outpatient status under this section without having been evaluated by the county mental health director or a designee. If, however, it shall appear to the court that the sanity of the defendant has been recovered fully, the defendant shall be remanded to the custody of the sheriff until the issue of sanity shall have been finally determined in the manner prescribed by law. A defendant committed to a state hospital or other treatment facility or placed on outpatient status pursuant to Title 15 (commencing with Section 1600) of Part 2 shall not be released from confinement, parole, or outpatient status unless and until the court which committed the person shall, after notice and hearing, find and determine that the person's sanity has been restored. Nothing in this section shall prevent the transfer of such person from one state hospital to any other state hospital by proper authority. Nothing in this section shall prevent the transfer of the patient to a hospital in another state in the manner provided in Section 4119 of the Welfare and Institutions Code.

(c) If the defendant is committed or transferred to a state hospital pursuant to this section, the court may, upon receiving the written recommendation of the medical director of the state hospital and the county mental health director that the defendant be transferred to a public or private treatment facility approved by the county mental health director, order the defendant transferred to that facility. If the defendant is committed or transferred to a public or private treatment facility approved by the county mental health director, the court may, upon receiving the written recommendation of the county mental health director, order the defendant transferred to a state hospital or to another public or private treatment facility approved by the county mental health director. Where either the defendant or the prosecuting attorney chooses to contest either kind of order of transfer, a petition may be filed in the court requesting a hearing which shall be held if the court determines that sufficient grounds exist. At that hearing, the prosecuting attorney or the defendant may present evidence bearing on the order of transfer. The court shall use the same procedures and standards of proof as used in conducting probation revocation hearings pursuant to Section 1203.2.

(d) Prior to making an order for transfer under this section, the court shall notify the defendant, the attorney of record for the defendant, the prosecuting attorney, and the county mental health director or a designee.

(e) If the defendant is confined in a state hospital or other treatment facility as an inpatient or is on parole under the provisions of subdivision (a) or (b) of Section 1611, the medical director of the facility shall, at six-month intervals, submit a report in writing to the court and the county mental health director of the county of commitment or a designee setting forth the status and progress of the defendant. The court shall transmit copies of these reports to the prosecutor and defense counsel.

(f) When directing that the defendant be confined in a state hospital pursuant to subdivision (a), the court shall select the state hospital in accordance with the policies established by the Department of Mental Health.

§ 1026.1. Release; grounds.

A person committed to a state hospital or other treatment facility under the provisions of Section 1026 shall be released from the state hospital or other treatment facility only under one or more of the following circumstances:

(a) Pursuant to the provisions of Section 1026.2.

(b) Upon expiration of the maximum term of commitment as provided in subdivision (a) of Section 1026.5, except as such term may be extended under the provisions of subdivision (b) of Section 1026.5.

§ 1026.2. Application for release because of restoration of sanity; persons who may petition; summary of treatment program; designation of facility; minimum confinement before or between applications; burden of proof; recommendation.

Text of section operative until Jan. 1, 1986, and on and after Jan. 1, 1989.

(a) An application for the release of a person who has been committed to a state hospital or other treatment facility, as provided in Section 1026, upon the ground that sanity has been restored, may be made to the superior court of the county from which the commitment was made, either by the person, or by the medical director of the state hospital or other treatment facility to which the person is committed or by the county mental health director where the person is committed or by the county mental health director where the person is on outpatient status under Title 15 (commencing with Section 1600) of Part 2. The court shall give notice of the hearing date to the prosecuting attorney, the county mental health director or a designee, and the medical director or person in charge of the facility providing treatment to the committed person at least 15 judicial days in advance of the hearing date.

§ 1026.5. Maximum term of commitment.

(a) (1) In the case of any person committed to a state hospital or other treatment facility pursuant to Section 1026 or placed on outpatient status pursuant to Section 1604, who committed a felony on or after July 1, 1977, the court shall state in the commitment order the maximum term of commitment, and the person may not be kept in actual custody longer than the maximum term of commitment, except as provided in this section. For the purposes of this section, "maximum term of commitment" shall mean the longest term of imprisonment which could have been imposed for the offense or offenses of which the person was convicted, including the upper term of the base offense and any additional terms for enhancements and consecutive sentences which could have been imposed less any applicable credits as defined by Section 2900.5, and disregarding any credits which could have been earned pursuant to Article 2.5 (commencing with Section 2930) of Chapter 7 of Title 1 of Part 3.

(2) In the case of a person confined in a state hospital or other treatment facility pursuant to Section 1026 or placed on outpatient status pursuant to Section 1604, who committed a felony prior to July 1, 1977, and who could have been sentenced under Section 1168 or 1170 if the offense was committed after July 1, 1977, the Board of Prison Terms shall determine the maximum term of commitment which could have been imposed under paragraph (1), and the person may not be kept in actual custody longer than the maximum term of commitment, except as provided in subdivision (b). The time limits of this section are not jurisdictional.

In fixing a term under this section, the board shall utilize the upper term of imprisonment which could have been imposed for the offense or offenses of which the person was convicted, increased by any additional terms which could have been imposed based on matters which were found to be true in the committing court. However, if at least two of the members of the board after reviewing the person's file determine that a longer term should be imposed for the reasons specified in Section 1170.2, a longer term may be imposed following the procedures and guidelines set forth in Section 1170.2, except that any hearings deemed necessary by the board shall be held within 90 days of September 28, 1979. Within 90 days of the date the person is received by the state hospital or other treatment facility, or of September 28, 1979, whichever is later, the Board of Prison Terms shall provide each person with the determination of the person's maximum term of commitment or shall notify such person that a hearing will be scheduled to determine the term.

Within 20 days following the determination of the maximum term of commitment the board shall provide the person, the prosecuting attorney, the committing court, and the state hospital or other treatment facility with a written statement setting forth the maximum term of commitment, the calculations, and any materials considered in determining the maximum term.

(3) In the case of a person committed to a state hospital or other treatment facility pursuant to Section 1026 or placed on outpatient status pursuant to Section 1604 who committed a misdemeanor, the maximum term of commitment shall be the longest term of county jail confinement which could have been imposed for the offense or offenses which the person was found to have committed, and the person may not be kept in actual custody longer than this maximum term.

(4) Nothing in this subdivision limits the power of any state hospital or other treatment facility or of the committing order to release the person,

conditionally or otherwise, for any period of time allowed by any other provision of law.

(b) (1) A person may be committed beyond the term prescribed by subdivision (a) only under the procedure set forth in this subdivision and only if such person has been committed under Section 1026 for a felony, and who by reason of a mental disease, defect, or disorder represents a substantial danger of physical harm to others.

(2) Not later than 180 days prior to the termination of the maximum term of commitment prescribed in subdivision (a), the medical director of a state hospital or other treatment facility shall submit to the prosecuting attorney his or her opinion as to whether or not the patient is a person described in paragraph (1). If requested by the prosecuting attorney, the opinion shall be accompanied by supporting evaluations and relevant hospital records. The prosecuting attorney may then file a petition for extended commitment in the superior court which issued the original commitment. Such petition shall be filed no later than 90 days before the expiration of the original commitment unless good cause is shown. Such petition shall state the reasons for the extended commitment, with accompanying affidavits specifying the factual basis for believing that the person meets each of the requirements set forth in paragraph (1).

(3) When such a petition is filed, the court shall advise the person named in the petition of the right to be represented by an attorney and of the right to a jury trial. The rules of discovery in criminal cases shall apply.

(4) The court shall conduct a hearing on the petition for extended commitment. The trial shall be by jury unless waived by both the person and the prosecuting attorney. The trial shall commence no later than 30 calendar days prior to the time the person would otherwise have been released, unless such time is waived by the person or unless good cause is shown.

(5) The person shall be entitled to the rights guaranteed under the federal and state Constitutions for criminal proceedings. All proceedings shall be in accordance with applicable constitutional guarantees. The state shall be represented by the district attorney who shall notify the Attorney General in writing that a case has been referred under this section. If the person is indigent, the county public defender or State Public Defender shall be appointed. The State Public Defender may provide for representation of the person in any manner authorized by Section 15402 of the Government Code. Appointment of necessary psychologists or psychiatrists shall be made in accordance with this article and Penal Code and Evidence Code provisions applicable to criminal defendants who have entered pleas of not guilty by reason of insanity.

(6) If the court or jury finds that the patient is a person described in para-

graph (1), the court shall order the patient recommitted to the facility in which the patient was confined at the time the petition was filed. Any such commitment shall be for an additional period of two years from the date of termination of the previous commitment.

(7) A person committed under this subdivision shall be eligible for release to outpatient status pursuant to the provisions of Title 15 (commencing with Section 1600) of Part 2.

(8) Prior to termination of a commitment under this subdivision, a petition for recommitment may be filed to determine whether the patient remains a person described in paragraph (1). Such recommitment proceeding shall be conducted in accordance with the provisions of this subdivision.

(9) Any commitment under this subdivision places an affirmative obligation on the treatment facility to provide treatment for the underlying causes of the person's mental disorder.

MONTANA'S CRIMINAL PROCEDURE LAW

Chapter 14

Mental Competency of Accused
(Selected Relevant Sections)

Part 1
Relevance of Mental Disease or Defect

46-14-101. Mental disease or defect. As used in this chapter, the term "mental disease or defect" does not include an abnormality manifested only by repeated criminal or other antisocial conduct.

46-14-102. Evidence of mental disease or defect admissible to prove state of mind. Evidence that the defendant suffered from a mental disease or defect is admissible whenever it is relevant to prove that the defendant did or did not have a state of mind which is an element of the offense.

Part 2
Procedure When Mental Disease or Defect an Issue

46-14-201. Requirement of notice—form of verdict and judgement.

(1) Evidence of mental disease or defect is not admissible in a trial on the merits unless the defendant, at the time of entering his plea of not guilty or within 10 days thereafter or at such later time as the court may for good cause permit, files a written notice of his purpose to rely on a mental disease or defect to prove that he did not have a particular state of mind which is an essential element of the offense charged. Otherwise, except on good cause shown, he shall not introduce evidence of mental disease or defect in his case in chief expert testimony in support of that defense.

(2) When the defendant is found not guilty of the charged offense or offenses or any lesser included offense for the reason that due to a mental disease or defect he could not have a particular state of mind that is an essential element of the offense charged, the verdict and the judgement shall so state.

46-14-221. Determination of fitness to proceed—effect of finding of unfitness—expenses.

(1) The issue of the defendant's fitness to proceed may be raised by the defendant or his counsel or by the county attorney. When the issue is raised, it shall be determined by the court. If neither the county attorney nor counsel for the defendant contests the finding of the report filed under 46-14-203, the court may make the determination on the basis of the report. If the finding is contested, the court shall hold a hearing on the issue. If the report is received in evidence upon the hearing, the parties have the right to summon and cross-examine the psychiatrists who joined in the report and to offer evidence upon the issue.

(2) If the court determines that the defendant lacks fitness to proceed, the proceeding against him shall be suspended, except as provided in subsection (4) of this section, and the court shall commit him to the custody of the director of the department of institutions to be placed in an appropriate institution of the department of institutions for so long as the unfitness endures. The committing court shall, within 90 days of commitment, review the defendant's fitness to proceed. If the court finds that he is still unfit to proceed and that it does not appear that he will become fit to proceed within the reasonably forseeable future, the proceeding against him shall be dismissed, except as provided in subsection (4) of this section, and the county attorney shall petition the court in the manner provided in chapter 20 or 21 of Title 53, whichever is appropriate, to determine the disposition of the defendant pursuant to those provisions.

(3) If the court determines that the defendant lacks fitness to proceed because he is developmentally disabled as provided in 53-20-102(4), the proceeding against him shall be dismissed and the county attorney shall petition the court in the manner provided in chapter 20 of Title 53.

(4) The fact that the defendant is unfit to proceed does not preclude any legal objection to the prosection which is susceptible to fair determination prior to trial and without the personal participation of the defendant.

(5) The expenses of sending the defendant to the custody of the direction of the department of institutions to be placed in an appropriate institution of the state department of institutions, of keeping him there, and of bringing him back are chargeable to the state but the state may recover them from the estate of the defendant.

Part 3
Disposition of Defendant

46-14-301. Commitment upon finding of not guilty by reason of lack of mental state—hearing to determine release or discharge.

(1) When a defendant is found not guilty for the reason that due to a mental disease or defect he could not have a particular state of mind that is an essential element of the offense charged, the court shall order a predisposition investigation in accordance with 46-18-112 and 46-18-113, which must include an investigation of the present mental condition of the defendant. If the trial was by jury, the court shall hold a hearing to determine the appropriate disposition of the defendant. If the trial was by the court, the court may hold a hearing to obtain any additional testimony it considers necessary to determine the appropriate disposition of the defendant. In either case, the testimony and evidence presented at the trial shall be considered by the court in making its determination.

(2) The court, upon finding that the defendant may not be discharged or released without danger to others, shall order the defendant committed to the custody of the superintendent of the Montana state hospital to be placed in an appropriate institution for custody, care, and treatment.

(3) A person committed to the custody of the superintendent shall have a hearing within 180 days of his confinement to determine his present mental condition and whether he may be discharged or released without danger to others. The hearing shall be conducted by the court which ordered the commitment unless that court transfers jurisdiction to the third judicial district. The court shall cause notice of the hearing to be served upon the person, his counsel, and the prosecuting attorney. Such a hearing shall be deemed a civil proceeding, and the burden shall be upon the defendant to prove by a preponderance of the evidence that he may be safely released.

(4) According to the determination of the court upon the hearing, the defendant shall be discharged or released on such conditions as the court determines to be necessary or shall be committed to the custody of the superintendent of the Montana state hospital to be placed in an appropriate institution for custody, care, and treatment.

46-14-311. Consideration of mental disease or defect in sentencing. Whenever a defendant is convicted on a verdict or a plea of guilty and he claims that at the time of the commission of the offense of which he was convicted he was suffering from a mental disease or defect which rendered him unable to appreciate the criminality of his conduct or to conform his conduct to the requirements of law, the sentencing court shall consider any relevant evidence presented at the trial and shall require such additional evidence as it considers necessary for the determination of the issue, including examination of the defendant and a report thereof as provided in 46-14-202 and 46-14-203.

46-14-312. Sentence to be imposed.

(1) If the court finds that the defendant at the time of the commission of the offense of which he was convicted did not suffer from a mental disease or

defect as described in 46-14-311, it shall sentence him as provided in Title 46, chapter 18.

(2) If the court finds that the defendant at the time of the commission of the offense suffered from a mental disease or defect as described in 46-14-311, any mandatory minimum sentence prescribed by law for the offense need not apply and the court shall sentence him to be committed to the custody of the director of the department of institutions to be placed in an appropriate institution for custody, care, and treatment for a definite period of time not to exceed the maximum term of imprisonment that could be imposed under subsection (1). The authority of the court with regard to sentencing is the same as authorized in Title 46, chapter 18, provided the treatment of the individual and the protection of the public are provided for.

(3) A defendant whose sentence has been imposed under subsection (2) may petition the sentencing court for review of the sentence if the professional person certifies that the defendant has been cured of the mental disease or defect. The sentencing court may make any order not inconsistent with its original sentencing authority except that the length of confinement or supervision must be equal to that of the original sentence. The professional person shall review the defendant's status each year.

46-14-313. Discharge of defendant from supervision. At the expiration of the period of commitment or period of treatment specified by the court under 46-14-312(2), the defendant must be discharged from custody and further supervision, subject only the law regarding the civil commitment of persons suffering from serious mental illness.

Index

Abolition of insanity defense, 34, 38
  constitutional issues in, 123
  in different states, 40
  historical aspects of, 121–123
  impact of, 145, 147, 149, 151
  in Montana, 8–9, 14, 23, 27, 28,
      121–137, 141
    and acquittal rate, 128–129
    collection of data on, 124–125
    competency for trial in, 129–130,
      131, 133, 136
    confinement and release proce-
      dures in, 124, 133–136, 137
    and defendant characteristics,
      127–128, 131–133
    mental health-related outcome in,
      131–133, 134, 135
    and plea rate, 125–127, 136
Acquittals, insanity, 27, 28, 175
  and burden of proof, 65–67, 78–81
  confinement after. *See* Confinement
      and release procedures
  data collection procedures for, 26
  defendant characteristics of, 29–31
    in California, 56–57
    in Georgia, 70–71
    in New York, 77–81
  after guilty but mentally ill verdict,
      106

  of Hinckley. *See* Hinckley acquittal
  in Montana, 125–126, 128–129
  plea data compared to, 9–10
  public reaction to, 2, 26, 32, 39
  and test of insanity, 48–49, 50, 53–
      55, 61
    in violent crimes, 56, 57
  variations in, 148
Adjudication methods
  in California, 57
  in Georgia, 71–72, 107–108, 112–
      114
    and burden of proof, 72
  in Montana, 127–128, 133
  in New York, 81, 96
    and burden of proof, 81
Adjudication reforms, 13, 14–15, 141,
      142–143
Age of defendants, 30, 56, 71
  in California, 56
  in Georgia, 71, 111
  in Montana, 127, 131, 132
  in New York, 80, 95
Ake v. Oklahoma, 38, 161
Alabama, 19, 37, 39, 40, 42
Alaska, 37, 40, 42
American Bar Association, 5, 65,
      101
  on tests of insanity, 2, 46–47

American Law Institute test of
   insanity, 13, 14, 33, 38, 41, 46
   in California, 8, 45, 47, 49, 141
American Psychiatric Association, 47,
   65–66
Arizona, 37, 40, 42
Arkansas, 37, 40, 42

Baxstrom v. Herold, 18, 105, 161
Benham v. Edwards, 33, 104–105,
   109, 110, 111, 112, 144, 161
Benhan v. Ledbetter, 105, 161
Berkowitz, David, 1, 5
Berwid, Adam, 18, 87
Blameworthiness, 4, 122
Bolton v. Harris, 33, 39, 86, 161
Burden and standard of proof. *See*
   Proof, burden and standard of

California, 16, 19, 37, 40, 42
   confinement and release procedures
      in, 52, 58–61, 62, 146–147
      determinate sentencing in, 52–53,
         55, 62, 94
   defendant characteristics in, 56–58
   penal code in, 202–207
   plea rate in, 5, 28, 47, 49, 50–53,
      61, 62
      in violent crimes, 56, 57
   plea success in, 28, 53–55, 57
   research project in, 7, 8, 167–170
      analysis of data in, 179, 180, 181
      collection of data in, 22–23, 25,
         26, 49–50, 174, 176
   test of insanity in, 45–62. *See also*
      Tests of insanity, in California
   timing of reforms in, 169
California v. Horn, 47, 161
Case laws, 18–19
Case records, 24, 25, 26, 27, 173, 174
Chapman, Mark David, 5
Colorado, 37, 40, 42
Competency to stand trial, 9, 23
   in Montana, 129–130, 131, 133,
      136
Computerized records, 24, 25, 26,
   174
Confinement and release procedures,
   13–14, 15, 35–36
   automatic and indefinite confine-
      ment, 35, 39–41, 103, 122
   and burden of proof, 35, 39–41, 85
      in Georgia, 73–74
      in New York, 81–84

   in California, 52, 58–61, 146–147
      determinate sentences in, 52–53,
         55, 62, 94
   constitutional issues in, 33
      in California, 52
      in Georgia, 103, 104, 105
      in New York, 88
   cost issues in, 6
   and crimes after release, 4, 147
   in different states, 40
   for felons, compared to insanity
      defendants, 30, 31
   in Georgia, 104–105, 109–110
      and burden of proof, 73–74
      in guilty but mentally ill verdict,
         115–119, 120
   for guilty but mentally ill, 103, 104,
      115–119, 120
   Hinckley acquittal affecting, 86
   in Montana, 124, 133–136, 137
   in New York, 8, 14, 34, 86–101
      and burden of proof, 81–84
      and defendant characteristics, 93,
         95–96
      historical aspects of, 86–88
      hospitalization in, 96–97
      impact of changes in, 98–101,
         143–144, 147
      Insanity Defense Reform Act of
         1980 on, 86, 88–90, 101
      length of, 97–98, 99
      outpatient programs in, 97, 98
      and plea bargains, 89, 95, 96, 97,
         100
      and plea rate, 91–92, 100
      and plea success, 93–95
      safety concerns in, 88, 89–90, 101
   premature release, 15, 146, 147
   public opinion on, 4, 34, 87, 101,
      146, 147
   research on, 23, 180, 181
Connecticut, 37, 40, 42
Constitutional issues, 33, 41, 123
   in burden of proof, 64–65
   in confinement conditions, 33
      in California, 52
      in Georgia, 103, 104, 105
      in New York, 88, 90, 101
Cost issues in reforms, 6–7
County information, 3, 9–10, 21, 168, 170
   collection of, 21–23, 173–175
Court dockets, 24, 25, 173, 174
Criminal Lunatics Act of 1800, 2, 32,
   122

Dahmer, Jeffrey, 1, 38, 138, 152
Data abstraction, 23–24, 172–176
    form for, 183–187
Data analysis, 178–181
Data collection, 20–27, 170–178
    in California, 49–50, 174
    in Georgia, 67, 105, 174
    in Montana, 124–125, 174
    in New York, 74, 90, 174
Data management, 176–178
Davis v. United States, 64, 161
Death penalty, in Georgia, 116, 117
Defendant characteristics, 29–31, 140
    in California, 56–58
    in Georgia, 70–73, 111, 113–115
    in Montana, 127–128, 131–133
    in New York, 77–81, 95–96
        and confinement conditions, 88,
            89–90, 93
Delaware, 37, 40, 42
Diagnosis of mental illness in
        defendants, 30, 31
    in California, 56
    in Georgia
        and burden of proof, 70–71, 72–
            73, 84
        and GBMI, 113–115
    in Montana, 127, 131–133
    in New York
        and burden of proof, 78, 84
        and commitment and release, 95,
            97
Diminished capacity defense, 41
Disposition methods. *See* Dispositional
        reforms
    in California, 57
    in Georgia reforms, 71–72, 107–108,
        112–114
    in Montana, 133
    in New York reforms, 81, 96, 141
Dispositional reforms, 13, 15, 86, 90,
    101, 141, 143–144
District of Columbia, 37, 39, 40, 42
    test of insanity in, 46, 48
*Dixon v. Attorney General of the
        Commonwealth of Pennsylvania*,
    19, 161
Due process concerns, 33, 41, 44
    in burden of proof, 64, 65
    in confinement, 4, 88, 90, 101, 104–
        105
Durham test, 33, 38, 46, 48, 49
Durham v. United States, 46, 161

Equal protection, 33, 41, 52, 88
Ethnicity of defendants, 30
    in California, 56
    in Georgia, 71, 111, 113–114
    in Montana, 127, 131, 132
    in New York, 80, 95
Expert testimony, 13

Florida, 20, 37, 40, 42
Foucha v. Louisiana, 150, 161

Gender of defendants, 30, 31
    in California, 56
    in Georgia, 71, 111, 113–114
    in Montana, 127, 131, 132
    in New York, 79, 80, 81, 95, 97
Georgia, 37, 40, 42
    burden and standard of proof in, 8,
        13, 63, 66, 67–74, 84–85, 141
        and confinement patterns, 73–74
        and defendant characteristics, 70–
            73
        impact of changes in, 74, 142–143
        and plea rate, 67–68, 69
        and plea success, 69–70
    confinement and release procedures
        in, 104–105, 109–110
        and burden of proof, 73–74
        for guilty but mentally ill, 115–
            119, 120
    criminal procedure law in, 191–194
    guilty but mentally ill in, 102–120.
        See also Guilty but mentally ill,
        in Georgia
    plea rate in, 28
        and burden of proof, 67–68, 69, 84
        in guilty but mentally ill, 105–
            108, 119–120
    plea success in, 28, 54, 108–111
        and burden of proof, 69–70
    research project in, 7, 8, 167, 168, 170
        analysis of data in, 179, 180, 181
        county-level data in, 173
        sources of data in, 21, 23, 25, 26, 174
        timing of reforms in, 169
Guilty and mentally ill, 38, 131
Guilty but insane, 38
Guilty but mentally ill, 8, 14–15, 35,
    38, 151
    confinement and release of, 103, 104
        in Georgia, 115–119, 120
    in different states, 37, 40, 103, 104
    in Georgia, 8, 14, 34, 84, 102–120, 141

confinement of, 115–119, 120
defendant characteristics in, 111,
   113, 114
impact of reforms concerning,
   144–145, 148, 149
plea rate, 105–108, 119–120
plea success, 108–111
Hinckley acquittal affecting, 102,
   119, 139, 144
historical aspects of, 102–105
in Michigan, 6, 34, 38, 102, 103,
   104, 120
research project in, 7, 8, 167–170
   analysis of data in, 179, 180,
      181
   collection of data in, 23–26, 67,
      173, 174, 175
timing of reforms in, 169

Hawaii, 37, 40, 42
Hinckley acquittal, 1–2, 3, 5, 138–
   140
   burden of proof in, 63–64
   political response to, 3, 139–140
   public reaction to, 2, 12, 32, 39,
      126–127
   reforms after, 7, 8, 9, 12, 34, 35–39,
      139
      on burden of proof, 66–67
      on confinement, 86
      on guilty but mentally ill, 102,
         119, 139, 144
      on tests of insanity, 46–47, 139
History of insanity defense
   in California, 45–46
   in Georgia, 102–105
   in Montana, 121–123
   in New York, 86–88
Hospitalization of defendants
   in California, 58–60
   in Georgia, 73, 115, 116
   in Montana, 124, 133, 134
   in New York, 82, 96–97

Idaho, 37, 38, 40, 42, 123
Illinois, 37, 40, 42, 103, 104
In re Moye, 52, 62, 161
In re Torsney, 87, 161
In re Winship, 64, 161
Incompetency to stand trial, 9, 23
   in Montana, 129–130, 131, 133,
      136
Indiana, 33, 37, 40, 42, 120

Insanity Defense Reform Acts
   of 1980, 86, 88–90, 101, 143
   of 1984, 41, 47
Iowa, 37, 40, 42

Jackson v. Indiana, 105, 161
Jones v. United States, 39, 41, 105,
   161
Judge, or bench trials
   in California, 55, 57
   in Georgia, 72, 107, 108, 113, 114
   in Montana, 127–128
   in New York, 81, 95, 96, 97
Jury trials, 48–49
   in California, 55, 57
   in Georgia, 72, 107, 108, 112, 113, 114
   in Montana, 127–128
   in New York, 81, 95, 96, 97

Kansas, 37, 39, 40, 42
Keedy, Michael, 124
Kentucky, 37, 40, 42

Lanterman-Petris-Short Act, 16, 19
Legislative reforms, 12–15, 34
   balance between individual rights
      and safety concerns in, 41, 88–
      90, 149–152
   Hinckley acquittal affecting, 34, 139
Legislators, misperceptions of, 5
Leland v. Oregon, 64–65, 161
Life sentences, in Georgia, 116, 119
Louisiana, 37, 40, 42, 123

Maine, 37, 40, 42
Maryland, 37, 40, 42, 48
Massachusetts, 19–20, 37, 39, 40, 42
McNaughtan standard, 13, 14, 33, 36–
   38, 41, 45–46
   in California, 8, 45, 47, 49, 141
Meese, Edward, 3, 4–5
Mental health advocacy movement, 2,
   32, 87
Michigan, 6, 33, 34, 37, 39, 40, 42
   guilty but mentally ill in, 6, 34, 38,
      102, 103, 104, 120
Minnesota, 37, 40, 42
Mississippi, 37, 39, 40, 42, 123
Missouri, 37, 40, 42, 167, 168, 169
Montana, 37, 38, 40, 42
   abolition of insanity defense in,
      121–137. *See also* Abolition of
      insanity defense, in Montana

Montana (*continued*)
    competency for trial in, 129–130,
        131, 133, 136
    criminal procedure law in, 208–211
    guilty and mentally ill in, 131
    plea rate in, 27, 28, 125–127, 136
    plea success in, 28, 128–129
    research project in, 7, 8, 167–170
        analysis of data in, 179, 180, 181
        collection of data in, 25, 26, 124–
            125, 171, 174
    timing of reforms in, 169
Murder cases, 151
    in California, 59, 60
    in Georgia, 113–115, 116, 117, 118
    in Montana, 127, 132, 133
    in New York, 81–84, 98

Nebraska, 37, 40, 42
Nevada, 37, 40, 42
New Hampshire, 37, 40, 42, 46
New Jersey, 33, 37, 42
    reforms in, 39, 40, 169, 177–178
    research project in, 7, 167, 170
        collection of data in, 174, 181
New Mexico, 37, 40, 42
New York, 37, 40, 42
    burden and standard of proof
        reform in, 8, 13, 63, 66, 74–85,
            141
        and confinement patterns, 81–84
        and defendant characteristics, 77–
            81
        impact of changes in, 84–85, 142–
            143
        and plea rate, 74–76, 84–85
        and plea success, 76–77, 80, 81
    confinement procedures in, 86–101.
        See also Confinement and
        release procedures, in New
        York
    criminal procedure law in, 195–201
    dispositional reforms in, 86, 90,
        101, 141, 143–144
        and confinement patterns, 96–98
        and defendant characteristics, 95–
            96
        impact of changes in, 98, 99
        and plea rate, 91–92, 100
        and plea success, 93–95, 100
    impact of reforms in, 142–144, 147
    mass patient transfer in, 18
    plea bargains in, 81, 89, 95, 96, 97,
        100

plea rate in, 5, 27, 28
    and burden of proof, 74–76, 84–85
    and confinement, 91–92, 100
plea success in, 28, 54
    and burden of proof, 76–77, 80, 81
    and confinement procedures, 93–95
research project in, 7, 8, 167, 168,
    170
    analysis of data in, 179, 180, 181
    county-level data in, 173
    sources of data in, 23, 24, 25, 26,
        174
timing of reforms in, 169
Nonviolent crimes
    in California, 54–55, 59, 61
    in Georgia
        burden of proof in, 73, 74
        guilty but mentally ill in, 108–
            109, 111, 116, 117
    in Montana, 134, 135, 136
    in New York
        burden of proof in, 83
        commitment and release reform
            in, 93–95, 98, 99, 100
North Carolina, 20, 37, 40, 42
North Dakota, 37, 40, 43

Ohio, 34, 37, 40, 43
    research project in, 7, 167, 170,
        174, 177
    timing of reforms in, 169
Oklahoma, 37, 38, 40, 43
Ontario, 20
Oregon, 20, 37, 40, 43, 48

Patterson v. New York, 65, 161
Pennsylvania, 37, 40, 43, 167, 168,
    169
    guilty but mentally ill in, 103
    mass patient transfer in, 19
People v. McQuillan, 33, 86–87, 103,
    105, 161
Plea bargains
    in California, 55, 57
    in Georgia
        and burden of proof, 71, 72
        and guilty but mentally ill, 107–
            108, 112–113, 115, 120
    in Montana, 127–128
    in New York
        and burden of proof reform in,
            81, 89
        and commitment and release
            reform in, 95, 96, 97, 100

Plea rate, 27, 28, 175, 178
  acquittal rates compared to, 9–10
  in California, 5, 28, 47, 49, 50–53, 61, 62
    in violent crimes, 56, 57
  in Georgia, 28
    and burden of proof, 67–68, 69, 84
    of guilty but mentally ill, 105–108, 119–120
  misperceptions on, 5–7, 150, 152
  in Montana, 27, 28, 125–127, 136
  in New York, 5, 27, 28
    and burden of proof, 74–76, 84–85
    and commitment and release reform, 91–92, 100
  sources of data on, 20, 21, 24–26, 174
  variations in, 148
Plea success, 26, 27–28, 65, 140, 175, 179
  in California, 28, 53–55, 57
  in Georgia, 28, 54
    and burden of proof, 69–70
    in guilty but mentally ill, 108–111
  in Montana, 28, 128–129
  in New York, 28, 54
    and burden of proof, 76–77, 80, 81
    and commitment and release reform, 93–95
Political response to Hinckley acquittal, 3, 139–140
Proof, burden and standard of, 7, 8, 13, 14, 35, 63–85, 141, 146, 151
  and confinement patterns, 35, 39–41
    in Georgia, 73–74, 85
    in New York, 81–84, 85
  constitutional issues in, 64–65
  in different states, 37, 40
    in Georgia, 67–74. *See also* Georgia, burden and standard of proof in
  in Hinckley case, 63–64
  history of, 64–65
  impact of changes in, 74, 84–85, 142–143, 146
  legal debates concerning, 63–67
    in New York, 74–85. *See also* New York, burden and standard of proof in
  number of reforms concerning, 36
  and plea rate, 65, 66, 67–68, 69, 84–85

and plea success, 65, 69–70, 76–77, 80, 81
Proposition 8, in California, 47, 61
Public opinion, 4, 5, 32–33, 138
  on acquittals, 2, 32, 39, 126–127
  in California, 61, 62
  on confinement conditions, 4, 34, 87, 101, 146, 147
  misperceptions in, 5, 150, 152

Reagan, President Ronald, 1–2, 46, 64, 126
Reform, use of term, 12
Research on insanity defense, 7–10
  abstraction of data in, 23–24, 172–176
    form for, 183–187
  on acquittals, 26, 175, 178, 179
    analysis of data in, 178–181
  on case law impact, 18–19
  collection of data in, 20–27, 170–178
    in California, 25, 49–50, 174
    in Georgia, 25, 67, 105, 174
    in Montana, 25, 124–125, 174
    in New York, 25, 74, 90, 174
  and confinement data, 23, 180, 181
  in counties, 3, 9–10, 21, 168, 170
    collection of data on, 21–23, 173–175
  framework of, 15–18
  future issues for, 148–149
  identification and selection of cases in, 24, 26, 173
  management of data in, 176–178
  methodology in, 165–181
  need for, 140–141, 152
  plea data in, 20, 21, 175, 178
    compared to acquittal data, 9–10
  sources of, 20, 21, 24–26, 174
  rationale of project, 165–166
  in states, 167–170, 174
    in multistate studies, 16, 17
    in single state studies, 16
    sources of data on, 21, 23, 174, 175–176
  on statutory reform impact, 19–20
Responsibility, criminal, 3–4, 33, 35, 46, 122
Rhode Island, 37, 40, 43
Rivera v. Delaware, 65, 161

Safety concerns, 145–146, 147
  balanced with individual rights, 41,
    88–90, 149–152
  in confinement and release proce-
    dures, 88, 89–90, 101
Senate hearings, 139–140
South Carolina, 37, 40, 43
South Dakota, 37, 40, 43
Specter, Arlen, 140
Standard of proof. *See* Proof, burden
  and standard of
State v. Field, 33, 161
State v. Krol, 33, 161
States
  reforms in, 40
  research on, 167–170, 174
    in multistate studies, 16, 17
    in single state studies, 16
    sources of data in, 21, 23, 174,
      175–176
  status of insanity defense in, 37
  statutory and case law citations in,
    42–43
  variations in insanity defense cases,
    148, 150
Statutory reforms, 12–15, 34
  research on, 19–20
Systems analysis of insanity defense
  reform, 11–31, 151–152

*Tarasoff v. The Regents of the
  University of California*, 19, 161
Tennessee, 37, 40, 43
Tests of insanity, 8, 13, 14, 33, 34
  of American Law Institute, 13, 14,
    33, 38, 41, 46, 141
  in California, 8, 45, 47, 49, 141
  burden of proof in, 41
  in California, 8, 13, 45–62, 141
    and confinement patterns, 58–
      60, 61, 146–147
    and defendant characteristics, 56–
      58
    impact of changes in, 47–49,
      142, 146–147
    and plea rate, 50–53
    and plea success, 53–55
  in different states, 37, 40
  Durham, 33, 38, 46, 48, 49
  federal legislation on, 41
  Hinckley acquittal affecting, 46–47,
    139

historical development of, 45–46
McNaughtan standard in, 8, 13, 14,
  33, 36–38, 41, 45–46, 141
number of reforms concerning, 36–
  38
in Wyoming, 45, 47–48, 49
Texas, 37, 40, 43
Torsney, Robert, 87
Trial procedures, 35, 38, 40

Utah, 37, 38, 40, 43, 123, 136

Verdict stage, 13
Vermont, 37, 40, 43
Victim crimes
  in California, 56
  in Georgia, 72, 112, 113, 114
  in Montana, 127–128, 133
  in New York, 80–81, 95
Violent crimes
  in California, 54–55, 56, 57
    confinement in, 58, 59, 60
  in Georgia
    burden of proof in, 71, 72, 73, 74
    confinement in, 73, 74, 116, 117,
      118
    guilty but mentally ill in, 108–
      109, 110–111, 113–115, 119
  in Montana, 127, 132, 133
    confinement in, 134, 135
  in New York
    burden of proof in, 79–80
    commitment of release reform in,
      93–94
    confinement in, 81–84, 97–98,
      99
Virgina, 37, 39, 40, 43

Washington, 37, 123
  reforms in, 40, 169, 177–178
  research project in, 7, 167, 170,
    174, 181
Washington, D. C., 37, 39, 40, 42
  test of insanity in, 46, 48
West Virginia, 37, 40
Wisconsin, 37, 38, 43
  reforms in, 40, 169, 177–178
  research project in, 7, 167, 170,
    174, 181
Wyatt v. Stickney, 19, 161
Wyoming, 37, 40, 43
  test of insanity in, 45, 47–48, 49